SEA OF JAPAN

Mukden

KOREA

Wei-hai-wei

aochow
Tsingtao
ANMEN BAY

J A P A N

D0847663

Shanghai

EAST

OCEAN

TAIWAN

MARIANA ISLANDS

nila

PHILIP

Syracuse, New York

CAROLINE

ISLANDS

PRINTED IN U.S.A.

palacios

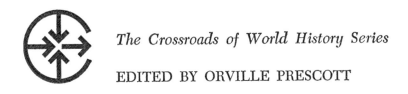

The Crossroads of World History Series

EDITED BY ORVILLE PRESCOTT

SINGAPORE

The Battle That Changed the World

The Crossroads of World History Series

SINGAPORE

The Battle That Changed the World

JAMES LEASOR

Garden City, New York

DOUBLEDAY & COMPANY, INC.

1968

Grateful acknowledgement is made to the following publishers and agents for permission to quote from copyrighted works under their control:

Angus & Robertson, Ltd., for excerpts from *Why Singapore Fell* by H. Gordon Bennett. Used by permission.

Jonathan Cape, Ltd., for excerpts from *Who Dies Fighting* by Angus Rose. Used by permission.

Chatto & Windus, Ltd., for excerpts from *Eastern Epic* by Compton Mackenzie. Used by permission.

Curtis Brown, Ltd., for excerpts from *Death of the Battleship* by Richard Hough. Published in England by William Collins Sons & Co., Ltd., as *The Hunting of Force Z*. Used by permission.

David Higham Associates, Ltd., for excerpts from *War in Malaya* by A. E. Percival. Used by permission.

Houghton Mifflin Company, for excerpts from *The Gathering Storm, The Grand Alliance,* and *The Hinge of Fate* by Winston Churchill. Used by permission.

Little, Brown and Company, for lines from "The Japanese" from *Verses from 1929 On* by Ogden Nash, copyright 1935 by The Curtis Publishing Company. Used by permission.

New American Library, Inc., for excerpts from *Life and Death of a Japanese General* by John Deane Potter. Used by permission.

W. W. Norton & Company, Inc. and William Collins Sons & Co., Ltd., for excerpts from *Trenchard: Man of Vision* by Andrew Boyle. Used by permission.

St. Martin's Press and Ure Smith Pty., Ltd., for excerpts from *Singapore: The Japanese Version* by Masanobu Tsuji. Used by permission.

Doubleday & Company, Inc., and Frederick Muller, Ltd., for excerpts from *Fortress: The Story of the Siege of Singapore* by Ken Attiwill. Published in England as *The Singapore Story*. Copyright © 1959 by Kenneth Attiwill. Used by permission.

ACKNOWLEDGEMENTS

It is rare for independent accounts of any event or incident to agree in all particulars. Different witnesses, each acting in good faith, can give completely conflicting accounts of what happened.

One realises the truth of this in writing about an event that has taken place within living memory. Accounts of those who were there, even some most closely involved, are frequently at variance; and discrepancies grow with the passing of the years, for time dims some memories while sharpening others.

In writing this book, I have endeavoured to consult accounts that were written as close in time as possible to the events they describe, rather than to rely on human memory for descriptions and impressions of what happened more than a quarter of a century ago.

Many people helped with their papers, diaries and accounts, and others have helped me about specific incidents, episodes and interpretations. I would like to acknowledge my debt to: Sir Jonathan Backhouse, Bart.; Mr. Edward Barford, M.C.; Mr. W. G. C. Blunn; Vice-Admiral Sir Ronald Brockman, C.S.I., C.I.E., C.B.E.; Mr. E. V. E. Day; Mr. Lionel W. Donough, O.B.E.; Col. W. H. P. Gardiner; Mr. S. K. Gaw; Mr. D. B. Gibson of the India Office Library; Sir Franklin Gimson, K.C.M.G.; Mr. Tony Houghton; the staff of the London Library; Admiral of the Fleet Viscount Mountbatten of Burma, K.G., P.C., G.C.B., G.C.S.I., G.C.I.E., G.C.V.O., D.S.O.; Mr. C. D. Overton, Commonwealth Relations Office Library; Mrs. Jack Rufus; Mrs. Joan St. George Saunders; Cecilia, Lady Sempill and Mrs. Elizabeth Taylor.

In addition to the above, I would like to express my appreciation to four others who helped me, but who have died since I started work on this book: Lord Beaverbrook, P.C.; Lord Hankey, G.C.B., P.C., G.C.M.G., G.C.V.O., Minister Without Portfolio in the War Cabinet; General Sir Leslie Hollis, K.C.B., K.B.E., Senior Assistant Secretary in the War Cabinet Office; and Lieutenant-General A. E. Percival, C.B., D.S.O., M.C., General Officer Commanding Malaya 1941–1942.

I am grateful to Lady Shenton Thomas for making available to me the late Sir Shenton Thomas' papers concerning the *Official History of the War in the Far East*, and to Dr. J. B. van Cuylenburg, who kindly let me use his own most detailed account of life in Singapore from the early years of this century until after the Second World War.

Many other people have helped with details and recollections of Malaya and Singapore before, during and after the war, but for personal reasons have asked to remain anonymous. I would also like to record my appreciation for their co-operation and advice. Any errors remaining are my own.

J.L.

SINGAPORE

Sunday in Singapore

LATE on a wet Sunday afternoon, Chinese New Year Day, February 15, 1942, twenty-five years ago, two generals—one British, one Japanese—faced each other across a white-clothed table in the assembly plant of the Ford Automobile Works outside Singapore.

The Englishman was tall and thin and fifty-five, Lieutenant-General Arthur Ernest Percival. He commanded the 85,000 British, Indian and Australian troops who, since the previous December, had fought a doomed and retreating rearguard action down the Malay peninsula, and now stood besieged in Singapore Island, 1100 yards south of the mainland.

The Japanese general, Tomoyuki Yamashita, was two years older, a short and heavily built man, with a pudgy face expressionless as a bladder of lard. Leading a fighting force numerically a third of the defending army, Yamashita had brought one of the most brilliant attacking campaigns in military history to this moment of triumph.

Now scores of Japanese officers, cameramen and newspaper reporters crowded the concrete floor to watch Percival sue for surrender.

More than a million bewildered civilian refugees, overwhelmingly Asiatic, had fled south to Singapore for safety. For years, almost every reference to Singapore had described it as a "bastion of the Empire" or "The Gibraltar of the East." Even its name—literally Lion Gate,[1] in the Sanskrit—seemed synonymous with strength and its importance to Britain; the British lion, British interests. But it was none of these. Unlike the Japanese, the refugees did not know that, although more than £63,000,000

---

[1] In the eleventh century, the Eastern ruler Rajendracola Deva the First gave the island this name to commemorate the lion-like courage of his men who had seized it in battle.

had been spent over a period of twenty years on building the gigantic naval base on the north coast of Singapore Island, this complex treasure-house of stores and equipment was only a base and not a fortress. Once the mainland had fallen it was as indefensible as the Isle of Wight would be if England succumbed to an invader; as naked as Long Island if the East Coast of the U.S.A. were occupied by an enemy power.

Now, broken in spirit, their belongings and their homes abandoned, the refugees crowded into the beaten city, thirty to a room. Many were Chinese who, richer and more industrious than the easy-going Malays, grouped together, fearing not only the Japanese, but also the envy of the Malays, who outnumbered them two to one.

With five out of every six gallons of water pumped into the island's two reservoirs pouring to waste through bombed conduits; with sewers smashed, drains clogged by the unburied dead, putrefying carcasses of dogs and mules fouling the canals, the risk of epidemic was very real.

Gangs of armed looters—some of them British and Australian deserters—roamed the streets in search of plunder; abandoned cars and trucks, many with bodies still in them, others ablaze, blocked the roads already piled with debris from bombed houses.

The defenders had little ammunition left; the only gasolene they now controlled was in the tanks of their trucks. Black smoke darkened the sky from the huge oil storage tanks, built for the British Navy that Percival's men had set ablaze to deny them to the Japanese. The rain brought down flecks of oil from the sky. The locals called it black rain. It seemed another evil omen; funeral flames for a dying empire.

Dazed by the incredible superiority of the Japanese, the defenders' will to win had withered. Out-gunned, out-generalled, and exhausted, with cohesion and command gone, they had fallen farther back for each of the campaign's seventy days and nights. Now they stood with only the sea behind them.

The Japanese had planned their campaign to the day. They determined to capture Singapore by Kigensetsu, the anniversary of the crowning of the first Japanese emperor, on February 11, 600 B.C.

And on February 11, four days before the surrender, Yamashita had a letter urging immediate capitulation dropped from a plane in a signal communication tube with red and white streamers. Percival sent back no answer. He was sure that reinforcements, an aircraft carrier with fighter planes, was on the way; he still believed he could hold out until they arrived.

On the following Sunday morning he called a conference with the Director-General of Civil Defence, the Inspector-General of Police, plus his own staff officers. He believed he had two alternatives—either to launch a counter-attack at once to capture the reservoirs and the supply dumps that had fallen into Japanese hands and drive the enemy off the heights of Bukit Timah from which it fired down on Singapore; or to surrender. But the defenders were too exhausted, too shattered by the long retreat for another counter-attack. This left only the second choice: surrender. At least surrender might spare the city some of the horrors that had visited Hong Kong when the Japanese had raped and murdered civilians after its capture.

Accordingly, he sent out two staff officers, carrying a white flag, to the Japanese command. They were met by a staff officer, Sugita, who spoke English, and, in fact, had actually written the note urging surrender. He produced conditions of surrender which the Japanese had prepared in advance. Percival was to be spared no humiliation, he was to come in person to admit his defeat.

Percival arrived at about six o'clock in a civilian car—his original staff Humber had been bombed—with the Union Jack and a white flag attached to the door pillars. They stopped at the crossing of three roads at Bukit Timah, and Sugita led them into the Ford factory. The concrete floor had been cleaned and places marked out in chalk for the Japanese senior officers who would witness, and the war reporters and cameramen who would record, the greatest disaster to the British Empire since Cornwallis surrendered Yorktown in the American War of Independence.

Percival wore khaki shorts and shirt, a webbing belt and a steel helmet. He was unarmed. The two officers who accompanied him, the Adjutant General and a major, also wore tropical uniform, but with brown leather Sam Browne belts and revolvers. One carried the white flag; the other, the Union Jack from the car.

Colonel Masanobu Tsuji, the planning officer largely responsible for the Japanese campaign which had brought such victory to their arms, described their faces as "pale and their eyes bloodshot."

Percival and Yamashita shook hands formally and sat down at opposite sides of the table. The air in the factory was sharp with cordite and the fumes of burning oil. The Japanese interpreter was poor, and possibly awed by the solemnity of the occasion. As Yamashita's adjutant wrote later in his diary: "Yamashita wanted to say a few kind words to Percival while he was shaking hands with him, as he looked so pale and thin and ill. But he could not say anything because he does not speak English, and he realised how difficult it is to convey heartfelt sympathy when the words are being interpreted by a third person."

For the two generals, their meeting was strictly military. Neither could realise its historical importance. At the start of the campaign, each Japanese soldier had been issued with a pamphlet that set out Japan's reasons for fighting the British and Americans. Her claim was that she would liberate East Asia from white invasion and oppression, for since "we Japanese, as an Eastern people, have ourselves for long been classed alongside the Chinese and the Indians as an inferior race, and treated as such, we must at the very least, here in Asia, beat these Westerners to submission, that they may change their arrogant and ill-mannered attitude.

"The present war is a struggle between races, and we must achieve the satisfaction of our just demands with no thought of leniency to Europeans, unless they be the Germans and Italians."

Even so, neither general could realise that this surrender

marked the end of the legend of the white man's inherent
supremacy over the coloured man—the Western rulers, the
Eastern ruled—that had lasted, virtually unchallenged, for centuries.

An outnumbered Asiatic army, arriving in Malaya with bicycles for transport, living rough on rice, looting what else they
needed as they advanced, had humiliated an infinitely more
complex Western army.

The psychological damage was even greater than the military
defeat—and this had been grotesque enough. Despite General
Percival's comforting belief that his men had inflicted heavy
losses on the enemy, the Japanese had lost only 3378 wounded
and 1715 dead in the battle of Singapore—a small price for
the greatest defeat an Asian army had inflicted on Europeans
since the bearded horsemen of Genghis Khan had swept from
the east to the gates of Vienna more than seven centuries before.

Under the lowering Singapore sky lit by the funeral pyres
of the British Empire—an empire vaster than the Greek, more
gentle and enduring than the Roman—a door closed on centuries
of white supremacy, and another opened on an unknown and
uncertain future, not only for the West in the East, but also
for the East itself.

From then on, the East would clamour for "independence"
and "freedom" from Western political and economic domination,
only to find too late that this independence was illusory, this
freedom only the freedom to sink into a morass of debt.

The political vacuum left in Asia when the West retreated
would be filled by Communism or its threat. As a direct result
of the surrender of Singapore, the stabilising influence of the
West would be removed. Added to the American belief in the
evils of colonialism it would eventually and ironically result in
young Americans and Australians, not even born at the time of
that Sunday meeting in 1942, dying in Vietnam in a rearguard
action to preserve the South of that country from the encroaching
Communism of the North.

Today, could any American who in the past had criticised or
resented European colonial empires in the East doubt that that

Sunday in Singapore marked the end of the most stable period that the East—and the West in the East—had ever known?

But then all this lay ahead, unseen; and even had Percival guessed what would follow surrender, there was nothing more he could do.

Physically the antithesis of each other, the victorious and the vanquished generals typified the cadres of command of their countries; Japan, apparently on the brink of grasping an empire; Britain, about to lose one. Their training, their characters, their tactics were also curiously contrasting.

From the age of eleven, Yamashita, the son of a Japanese village doctor, had been trained as a soldier, first at the School of the Southern Sea, then at the Central Military Academy in Tokyo.

He became an Assistant Military Attaché in the Japanese Embassy in Berne, where Captain Hideki Tojo, later to be Yamashita's Prime Minister during the Second World War, was a colleague.

During the Young Officer's Rebellion in Japan in 1936, Yamashita, by then Chief of Military Affairs in the Army, played a leading part in averting virtual civil war. The young officers accused politicians and businessmen of trying to reduce the size and efficiency of their army instead of modernizing it to European standards. Also, they resented the widespread poverty throughout Japan, and the gradual eroding of their own social position. Senior officers wanted the most rigorous punishment for all the young officers involved in the rebellion. Yamashita urged leniency. Because of this, some superiors felt that he was siding with the rebels, and he was posted to Korea for eighteen months until criticism of his action cooled. Convinced that this was the end of his military career, he admitted later: "I felt I had no future in the Army, so I was always in the front line, where the bullets flew thickest. I sought only a place to die." That he survived made him a legendary leader.

In 1940, Yamashita was appointed Inspector General of the Japanese Air Force, and in this capacity he visited Hitler and Mussolini to study their methods of war. Publicly he declared, "I feel that Hitler's mind is spiritual, transcending material plans."

Privately he was less impressed, thought that the Führer was
"like a clerk."

On Yamashita's return to Japan, he was immediately given
command of the Twenty-fifth Army, then training to invade
Malaya and conquer Singapore, Britain's base that commanded
the sea approaches to Japan, Australia and New Zealand.

Yamashita trained his men on Hainan Island in conditions
approaching those of Malaya. They carried out innumerable
landings, lived rough, learned to travel with the minimum of
impedimenta. Each received a booklet, already referred to,
"Read this alone and the War can be won," which, in addition
to giving reasons for attacking Malaya, contained more immediately valuable hints on health in that country's humid climate,
care of weapons, and how to live off the land. On December 7
—simultaneously with the attack on Pearl Harbor—the attack
on Malaya began.

By that date, the majority of the British defenders still had
no clear idea why they had been posted to Malaya, away from
a war in Europe already more than two years old; away from
Britain under threat of German invasion, where, night after
night, their homes were being bombed. No one had thought it
necessary to produce an equivalent of the Japanese pamphlet for
them. Morale was poor, and for this Percival must bear some
share of blame.

Agreed, he could not help the fact that his troops were mainly
raw, that too many staff officers were mediocre, but training
was still geared to peace and not to war. Major Spencer Chapman, later to fight for most of the war behind the Japanese
lines, had arrived in 1941 to find "the High Command . . .
not in the least interested in guerilla warfare in any of its
forms."[2]

Unlike Yamashita, Percival was not cast in a character's mould.
He was correct, courageous—and colourless. Too many of his
soldiers did not even know what he looked like.

He held the D.S.O., and bar, the M.C., the French Croix
de Guerre, but in this situation personal bravery was not enough.

[2] *The Jungle Is Neutral* by F. Spencer Chapman.

The son of a Hertfordshire land agent, Percival had been educated at Rugby, where he played in the scrum and then joined a city firm as a clerk. Although twenty-seven when the First War began, he immediately enlisted as a private soldier. Within a month he was commissioned. By thirty he was a colonel commanding a front-line battalion. After the war, he made the army his career.

In 1921, posted to Ireland during "the troubles" he sent back a report on conditions which so impressed Churchill, then War Minister, and Lloyd George, the Prime Minister, that Churchill recommended him for a Staff College course, although he was over-age.

In fact, Percival became a distinguished student at the Camberley Staff College, at the Royal Naval College in Greenwich, and at the Imperial Defence College, while Yamashita, never a man for paper work, experienced the greatest difficulty in passing his entrance exam for the Tokyo War College, and was only allowed to enrol after several attempts.

But while Percival as a staff officer in Malaya in 1936, and as Army Commander five years later, could produce perfect proposals on paper, either for defence or attack, he lacked the ability to translate these paper plans successfully into performance. It was one thing to describe flanking movements, phased withdrawals and counter-attacks in a report; quite another to stage them in streaming rain, with bewildered, depressed troops —and many Indians under his command who had never seen a tank until they came face to face with one of Japanese make.

A tactical exercise without troops lacked the hard reality of men fleeing under crushing air superiority, the panic that left too many strategic bridges unblown during the retreat, and the almost complete breakdown of communications which made the civilian telephone line and the railway a main link between Percival's headquarters in Singapore and his fighting troops hundreds of miles up-country.

Percival's service in the '20s and '30s was in a country at peace; a spell in Nigeria, then as a battalion commander, then various staff appointments. Yamashita spent these years in the crucible of war with China, fighting in Manchuria, in Korea.

For the twenty years since 1921, when at American and Canadian pressure Britain abrogated the Anglo-Japanese Treaty, Japan smouldered under what she considered an intentional slight and humiliation, and became Britain's only potential enemy in the East.

The original purpose of the 1902 Anglo-Japanese alliance was to protect Japan, as a small country, against Russian ambitions and aggression. In fact, the war against Russia, which came three years later, ended with a decisive Japanese victory and, in the words of Churchill, "Japan now took her place among the Great Powers. The Japanese were themselves astonished at the respect with which they were viewed."

During the First World War, Japan sided with the Allies, but took little active part beyond seizing German possessions in the East. After the Russian Revolution, she moved into Siberia and had territorial ambitions in Manchuria, and North China, so that instead of being the underdog, she was now regarded as a potential bully.

At the Washington Disarmament Conference in 1921, the opportunity was taken to limit Japanese influence. America and Canada were eager for this because they were worried about the increase of Japanese immigration.

Churchill wrote that it was "with sorrow" that the treaty ended, "but as we had to choose between Japanese and American friendship, I had no doubts what our course should be."

This course ended in collision, for although the treaty was replaced with a vaguely phrased agreement, Japan felt she had lost face, and this feeling bred bitter resentment.

Because of Singapore's geographic position it was selected as the focus of British Far Eastern defence. Japan, in her crowded islands, cast envious eyes at the open spaces of Australia—and indeed Yamashita had a plan to land there. Singapore, lying between Australia and India, was—in those years of naval strategy and vestigial air power—an obvious choice as a pivot of defence; and since Japan was Britain's only conceivable enemy, a

Japanese attack on Singapore became a stock exercise for students in British Staff Colleges.

Each year, students invariably agreed that the best way to subdue Singapore would be to land high up the coast in Malaya and then drive south to Singapore Island's unprotected north shore.

Each year, too, in the Tokyo War College, the same exercise was studied, and Japanese students reached the same conclusions. The seventy-day campaign, which ended in humiliation in the Ford factory on that wet Sunday afternoon was the result of these rehearsals. Japan had learned from every one; Britain learned from none.

Because of Middle East priorities for supplies and aid to Russia in 1941, Malaya and Singapore were bottom of the list. As Churchill admitted later, "The whole Japanese menace lay in a sinister twilight." The fighting war was in Europe and not in Asia.

Percival, appointed General Officer Commanding, Malaya, in March 1941, and ordered to fly to Singapore at three days' notice, found that his flying boat was grounded by a mechanical fault. Such was Britain's shortage of spare parts, so low was Percival's priority, that no replacement could be found, and so his urgent departure was postponed for a further five weeks until a passage in another flying boat was available. When he reached Singapore he discovered that his delay typified Whitehall's assessment of the Far East importance.

He asked for minimum requirements of two tank regiments and 48 infantry battalions, plus 556 aircraft. He received no tanks at all, only 33 infantry battalions, mostly raw troops, a few heavy guns and 141 aircraft. Some, like the Vildebeestes, were barely capable of 100 m.p.h. The British aircraft that could have saved Singapore went to Russia instead. Most were lost in the Arctic convoys sunk by Nazi submarines.

Percival accepted this stoically. As he told me later, "It wouldn't have been any good winning the war in the East and losing the war in the West. Supposing we had lost the war in the West and finished up with Germany supreme—and they might have been if they had knocked Russia out. Britain would have been occupied by Germany. Then what would have been the use of an Empire saved in the East?"

Before the war, Percival played cricket for the Gentlemen of Essex. In war, as in peace, he stuck to the rules; no complaints, no excuses, although the game was all but over.

Yamashita saw Malaya for the first time when he landed in December 1941. But his widespread espionage net—Japanese fishermen, plantation and mine managers, merchants, barbers, photographers (almost unbelievably, the official photographer for the Singapore naval base was Japanese)—all these were his eyes and ears.

In contrast, although the British had occupied Malaya for more than a century, their Intelligence network was abysmal. As an economy measure, the Army even ceased to have its own Intelligence Service there in 1940.

British Army liaison with civil authorities was so weak that during the first Japanese air raid over Singapore, the city lights were blazing because no one could find the man with the power-house key to turn them out.

Too many civilians remained unimpressed by the sombre march of events. Even on the eve of Singapore's surrender, a British gunnery officer was told he needed permission from the golf club committee before he could mount guns on the links.

Of all imperial peoples the British in the British Isles knew least about their possessions. They had controlled far countries for so long that the word "empire" became a music-hall joke among the mass of people; something to be spoken of with patronage or shame among the left-wing intelligentsia, or those who would like to be so regarded.

Too few had any idea of the enormous benefits that had accrued to the peoples of the East through colonization: the roads, the bridges, the railways built across thousands of miles of desert and mountains; the schools, the hospitals, the cities, the health programmes, the rule of law and the incorruptibility of justice.

If the British knew so little about their own empire, it is

not to be wondered at that other friendly countries, such as the United States, knew far less. As a nation of immigrants and refugees from political or religious persecution, superimposed on emigrants from Britain, and, as a former colony, strongly anti-colonial, they were understandably willing, in the absence of truth, to believe the loudest voices denigrating European achievements in the East.

In fact, Columbus had discovered America entirely by mistake. He was not searching for a new world, but, even then, for a new route to the rich old trading world of the East.

In the fifteenth and sixteenth centuries, the East was the source of spices on which Europeans relied to keep their meat fresh in winter. These spices—and silk and jewels—fetched great sums, for apart from the routine hazards of shipwreck, mutiny and death by scurvy, the traders risked massacre when landing in the East, and piracy on their way home.

By the sixteenth century, Britain, Portugal and France, as the main European trading nations, had founded trading posts in India and elsewhere in the East. To guard these enclaves they enlisted locals, whom they dressed in European style uniforms.

Sometimes, local rulers would only give permission for a trading post to be established if the company's army would join forces with his own forces against some neighbouring ruler with whom he had a dispute.

Gradually, from such small beginnings, European nations came to control enormous tracts of land, sometimes entire countries— as Britain with India, Burma and Malaya; Holland with Java; Portugal with parts of India. They did not seek to do this, and the countries thus acquired, often far larger than their own, were an expensive embarrassment, because the European trading companies, like overseas commercial concerns today, were there to trade, not to take on new and costly political commitments. But if they refused a local ruler's request for help, then he might appeal elsewhere, and they could be driven out altogether. So, like the badger that must dig or have his nails curve into his own flesh, their unwanted, unwished-for Eastern empires grew.

By the early nineteenth century, the Dutch were the leading traders in Malaya. An executive of the British East India Company, Stamford Raffles, feared that British merchants were in danger of being driven out of Malaya entirely, so he suggested founding a new port there through which could be channelled all trade the Dutch did not already control, and which could also be a useful clearing point for every sort of British merchandise. Various sites were suggested, and, in 1819, he landed with a friend on an almost uninhabited island, south of the mainland, thirteen miles wide and twenty-seven miles long. It was called Singapore and Raffles was much impressed by its possibilities.

"It has been my good fortune to discover one of the most safe and extensive harbours in these seas, with every facility for protecting shipping in time of war, etc.," he wrote home to London. "In short, Singapore is everything we could desire, and I may consider myself most fortunate in the selection; it will soon rise into importance . . ."

Raffles took over the island on behalf of his company from the Sultan of Johore who ruled the most southern state of Malaya, for an annual rent of 5000 Spanish dollars, with another 3000 Spanish dollars every year for the local chief on the island. In return for this, he had permission to build "factories"—trading offices—and warehouses.

The East India Company thought he had wasted their money. Raffles returned to England in poor health. He started the London Zoo; then, his constitution weakened by years in the East, he died and, after his death, the East India Company indulged in acrimonious correspondence with his widow, claiming that Raffles, in acquiring Singapore, had exceeded his brief, and as a result his estate owed the company £22,000.

But within a year of acquiring Singapore, immigration of Chinese and Malays to work in the port had raised the population from roughly 150 to 10,000. And for the next century, Singapore and Malaya, which came under British rule, knew peace and a rising prosperity, based on enormous natural deposits of tin, plus the export of coffee, sugar, pepper, tapioca, gutta-percha, timber, resins and cane.

The First World War passed by Singapore, but demands for rubber for tyres made Malaya rich, because the Malaya rubber plantations (also started by the British) produced a third of the world's natural rubber. Deposits of tin provided half of all the world's tin demands. Prosperity and peace brought their own feeling of perpetual safety, and indeed, as we have seen, the West had no potential enemy in the East until 1921.

The Washington Conference that replaced the Anglo-Japanese Treaty of 1902, with a vague pact of friendship between Britain, Japan and the United States, also limited the size and number of warships. Britain and the United States, the great maritime powers, would have the ratio of five each to only three for Japan, who felt she had been snubbed. She was already touchy about immigration difficulties in the United States, and since, in the East, face is all, Britain in Malaya, and America in the Philippines, had created a cruel and implacable enemy for themselves.

Within a year, the British Government, realising too late the latent hostility of Japan, decided to select a base in Southeast Asia from which the Royal Navy could, if necessary, defend Malaya, Borneo and also help to defend Australia and New Zealand. Hong Kong was indefensible; Sydney, unsuitable; Singapore was eventually selected.

Under a Conservative government in Britain work was to begin at once. Then an election put the Socialists in power. Their theory of "collective security," of action by the League of Nations as opposed to action by individual countries to safe-guard their individual interests, was more important to them than arms, so work stopped on the base.

After another election—which the Conservatives won—work began again.

Throughout the 1920s, into the early thirties this stop-start continued, and the base was only opened in 1938, seventeen years after the need for it had been recognised.

But even more serious for Singapore, and so eventually for all the West, was the constant bickering between Navy and Air Force—in America as much as in Britain—as to the relative merits of the battleship and the bomber.

Navy traditionalists were convinced that a capital ship's armaments could drive off any torpedo-carrying aircraft. The Royal Air Force disputed this vehemently. Their argument ended sullenly in an unhappy compromise: Singapore would have some planes, plus fifteen-inch naval guns embedded in concrete pointing out to sea.

This was the only direction from which it was believed an attack could come, because the War Office assured successive British Governments that no invasion could come overland because of the thick jungle.

So Singapore's enormous base, with a floating dock large enough to take the *Queen Mary*, food and stores to supply the entire Royal Navy for three months, seventeen football pitches, churches, cinemas, a whole housing development for the employees, was still only a base and not a defensive position.

In the thirties, the nearest Japanese base was 1700 miles away. The British calculated on being able to move their main fleet to Singapore from anywhere in the world within seventy days, and Singapore could surely hold out for that long. Also, in those days, no war plane could fly non-stop for 1700 miles.

But the planners in peace discounted two items: that French Indo-China, only 300 miles from Malaya's east coast, could be used by the Japanese; and that the British fleet might be involved in other oceans and so unable to sail. When France fell in 1940, Japan occupied French Indo-China; and by the following year the British Navy was desperately committed to protecting Atlantic convoys and to action in the Mediterranean. Thus the plan to defend Singapore was useless, but was still pathetically adhered to, because no one came up with anything better.

The Americans learned as little from their naval manoeuvres in 1932, held to test the defences of Pearl Harbor against a surprise attack. A U.S. fleet of nearly two hundred ships sailed from the Californian coast across the Pacific to the Philippines.

One section was to simulate an assault, the others would act as defence.

Admiral H. E. Yarnell, a believer in aerial attack, took the aircraft carriers *Saratoga* and *Lexington*, with four escorting destroyers, ahead of the main force. As he hoped, he ran into bad weather twenty-four hours from Pearl Harbor; the defenders, expecting a huge fleet, did not spot six isolated vessels on the vast and misty sea.

Before dawn, on Sunday morning, February 7, 1932, he was within sixty miles of Oahu. In darkness, he catapulted away 152 planes that flew in over Pearl Harbor from the northeast—exactly the same direction as the second and deadly flight of Japanese planes came on another Sunday morning, December 7, 1941, at the same time as the first air raids over Singapore, which, in time, is sixteen hours ahead of Pearl Harbor.

Each group of planes in 1932, as in 1941, had its own task, its own target. Had Yarnell's planes carried real bombs they could have sunk the U.S. fleet while the ships lay lazily at anchor on that Sunday morning—as easily as the Japanese bombers did nine years later.

The lessons went unlearned; they were make-believe manoeuvres; things would have been different if it had been war, said the defenders afterwards. But, in the event, nothing was different; the Japanese saw to that.

On that dummy run in February 1932, the Japanese had observers on the high points of Oahu; they had agents in fishing sampans; they had waiters in bars and barbers in saloons to note what navy sailors and airmen said afterwards about the attack.

Their reports went back to Tokyo, for the Japanese Intelligence system was as efficient as their aircraft, and in their years of preparation, the Japanese built up as magnificent an espionage network in Pearl Harbor as they had throughout Malaya to advise them of what resistance to expect and where. Japanese fishing fleets would regularly appear off Malaya's coastline—as nowadays Russian trawlers carrying highly sophisticated electronic equipment, quite unnecessary for the landing of fish, sail inexplicably close to Western military targets, along American and European coasts.

Japanese photographers in most Malayan towns also offered cut rates to British soldiers for the privilege of developing and printing their photographs; some might be of military significance.

Singapore boasted many Japanese masseurs and barbers, plus Japanese-owned toy shops and Japanese shops selling fine silk. Other Japanese managed rubber plantations and tin mines.

Many of these key Japanese nationals went home quietly to Japan in November 1941. They returned the following month in uniform with the invading Japanese army as guides and translators.

The Japanese attacked Malaya on December 7, along the narrowest point of the Malay peninsula. This, the Kra Isthmus, should also have been the easiest to defend against attack, but it lies just north of the Siamese border.

The British had planned to cross this border and hold this vital neck of land, but they were under strict orders not to cross into Siam territory unless they were certain the Japanese were heading for Malaya. Although reconnaissance planes had seen the Japanese fleets of cargo vessels, and landing craft packed with troops, heading toward the peninsula, obviously they could not be totally certain they were a genuine invading force.

Britain was anxious not to appear the aggressor against Japan, because there was no guarantee that the United States would come into the war unless Japan attacked them. The fact that Japan attacked Pearl Harbor simultaneously with Singapore meant that she was doomed for defeat. Otherwise, it is likely that she could have kept her conquests.

In the autumn of 1941, Churchill wished to send a fleet to the Far East to deter Japan from any planned aggression. But the aircraft carrier designated for this purpose ran aground in trials off Jamaica, so the fleet consisted of two British capital ships, *Repulse* and *Prince of Wales*, plus a motley collection of old, slow vessels scratched together from other oceans.

This plan might have succeeded in an earlier age, but without air cover it could have only one outcome. The *Repulse* and *Prince of Wales*, pride of the Royal Navy, were sunk within hours of their first engagement. The arguments as to the relative values of bombs and battleships ended with them.

Meanwhile, fighting down the humid jungles of Malaya, where the nights were loud with the whine of mosquitoes, the rusty rachets of crickets, the strange calls of wild animals, all under streaming rain, the British, Australians and Indians fell back before the Japanese.

When they offered strong resistance, at a crossroads or a contour, the Japanese invaders simply by-passed them. Without air cover, without strong leadership, without faith in why they were fighting, the defenders' rearguard action soon became a retreat. Bridges that should have been destroyed were left unblown; either the Japanese or fifth columnists cut electric charge wires, or charge wires, laid too hastily, did not connect, or rain damped the fuses.

Atmospheric conditions ruined radio reception of army sets; runners and despatch riders were ambushed; messages never got through. And all the while, back and back fell the defenders, while the Japanese, landing on beaches on both sides of the peninsula, using dozens of small craft they captured in Penang harbour, seemed to be everywhere and so appeared omnipotent.

On through the steamy jungles, which British military maps marked hopefully as "unpenetrable," the Japanese came, often disguised as Malayans; others floated along rivers on logs or in canoes; thousands cycled down the long straight roads to Singapore. Ironically, they had only school atlases for maps so they did not know that the British War Office considered the jungles through which they came such a serious barrier to their progress.

They seized airfields, empty because the retreating defenders had no planes to fly from them, and used them for their own. Instead of bringing trucks, they captured British vehicles and used them.

They fought because they knew what they were fighting for —Japanese domination, Japanese superiority. Thirty-six years earlier, the Japanese Navy, then unknown and derisory, had beaten the Russian Navy, which had outnumbered it in ships and men. Now they were beating the West whose army also outnumbered theirs. And with every new success, the Japanese appeared more invincible, until, to the depressed, retreating defenders, they appeared as unbeatable supermen.

The British, Indian and Australian defenders of Malaya were all far from home, in a humid, alien country which for a hundred years had not known close involvement in any war. The local people did not feel themselves personally involved in the conflict; it was a struggle between other races as to who should rule them.

As General Percival later told this writer: "The civilian population were rather naturally saying to themselves: 'Who's coming out top dog here?' So there wasn't very much help from them."

Worse, many Asiatics went over to aid the Japanese actively. Groups of Australians and Europeans, escaping after the surrender, either in small boats to other islands, or trekking through the jungle, were intercepted and handed over to face almost certain death.

Churchill and Sir John Dill, the Chief of the Imperial General Staff, had both advocated that a strong defensive line be made across Johore, the southernmost state in Malaya, overlooking the channel to Singapore Island. Churchill could see the danger of using up men and material in a retreat. Percival, on the other hand, was playing for time, hoping for reinforcements. He lost the men, the equipment and the game.

His troops streamed across the concrete causeway into Singapore, leaving the tower in the palace of the Sultan of Johore as a lookout point for General Yamashita, from which he directed the final assault.

Worse, the causeway with its railway line and road was not effectively demolished. At low tide, water was only four feet deep; even the Japanese could wade across—and they did.

Now, too late, the force of the fallacy about Singapore's impregnability was realised in Whitehall. The big guns all pointed south and east, to sea; there were none pointing north in the direction of the enemy. As Churchill wrote when he was informed that there were no permanent fortifications on the north of the island: "Even more astounding, no measures worth speaking of had been taken by any of the commanders since the war began. . . . The possibility of Singapore having no landward defences no more entered into my mind than that of a battleship being launched without a bottom."

General Percival controlled so few planes that he had to borrow a private aircraft to fly from Singapore to the front. Usually, he visited it by train. His main communication with front-line commanders was through the peacetime civil telephone system. His generals could be cut off in a mid-report so that a private subscriber might make a local call.

Indian and Malay labourers and coolies fled early on from the docks. Troops had to unload their own guns and then trundle them into action. Some Hurricane fighter aircraft was never uncrated at all.

Ironically, the Japanese, the world's premier technical imitators, had copied those qualities of character that had made the West great: enterprise, audacity, disregard for ridiculous rules, and (the ultimate indignity) even their plan to land in the north and move south.

It was a battle of East and West, coloured and white, between those who had to win and those who feared they could lose. And in losing that battle they also lost so much more as well. They lost their psychological superiority, their belief in their right to rule; and when they had lost that, there was little else left to lose.

Curiously, Yamashita suspected that Percival was playing for time in making his request for surrender. Accordingly, he ringed the Ford factory with a thousand armed soldiers in case the meeting was simply a trick to extract one last advantage.

Sir Archibald Wavell, then Commander-in-Chief of the Far East, said later that three more weeks might have changed the outcome. Percival told me that if he could have held out for only two more weeks, reinforcements would have arrived and counter-attacks begun. Yamashita put the time at one week. He desperately needed a quick campaign, because of his own supply difficulties. His men were down to one hundred rounds of ammunition when they entered Singapore. Shells for his big guns were so scarce, food and petrol stores so low, that his officer in charge of supplies, Colonel Ikatini, begged him to delay the assault on the city. Instead, Yamashita opened up an immense but brief barrage, gambling everything on its psychological effect on the defenders after seventy days in retreat.

Both Percival and Yamashita began that Sunday in prayer. Percival received Holy Communion at his headquarters; Yamashita bowed solemnly in the direction of the Emperor's palace in Tokyo.

Characteristically, they also ended that climactic day in prayer. Percival prayed privately; it happened to be his daughter's twelfth birthday. He had fought his best with the best his government had given him. Now he prepared to bear captivity, the defeat of his army, the ruin of his career, with courage and no complaint.

Late that night, Yamashita walked alone to the edge of the ruined city. The Japanese flag waved above Cathay Building, the highest building in Singapore. Yamashita bowed in the direction of his Emperor. Like some old Roman legionary of the past, far from home, he had done that which he had set out to do. *Quod erat demonstrandum.*

In fact, he had done far more. Agreed, within three years the ever-turning wheel of fortune would revolve, and Percival, released from a Manchurian prison camp, would watch Yamashita in turn surrender to the Americans in Manila—to be sentenced to death, on December 7, 1945, the fourth anniversary of the attack on Singapore.

But for the West, and its influence in the East, that came too late.

Yamashita, by his victory in Singapore, had cut the arteries of an empire, of all the European empires. On that Sunday, centuries of white supremacy began to bleed away. Nothing in the relationship between East and West, Orient and Occident, would ever be the same.

Chapter One

THE MAN who founded Singapore, Thomas Stamford Raffles, was in many ways a prototype of a new generation of empire-builders. Hard-working, burning with ambition and high ideals, he was a self-made man who owed nothing to aristocratic connections and little to formal education. He was born in 1781 aboard the merchant ship of which his father was then captain, off the coast of Jamaica. His family's later poverty forced him to leave school at fourteen and to start work as an "extra clerk"—virtually an office boy—at the offices of the East India Company in Leadenhall Street.

"I have never ceased to deplore the necessity which withdrew me so early from school," he wrote years later. "I had hardly been two years at a boarding school, when I was withdrawn, and forced to enter on the busy scenes of public life, then a mere boy."[1]

He worked in the London office for ten years, and although there were already signs that his health was not good (at one time it was feared that he had consumption) his "peculiar qualifications" earned him rapid promotion, "notwithstanding the claims of others, who possessed an interest of which he could not boast."

At the same time, he devoted his spare time to mastering French and studying zoology and botany. In 1805, Raffles went East for the first time as Assistant Secretary to the new administration in Malaya. Unlike many other Europeans who served overseas for years and yet never learned more than a few words of the language, Raffles studied Malay on the voyage, and on his arrival threw himself into the study of Malay history and lit-

[1] Quoted from *Memoirs of the Life and Public Service of Sir T. S. Raffles* by Lady Raffles.

erature. As a result, he soon made himself indispensable to the Governor, was promoted to Secretary, and proved to be so efficient in this post that, three years later, the Governor could write home of "the unwearied zeal and assiduity with which he has, since the formation of the establishment, devoted his talents to the furtherance of the company's interests; his unremitting attention to the duties of the most laborious office under this government, added to those of Registrar of the Recorder's Court, which, at the period of its establishment, he voluntarily and gratuitously undertook."

But working at such pressure in the dripping humidity of Penang proved too much for his frail constitution, and Raffles suffered two serious illnesses, the second almost fatal. As a result he was forced to spend some months of convalescence in the more wholesome climate of Malacca. On his arrival there he found to his dismay that the East India Company, influenced by Penang merchants who were jealous of Malacca's trade, was proposing to evacuate the population of twenty thousand and close the port; already the fortifications had been knocked down.

At the end of three months' leave, in October 1808, Raffles returned to Penang and lost no time in delivering to the Governor and Council a long report on the Malacca situation. In this brilliant document[2] he forcefully pointed out the strategic and commercial importance of Malacca, situated at the narrowest part of the Straits and commanding one of the two main trade routes to the Malay Archipelago and the Far East. Having read what Raffles had to say, the Council instantly decided to reserve its decision. Malacca was to be kept for the moment.

This Malacca report was Raffles' first important contribution to the development of the British Empire in the East. It was also clearly intended to procure for its author a more responsible and a more powerful position in the East India Company's service. But, to Raffles' annoyance and disappointment, the Company seemed unaccountably slow to recognise his qualities. At the end of the year he was still bogged down in his work of petty administration in Penang. True, the place was lively enough, although

[2] Quoted in *Raffles of the Eastern Isles* by C. E. Wurtzburg.

Mrs. Raffles seems to have enjoyed the round of parties more than her husband did; but greatness, Raffles knew, was not to be attained by dancing all night, and his ambition was spurring him on.

In a moment of despair he wrote to a friend in England: "I am convinced my health will never permit my holding this office many years. If therefore I am not to work for a seat in Council, or some quiet place in the Government, I must either fall a sacrifice or apply for the first vacancy in the Collectorship or other subordinate office. My constitution was always delicate; with care . . . it would last as long here as in England. Without it, it will soon break up. I am afraid they will work the willing horse to death. . . ."

But the willing horse was not, after all, fated to die unrecognised on the steamy island of Penang. A year after he had delivered his report on Malacca, Raffles heard from a friend in Calcutta, to whom he had sent a copy, that Lord Minto, the Governor-General of India since 1806, had seen the report and was "greatly pleased" with it. This was the opportunity of which he had dreamed. In June 1810, Raffles set sail for Calcutta where he had an interview with Lord Minto. The original purpose of his journey was to try and obtain from Minto the Governor-Generalship of the Moluccas, a not very important group of islands which had been accidentally captured by an English raiding party. But by the time he arrived, the appointment had been filled. Raffles, undeterred, drew to Lord Minto's attention the Dutch island of Java.

"On the mention of Java, his Lordship cast a look of such scrutiny, anticipation and kindness upon me, as I shall never forget. 'Yes,' said he, 'Java is an interesting island; I shall be happy to receive any information you can give me concerning it.'"

In fact, Lord Minto had been interested in Java for some months before he discussed it with Raffles. Although the government in London was anxious to contain Dutch influence in the East, it was prepared only to wound, not to kill. Part of Minto's instructions concerning Java, received in 1810, urged him to "subdue the Dutch Government, to destroy the fortifications, to distribute the ordnance, arms and military stores amongst the native chiefs and inhabitants, and then to retire from the country."

The East India Company was even more cautious. It did not want Java at all. If the Dutch could not make the island pay, then what use was it to the British?

Minto, like Raffles, regarded this attitude as feeble and un-enterprising; Java could be *made* profitable. In any case, it was there, under foreign domination, and Minto disliked that fact as much as did Raffles. Furthermore, when Napoleon annexed Holland there was a danger that the island would be used as a French base for operations against the British. This last factor overcame the prudence of the ministers in London; Minto was authorised to attack. All he needed now was a man who could provide him with detailed intelligence, enter into negotiations with local chiefs before the assault and organise an administration afterwards. In Raffles he found his man.

Raffles returned to Malacca as Agent to the Governor-General, with the task of preparing for an expedition against Java. He tackled this job with his usual stupendous energy. Java caught his imagination, and in one of his reports of Minto he wrote: "I have now only to congratulate your Lordship on the most splendid prospect which any administration has beheld since our first acquisition of India: the pacification of India completed, the tranquillity and prosperity of our Eastern possessions secured, the total expulsion of the European enemy from the Eastern Seas, and the justice, humanity and moderation of the British Govern-ment as much exemplified in fostering and leading on new races of subjects and allies in the cause of improvement as in the undaunted courage and resolution of British soldiers in rescuing them from oppression."[3]

The subsequent invasion of Java took place in June 1811, and was largely a ceremonial affair. Lord Minto himself sailed with the invading troops. The huge fleet landed unopposed. For a

[3] Quoted in *Raffles of Singapore* by Sir R. Coupland.

month there was sporadic fighting as the British advanced, then, on September 18, 1811, the Dutch Governor-General, Janssens, formally surrendered. Before leaving for Calcutta, Minto appointed Raffles Lieutenant-Governor of Java. "Whilst we are in Java," he told him, "let us do all the good we can."

Raffles set to work. He had inherited a bankrupt country with no proper administration. For five years he struggled heroically to repair the economy, to introduce justice and tax reform, to put Java on its feet. His reward was the hostility of the army, the apathy of the native population and, since his economic forecast proved over-optimistic, the distrust of the directors of the East India Company. In 1816, he was recalled to London, the directors declaring that Raffles had made the occupation of Java a "source of financial embarrassment to the British Government."

As ex-Governor of Java, Raffles was lionised by fashionable society, and made many new and influential friends. He wrote a history of Java, and dedicated it to the Prince Regent, who was sufficiently flattered to see that the author was knighted, after expressing his high sense of "the eminent services he had rendered to his country in the government of Java."

In spite of his apparent failure, Raffles had achieved far more than anyone supposed. In the words of his biographer, C. E. Wurtzburg: "He was the first to introduce into colonial administration the new liberalism of which, in Europe, England was the chief nursery. A chapter had been closed; it was Raffles who opened the new chapter. . . ."

It was British policy to maintain a strong Netherlands as a balance to French power, and, accordingly, the Dutch were now re-established in most of their old possessions in the East Indies, including Java and Malacca. Indeed, the only British stations left in the Malayan archipelago were Bencoolen, on the west coast of Sumatra, and Penang. It was to Bencoolen that Raffles, now Sir Stamford Raffles, was sent as Lieutenant-Governor in October 1817.

The post was intended as an honourable retreat for the ex-Governor of Java, but Raffles was not yet ready to retire without a struggle. At first, it did not look a very promising appointment;

Bencoolen had been neglected; it was not well situated for trade, and it had been badly hit by earthquakes.

"This is, without exception, the most wretched place I ever beheld," Raffles wrote shortly after his arrival. "I cannot convey to you an adequate idea of the state of ruin and dilapidation which surrounds me. . . . The natives say that Bencoolen is now a *tàna mati* (dead land). In truth, I could never have conceived any thing half so bad."

But Raffles was not easily discouraged, and immediately set about reform.

"We shall try and make it better: and if I am well supported from home, the west coast may yet be turned to account. You must, however, be prepared for the abolition of slavery; the emancipation of the country people from the forced cultivation of pepper; the discontinuance of the gaming and cock-fighting farms; and a thousand other practices equally disgraceful and repugnant to the British character and government. A complete and thorough reform is indispensable, and reductions must be made throughout."

These reforms were immediately put in hand, although the abandonment of the pepper monopoly and of the practice of farming out the gambling and cock-fighting rights, from which the Government drew much of its revenue, was not well received in London. At the same time Raffles, accompanied by his wife, embarked on a series of hazardous explorations into the interior of Sumatra, and he took what he regarded as the first step towards establishing British influence throughout the island by concluding a conditional treaty of alliance with the Sultan of Menangkabu. But the treaty was never ratified by the Bengal Government, and meantime the Dutch, now back in possession, were rapidly extending and strengthening their trading monopoly in all the ports of the archipelago, so that Raffles began to fear that British trade would be excluded altogether from the islands.

Before leaving England, Raffles had submitted to Canning (then president of the Board of Control) a memorandum proposing the foundation of a new port within the archipelago as a centre for all the native trade that was still free of Dutch control and as an *entrepôt* for British merchandise.

In 1818 he visited Lord Moira, who had now become the Marquess of Hastings, in Calcutta, and obtained his support for this project—provided it could be done without provoking the Dutch. Raffles had in mind the Riau Islands as being suitable for his purpose, but in case the Dutch forestalled him there, he persuaded Hastings to instruct him to "open a negotiation with the Chief of Johore" for a site in his dominions further south.

"It is expressly to be understood," Raffles' orders stated, "and it will be incumbent on you always to keep in mind, that the object in fixing upon a Post of this nature is not the extension of territorial influence but strictly limited to the occupation of an advantageous position for the protection of our commerce. These instructions are framed under an impression that the Dutch have not formed any establishment at Riau. In the event of their doing so at the period of your arrival, you will, of course, abstain from all negotiations and collision." On December 12, 1818, Raffles sailed from Calcutta.

When he reached Penang he found that the Dutch had indeed settled at Riau. He also found that the British Governor of Penang, Colonel Bannerman, was violently opposed to the whole enterprise. Bannerman was terrified of offending the Dutch, and determined not to get into trouble with the directors of the Company as he was certain that Raffles would, sooner or later. No doubt the Colonel was also jealous, but Raffles was undismayed, and sailed on to Malacca, where he picked up Major Farquhar, who had recently handed the town over to the Dutch.

Since Riau was ruled out as a site, the two men investigated the possibilities of the Carimon Islands, but a marine survey showed that they were unsuitable. Finally, on January 28, 1819, they landed on the almost uninhabited island of Singapore. The island was virtually unknown, but Raffles had heard of it in the course of his researches into Malay history, for it was the site of an ancient city whose ruins could still be seen.

"Here I am at Singapore," he wrote to a friend, "true to my

word, and in the enjoyment of all the pleasure which a footing on such classic ground must inspire. . . . This place possesses an excellent harbour, and every thing that can be desired for a British port in the island of St. John's, which forms the south-western point of the harbour.

"We have commanded an intercourse with all the ships passing through the Straits of Singapore. We are within a week's sail of China, close to Siam, and in the very seat of the Malayan Empire. This, therefore, will probably be my last attempt. If I am deserted now, I must fain return to Bencoolen, and become philosopher."

In another letter, he wrote: "Our station completely outflanks the Straits of Malacca, and secures a passage for our China ships at all times, and under all circumstances. It has further been my good fortune to discover one of the most safe and extensive harbours in these seas, with every facility for protecting shipping in time of war, &c.

"In short, Singapore is every thing we could desire, and I may consider myself most fortunate in the selection; it will soon rise into importance; and with this single station alone I would undertake to counteract all the plans of Mynheer; it breaks the spell; and they are not longer the exclusive sovereigns of the Eastern seas."

Raffles' instructions from Lord Hastings had been to establish a British post "with the consent of the native government," and without a quarrel with the "Netherlandish authorities." The local chief, the Temenggong of Johore, told Raffles that the Dutch had made no claim to Singapore and that the British could buy land for a factory there or in Johore. But the Temenggong was only a subordinate chief, owing allegiance to the Sultan of Johore, and the Sultan, whose seat was at Riau, was a Dutch puppet and so could not be expected to ratify an agreement granting land to the British.

Accordingly, Raffles decided to appoint a new Sultan and then negotiate with him. Such a move would mean that, technically at least, he was keeping to his brief. There was some justification for his action, because the Sultan, Abdu'r-Rahman, was a younger son who had been enthroned by the Underking of Riau in the absence of his elder brother Hosein at the time of their father's death in 1812.

The Underking, a member of the warlike Bugis race, originally from Celebes, who were at this time acquiring a dominant influence as the power behind the throne in several Malay states, claimed that he had merely acted in accordance with the old Malay custom that the new Sultan must be enthroned before the old one was buried. This may have been so, but no doubt his real motive in appointing a younger brother who would be dependent on himself, was to increase his own influence. In any case, Raffles, who in 1813 had himself recognised Abdu'r-Rahman as Sultan, now sent for Hosein, who arrived from Riau disguised as a fisherman.

On February 6 Hosein was installed at Singapore as Sultan of Johore, and on the same day Raffles signed a treaty with him under which the British were free to erect factories in return for annual payments of 5000 Spanish dollars to the Sultan and 3000 dollars to the Temenggong.

The new Sultan and the Temenggong were probably not displeased with their bargain, and it is likely that they knew of the liberality and justice of Raffles' administration in Java. But Java had, after all, been handed back to the Dutch, and they seem to have doubted the ability of the British to protect them. To insure themselves against possible Dutch vengeance, they therefore wrote a diplomatic letter to Timmerman Thyssen, the Dutch Governor of Malacca, explaining that they had acted under compulsion.

Thyssen was furious, and it was rumoured that he was about to attack; Bannerman, the Governor of Penang, refused to send troops to assist the colonists and wrote to Lord Hastings recommending a withdrawal. But Hastings had been encouraged by Raffles' enthusiastic account of Singapore, and replied firmly that "We think your Government entirely wrong in determining so broadly against the propriety of the step taken by Sir Stamford Raffles."

To the Dutch protests, he replied politely that he had tried too late to prevent Raffles establishing a post in the Eastern Archipelago, but that Singapore could not now be abandoned "on your demand without subscribing to the rights which you claim, and of which we are not satisfied, thereby awkwardly forestalling the judgment which was to have taken place at home."

In August, the Company's Secret Committee wrote to Lord Hastings that Raffles had disobeyed his instructions by risking a collision with the Dutch in the Straits of Malacca, and that his record had "rendered doubtful the expediency of employing him at all in any negotiation or undertaking in the Eastern Seas." But they would take no action before receiving the explanations of the Governor-General, and Lord Hastings was becoming increasingly convinced of the value of Singapore.

"We could not but expect," he replied, "that in the event of our securing a station which would baffle the injurious policy of our neighbours, they would not fail to impugn our right to take possession of such a spot by advancing some prior title to it."

The threatened Dutch attack never took place, and the astonishing growth of Singapore soon caused the Company to revise their opinion of the morality of taking it. Within a year, Malay and Chinese immigration had raised the population from about 150 to 10,000; in 1820, 35,000 tons of shipping used the port. By 1825, the value of its trade was more than double that of Penang and Malacca combined. There could be no question of withdrawal from so valuable an acquisition, and in 1824 the position was stabilised by an Anglo-Dutch treaty (the Treaty of London) under the terms of which Britain retained Singapore but surrendered Bencoolen and all claims in Sumatra in return for Malacca. The equator was recognised as the dividing line between the two spheres of influence, and there was little further friction.

Raffles himself was able to spend only a few months in Singapore before returning to his post at Bencoolen. He returned to Singapore once only, in October 1822, when he took over the government of the island for nine months before returning to England. He was aware that Singapore was his greatest achievement in the East; his three children had died in Bencoolen, and he now had little else to live for.

"Rob me not of this my political child," he wrote, "and you may yet see me at home in all my wonted spirits, and with an elasticity about me which will bear me up against all that party spirit can do to depress me."

There was much to do, for Major Farquhar, whom he had left as Resident, had disobeyed instructions and permitted slave trading, farmed out the cock-fighting and gambling rights, and sold some of the best land to speculators.

Land was, therefore, bought back for public buildings, slavery and the slave trade were absolutely and finally forbidden, and so was gambling, a reform that was to prove less durable. Raffles had new plans drawn up for controlling the development of the town, he instituted a new system of administration and introduced British law, and devised a system of revenue, with no tax on the trade. Singapore was to be a free port, open to the ships of every nation, free of duty.

Finally, in June 1823, Raffles left for London. He had intended to go into Parliament, but he was not well enough to do so. His years in the East, his struggles against his superiors ignorant of a situation so far away from London; frustration, disappointment, all against a background of an enervating climate, had undermined his constitution. He had to retire to the country, and this he did in 1825. He bought a small estate near Mill Hill, some miles to the north of London.

While in London he had found time to establish a Zoological Society, with himself as president, and to obtain from the Government a site in the Regents Park for "a collection of living animals, such as never yet existed in ancient or modern times." Raffles did not live long after this; he died in July 1826, the day before his forty-fifth birthday, of apoplexy. During his last year, he was harassed by a demand from the East India Company which he had served so well, for £22,000, for items of expenditure which had been sanctioned by the Bengal Government but never ratified by the directors in London. After his death, the Company settled with his widow for £10,000.

As Frank Swettenham, one-time Governor of the Straits Settlements and author of the standard history of British Malaya,
later pointed out, Raffles remained practically unheard of in
England, although it was entirely to him that the English owed
the possession of Singapore, "the gateway to the East, a naval
base of the highest importance, a great commercial centre and
the most prosperous of the British colonies. It led to the extension
of British influence in Malaya and South East Asia, and to the
opening up of Australia and New Zealand.

"No British party and no British Government can claim to
have taken any part in its acquisition, except by grudgingly
assenting to what had been done almost without their knowing,
and entirely against their wishes."

Indeed, for nearly a hundred years no one even knew where
Raffles was buried. Then his grave was accidentally discovered in
1914 in Hendon churchyard.

*   *   *

The British had come to the East for trade. They had settled,
and in order to continue trading, had absorbed whole countries.
Once these countries could manage their own affairs, then the
British would hand the governing of their affairs back to them,
and concentrate on her first concern: trade. That was the oft-
repeated intention, but gradually this attitude underwent a subtle
change. From being supremely confident, they suddenly began
to have doubts.

Would they not lose the prestige essential and endemic in an
imperial race if they admitted that the subject races, of different
coloured skin, were their equal as human beings?

Surely they could not be equal or they would not be subject to
alien rule; like the white men, they would be in charge of their
own countries, their own destiny.

In the very early twentieth century, the colour bar began as
a physical separation, and then moved to the intellectual plane,
with infinitely more dangerous results.

In the view of this writer, the Boer War in South Africa,

which aroused strong liberal protest in Britain, made the British realise for the first time, either consciously or subconsciously, that they were from a small northern island, a long distance away, and not markedly superior to other nationalities, save possibly in their abilities to navigate and to trade.

Although some administrators and some soldiers were men of genius, most were not. The fiascos of the Afghan war, the Crimea campaign, the Indian Mutiny and finally the Boer War, all within a space of roughly fifty years, however these disasters were disguised and camouflaged, showed that the British, while often being remarkably brave, could also be at least as inefficient and haphazard.

They were in any case numerically outnumbered by thousands to one in their Eastern possessions, and should the so-called subject peoples indulge in a concerted and co-ordinated rebellion, the issue could have only one outcome.

Agreed that reinforcements and gunboats would eventually arrive to avenge them, but not before weeks or even months had passed, such were the distances involved; and this delay would not help the unfortunate British minority. Thus the first seeds of doubt about their imperial mission began to grow.

There was also another reason. The opening of the Suez Canal in 1869 had reduced the distance from London to Bombay from 11,500 miles (the distance by way of the Cape) to 6400 miles, and this resulted in a quite unexpected change of attitude in British officials and merchants who were posted to the East. Whereas before this they had often regarded their posting as permanent, the dramatic cut in the distance between London and the East made them regard their stay there as being temporary. They would enjoy their time in India, in Malaya, in Burma, in China, but it was now only endured as a means to an early retirement back in Britain on a fine pension, and in a style of life for which they could not otherwise have hoped.

With improving communications, and speedier vessels, their wives and families accompanied them East, although their children were often sent home to England to school. Their wives had no knowledge of conditions in the East, and in the writer's own experience many who had spent ten or even twenty years in Asiatic countries would be curiously proud of the fact that they could not speak more than a few words of the local language. They would explain that to learn it was unnecessary; the only Asiatics with whom they came in contact—servants, shopkeepers and the like—could speak sufficient English for their purposes.

These wives also had no knowledge of indigenous customs or religions, and they did not feel their lack. Also, they resented the growing wealth of many Indians and Asiatics and so withdrew into their own enclaves behind high walls of snobbery and race. Gradually, as had happened to the empires of Greece and Rome, to China under the Dowager Empress, to the old Ottoman Empire, change and disaffection in the outer marches went unchecked, because they were unknown.

Where once there had been warmth and comradeship, now there was coolness, an invisible barrier based on fear and prejudice and ignorance. The old paternalism of the West gave way to a more rigid and formal association, built on false values and empty protocol.

The late Aga Khan once recalled how, at a party he gave for some British and Indian officials in Bombay, his cousin mentioned in the course of conversation that the Arabs had ruled Spain for five hundred years, but in the end had passed from that country. To his surprise, his British guests felt that they were being subtly insulted.

"We will not have such comparisons made," they said. "Our rule is permanent, not something that lasts a few centuries and then disappears. Even to think as you think is disloyal."[4]

Loyal or disloyal, their empire had, at that time, rather less than fifty years to run.

[4] *Memoirs of the Aga Khan.*

Chapter Two

DURING these years, Singapore grew with astonishing rapidity to become the most important commercial centre in Southeast Asia. As a result, trade at Penang and Malacca (which the British had acquired from the Dutch in exchange for Bencoolen in 1824) slowly declined. Penang's revenue never justified the top-heavy administration with which the island had been endowed when it became a presidency in 1805; therefore, in 1830, the administrative system was readjusted. Penang and Malacca became residencies responsible to the Govenor of Singapore, who, in turn, took orders from the Governor-General in India. It was at about this time that the term "Straits Settlements" became current, and the Governor became known as the Governor of the Straits Settlements.

It was the policy of the East India Company to avoid any interference or military commitments in the Malay States, and for some time the three British ports, with their growing and largely Chinese trading communities, continued as trading stations and as staging posts on the China route, more or less detached from the political affairs of the Malay peninsula. The wisdom of this policy seemed amply confirmed by an absurd incident which occurred in 1831. Owing to an official's mistake about the financial obligations of the little state of Naning (on the borders of Malacca) to the former Dutch Government, the Straits Government became involved in an admittedly unjust war which cost £100,000, and resulted in the annexation of a territory whose revenues never covered the cost of its administration.

Nonetheless, some interference did take place, largely in response to the growing power of Siam. In 1821, the Sultan of Kedah's fears were realised when his country was invaded by the Siamese. The Sultan fled to Penang and from this base continued to organise resistance to the invaders. This gave rise to a rather delicate situation, for the Siamese could be in a position to revoke the treaty by which Kedah had ceded Penang to the British, and the Company made urgent attempts to come to an arrangement with Siam. Two missions were sent to Bangkok; the second succeeded in 1826 in obtaining a treaty which gave the Company the right to trade with territories under Siamese control, in return for British recognition of the Siamese position in Kedah. The ex-Sultan of Kedah was not to be permitted to live in Penang, Perak, Selangor or Burma, and he was removed, protesting, to Malacca, while British ships patrolled the Kedah coast to prevent him from running arms to his supporters.

Meanwhile, the Siamese were attempting to extend their control to Perak, but this Governor Fullerton of Penang decided (apparently on his own initiative) to prevent. In 1822 he had sent ships which frustrated a sea invasion of Perak, and he now concluded a treaty with the Sultan of Perak, guaranteeing him British support against an attack from Siam or any of the Malay States. The states on the east coast, however, received no such guarantee. During the 1820s Siam gained virtually complete control over Kelantan, while Trengganu was forced to acknowledge Siamese suzerainty by sending tribute every three years.

For the ex-Sultan of Kedah, at least, there was a fairly happy ending. In 1842, the Siamese, tired of constant guerilla warfare, accepted his submission and reinstalled him as Sultan of a somewhat reduced state. As a punishment for his misbehaviour, the part of Kedah which is now called Perlis was partitioned off and became a separate state under its own Sultan. Both Perlis and Kedah remained tributaries of Siam.

On one other occasion there was a danger of a clash between British and Siamese forces. In 1858 a rebellion broke out in Pahang, led by a certain Wan Ahmad, brother of the reigning Bendahara. Wan Ahmad claimed that the previous Bendahara, their father, had intended his two sons to succeed him as joint rulers, but after four years of civil war the brothers still disagreed. Wan Ahmad fled to Bangkok, where he received support from the Siamese, who were no doubt anxious to extend their influence to Pahang. A Siamese invasion fleet was assembled at Trengganu; Governor Cavanagh of Singapore saw this as a threat to British trade with Pahang, and sent a warship, which shelled the fort at Trengganu. The situation might have developed into a war between Britain and Siam, but two months later the Bendahara himself died, and in the absence of any other candidate, Wan Ahmad succeeded him unopposed. He later dropped the inferior title of Bendahara for the title of Sultan, thus symbolising his independence, and for the rest of his reign contrived to remain on good terms with both Britain and Siam.

Among the Malays, piracy was long considered an honourable profession, and the rapid development of Singapore as a commercial centre also made it a lucrative one. One of the most notorious pirate lairs was the northwest coast of Borneo. In 1835, Europeans and Chinese businessmen in Bengal submitted a petition to the British Parliament in London and to the Government of India at Calcutta, complaining about their losses at the hands of Malayan pirates operating from Borneo. In reply to this petition, the British sent six warships to Singapore in 1836. These included a steamship called the *Diana,* and she could outmanoeuvre the pirate galleys, which could always escape the attentions of hostile sailing ships since they could be rowed fast and did not depend on the wind. Piracy decreased for a while, but revived in the 1840s. By this time, though, a remarkable character had arrived on the scene, an Englishman named James Brooke. He had fought in the first Anglo-Burmese War and been seriously wounded. In 1830 he sailed to China and was so impressed with the beauty of the Malay peninsula and outraged by the devastation caused by pirates that when his father died he fitted out his own yacht, the *Royalist,* of 140 tons, picked a crew, and in 1839 arrived in Borneo, ostensibly to carry out a programme of exploration and scientific research.

Brooke found the native state of Sarawak in revolt against the Sultan of Brunei. He made friends with the Sultan's uncle, Pangeran Muda Hashim, and in return for help in dealing with the hostile Dyaks of Sarawak, he was offered the governorship of that state. He completely stamped out the rebellion and won the confidence of the Malays and Dyaks who had long suffered under Brunei's misrule. Having established peace he set about introducing good government in Sarawak and trying to interest the British authorities, meanwhile, in Brunei, as a coaling station between the newly-acquired Hong Kong and Singapore. Coaling stations were essential in the early days of steam, because the ships ate up huge quantities of coal, the storage of which on board could take up far too much available cargo space. Brunei and Labuan both had excellent coal seams, and Brooke discovered that the Dutch had their eyes on the area for the same reason. In 1844 the Sultan, Omar, offered Labuan to Britain, and Brooke urged acceptance.

Two years later Brooke was in trouble. He had waged a vigorous and highly successful campaign against the pirates, and as a result many powerful Malayan nobles, whose economies had been shored up by the profits accruing from piracy, were in financial difficulties. This faction murdered Brooke's great friend, the Sultan's uncle, and tried to assassinate Brooke, but he escaped. With the help of Admiral Cochrane, he suppressed this revolt, and the Sultan, who had fallen temporarily under the influence of the nobles and whom Brooke now restored to his throne as a gesture of goodwill, ceded Sarawak to Brooke personally. At the same time Brooke received a letter from Lord Palmerston accepting Labuan. He returned to England in triumph as Raja Brooke of Sarawak, was knighted and made Governor of Labuan.

The Dutch objected to Brooke's actions in Borneo, and so did many English radicals. In 1849, at the request of Sultan Omar, Brooke smashed a huge pirate fleet of more than a hundred warboats at Batang Maru. Palmerston defended the action, but Gladstone and David Hume thought it disgraceful. Brooke was finally cleared by Royal Commission in 1854.

The Labuan settlement failed, but still Britain held on to the island. Brooke meanwhile continued in fairly solitary state as Raja of Sarawak, becoming worried in his later years about his status.

The British Government continued to refer to him as "Sir

James Brooke, Raja of Sarawak," treating him as an independent ruler, but showed no signs of wishing to take over Sarawak for the Crown. After being an independent ruler for twenty-two years Sir James retired to England. His nephew, Captain James Brooke Brooke, took over in Sarawak.

Apart from these sporadic incidents, diplomatic relations between the Straits Government and the various Malay States were confined to occasional visits by successive Governors to the Sultans of neighbouring states, followed by the periodic exchange of polite letters. Commercial relations, on the other hand, were fairly extensive. Johore, being situated so close to Singapore, was more subject than the other states to the impact of modern commercial civilisation, and, with the aid of Chinese capital from Singapore, its development was fairly rapidly carried out.

In Perak, Selangor and Sungei Ujong, Chinese merchants interested themselves in tin-mining, and by the 1850s there were large Chinese mining populations in certain districts of those states. An increasing number of these Chinese had been born in the Straits Settlements and were therefore British citizens.

Malaya in the early nineteenth century was very thinly populated: one estimate puts the total population of the peninsula at about 300,000. The arrival of a large Chinese mining community concentrated into a small area could easily unbalance the racial constitution of a district. Local chiefs were quick to see the advantages of mining concessions which brought them large revenues, but they often found themselves unable to control turbulent foreign populations which sometimes outnumbered their own Malay subjects.

In 1867, and again in 1872, large-scale warfare broke out in Perak between the members of two rival Chinese secret societies, the last outbreak at a time when the Malay government of the state was paralysed by a dispute over the succession to the Sultanate. At the same time, civil war was raging between Malay factions in Selangor, supported by Chinese groups on both sides. The Singapore Chamber of Commerce, whose members suffered most from the resulting disruption of trade, was loud in its complaints, but in November 1872 the Governor could still reply that "if persons, knowing the risks they run, owing to the disturbed state of these countries, choose to hazard their lives and properties for the sake of the large profits which accompany successful trading, they must not expect the British Government to be answerable if their speculation proves unsuccessful."

This statement was approved by Lord Kimberley, then Secretary of State for the Colonies. For although after the belated abolition of the East India Company in 1858 all the territories under its control had passed to the India Office, agitation by the members of the Singapore trading community, who resented being treated as a kind of uncomfortable appendage of India, led in 1867 to the transfer of the Straits Settlements to the Colonial Office. The policy of determined non-intervention did not long survive this change.

From 1872 to 1873 the situation in Perak and Selangor continued to deteriorate. The Chinese in Perak, deprived by the fighting of their normal livelihood, turned successfully to piracy, and terrorised shipping on the Larut River and in the Straits of Malacca. Nevertheless, we must look elsewhere for a complete explanation of the sudden drastic change in British policy which now took place.

Germany, since Bismarck's unification of the country in 1870, had been casting greedy eyes on Malaya and New Guinea, and it is probable that Lord Kimberley began to fear that if the British did not act in Malaya, the Germans would. Whatever the explanation, in November 1873, a new Governor, Sir Andrew Clarke, arrived in Singapore with instructions from the Colonial Office to enquire into conditions in the Malay States and report whether any steps could be taken to restore order there and to protect trade. In particular, he was to consider the possibility of appointing a British officer to reside in any of the states, with, of course, the full consent of the native government. Immediately after his arrival, Clarke set about solving the problems of Perak.

Apart from the Chinese wars, Perak had a succession problem. On the death of the previous Sultan in 1871, the chiefs had elected as their new Sultan a certain Ismail, who was only related to the royal house by marriage. They had overlooked the claims of two princes in the direct line of descent, from whom the choice should normally have been made, Raja Abdullah and Raja Yusuf.

The wealthiest of the chiefs involved was Ibrahim, the Mantri of Larut, the tin-mining district which was the centre of the Chinese wars. Ibrahim apparently bore a grudge against Abdullah, and at the election he gave his support to Ismail. In the following year, Abdullah, with the assistance of Yusuf, rebelled against Ismail and declared himself Sultan. He also wrote to the Straits Government asking for recognition, and in December 1873, no doubt as a means of obtaining recognition, he wrote to Sir Andrew Clarke asking for British protection for Perak and a British Resident "to show us a good system of government."

Clarke managed to persuade the leaders of the Chinese factions in Perak to accept his arbitration, and he then called a meeting of the Chinese leaders and the principal Malay chiefs.

This meeting took place on the island of Pangkor, near the estuary of the Perak River, in January 1874; as a result of it, the Chinese leaders signed an undertaking to keep the peace under a penalty of 50,000 Mexican dollars, and a commission was appointed to define the boundaries of the mining lands belonging to each group and to arrange for the release of prisoners, mainly women and children, held by each side. The Malay chiefs, including Ibrahim the Mantri, then signed an agreement (known as the Pangkor Engagement) recognising Abdullah as Sultan of Perak. This was hardly surprising since neither Ismail, the reigning Sultan, nor any of his supporters had seen much point in attending the meeting and the Mantri, who now gave his rather doubtful support to Abdullah, did so in order to achieve recognition of his own lucrative position in Larut.

Abdullah agreed to accept a British Resident, whose advice was to be asked for and acted upon in all questions except matters of Malay religion or custom. The Mantri's chief of police, an adventurous Englishman named Captain Speedy, was immediately appointed Assistant Resident, and James Birch, an official who had spent thirty years in the Colonial Service in Ceylon, was sent out in November as Resident. Thus, in Lower Perak, Abdullah now reigned as Sultan, supported by the local chiefs and by the British, while Sultan Ismail, refusing offers of a pension and a courtesy title, continued as before in Upper Perak. Yusuf, who had not been invited to Pangkor, sulked at home, threatening to bring in Siamese help to seize power for himself.

Birch, who now took up the post of Resident in Perak, had little experience of Malaya or sympathy with Malay customs, and did not even speak the language. He immediately antagonised the chiefs by removing their feudal rights to collect taxes and attempting to abolish the widespread system of debt-slavery, thus depriving them at once of income and property, without offering compensation.

Sultan Abdullah felt humiliated at being given orders by someone whom he regarded as a junior official, and when, in 1875, Birch arranged a meeting of the chiefs at which he hoped to persuade Ismail to hand over the regalia and recognise Abdullah as Sultan, Abdullah wrote secretly to Ismail and told him to do nothing of the kind, "otherwise Perak will be given over to the English, for my words have caused me to be much indebted to them." Understandably, the meeting was not a success.

In May of that year a deputation of chiefs went to Singapore to complain of the activities of the Resident. A new Governor, Sir William Jervois, was just taking over from Sir Andrew Clarke; Jervois refused to listen to complaints behind the back of his Resident. A seance was held, at which the Sultan himself acted as one of the mediums, and the spirits prophesied the death of Mr. Birch. More practically, one of the chiefs, the Maharaja Lela, offered to kill the Resident when he passed through his village of Pasir Salak.

Finally, after a visit to Perak where he saw for himself that things were going badly, Jervois proposed that the chiefs be pensioned off and the government taken over by British officials.

Abdullah signed these proposals, under threat that British recognition would be transferred to Yusuf if he did not. But he had now determined that Birch must go, and he sent a *kris*, a Malay dagger with a peculiarly curved blade, to the Maharaja Lela, in symbolic approval of the proposed murder.

In November 1875, Birch passed by boat through Pasir Salak, posting up proclamations of the new system of administration. He ignored a demonstration of armed force on the bank, and leaving his interpreter to post the proclamations on the wall of a Chinese goldsmith's shop in the village, he went to take his daily bath in a floating bath-house moored by the river bank. As the proclamations went up, the interpreter was stabbed, and Birch himself was speared to death through the walls of the bath-house.

A large British force, with reinforcements from India, was sent out to arrest the murderers. The Maharaja Lela and two others were convicted and hanged; three of the chiefs, including Sultan Abdullah, were exiled to the Seychelles, while Sultan Ismail went into exile in Johore. Of the important chiefs only Yusuf now remained, and he now became first Regent, and later Sultan, of Perak.

Although those opposed to the spread of British influence were now deprived of their leaders, much hostility had been aroused and there were serious problems of law and order. The next Resident, whose powers had been confined to the giving of advice, resigned within a year. He was succeeded by Hugh Low, who, by tact and persuasion, devised an administrative system on which that of all the protected Malay States was eventually based.

The chiefs were compensated for the loss of their feudal rights by being given administrative posts or pensions, as well as a percentage of the taxes gathered in their own districts; police duties were given to village headmen, and the police force was reduced. All appointments were made, all revenues collected, in the name of the Sultan; no action was taken without consulting local opinion. Over all stood a State Council, with

the Sultan as president, on which sat the Resident, the major
Malay chiefs, and representatives of the Chinese business community.

Perak prospered under the new dispensation; the state debt
of $800,000[1] was paid off in six years, and in 1888, the year
before Low retired, the revenue came to over $2,000,000, raised
largely by export duties on the rapidly expanding tin trade.

In the meantime, British Residents had been appointed to
two other states, Selangor and Sungei Ujong. Civil war had
broken out in Selangor between two rival groups of chiefs in
1866; factions of Chinese miners had joined in with enthusiasm
on opposite sides, and the Chinese leader in Kuala Lumpur was
offering $100 for every rebel head brought in. The Sultan him-
self was an old man who was reputed to have killed ninety-nine
men with his own hand, but he was now living in retirement
and peacefully pursuing his hobbies of gardening, hoarding tin
and smoking opium, preserving his own peace by showing equal
favour to both sides in the war.

He had, however, appointed his son-in-law, Kudin, a brother
of the Sultan of Kedah, as Viceroy of Selangor with the task of
restoring law and order, but initially the rebels merely resented
the intrusion of a foreigner and the situation deteriorated. Finally, Kudin managed to obtain the assistance of an army of
three thousand men from Pahang, and by 1873 he was beginning
to show progress.

The Sultan now asked for the appointment of a British Resident, and in September 1874 Frank Swettenham, a young civil
servant who had come out to Singapore as a cadet two years
previously, was sent to Langat to give informal advice to the
Sultan. Swettenham had studied the language and customs of
the country and the appointment was a success; Clarke therefore
appointed J. G. Davidson, an old friend and adviser of Kudin,
to the post of Resident in Selangor, leaving Swettenham as
Assistant Resident. The tact and good sense of these two offi-

[1] These are Mexican dollars; the value fluctuated between about 4/- and
2/- to the dollar. A Straits dollar, with a fixed exchange rate of 2/4d. to
the dollar, was introduced in 1906.

cials ensured that British protection was extended to Selangor unopposed.

Sungei Ujong, the third state to accept a British Resident, is one of the small states which make up the modern Negri Sembilan (the Nine Countries). As in Perak and Selangor, the situation was confused by the rivalries of the chiefs, who were financing their quarrels by levying arbitrary tolls upon the tin trade. In 1874, Clarke signed a treaty with one of these chiefs, the Dato Klana, by which the Dato Klana undertook to prevent interference with the river traffic in return for British protection; four months later he asked for the appointment of a British Resident.

No doubt his original intention was as much to increase his own authority with British support as to improve the condition of the country, and one of the new Resident's first duties was to provide the Dato Klana with military protection against the attacks of rival chiefs who resented this interference by the Straits Government. But the success of the new administration in improving security and communications, and therefore trade and revenue, ultimately persuaded the rest of the Nine Countries to follow the example of Sungei Ujong.

Thus by the end of his first year of office, Sir Andrew Clarke had succeeded in introducing British advisers, and a measure of British control, into three states covering most of the west coast of the peninsula. After the disaster in Perak, there was a period of reappraisal, and it was decided that no more Residents would be appointed until the success of these early experimental appointments was assured.

Then, in 1888, a British Chinese subject was stabbed in Pahang, apparently at the orders of the Sultan who, it was rumoured, coveted the man's wife. The Governor of the Straits Settlements, Sir Cecil Smith, went to Pahang to demand satisfaction, and (on the advice of the Sultan of Johore) the Sultan of Pahang apologised for the incident and asked for the appointment of a British Resident, doubtless in order to avoid the more serious consequences which were threatened.

Meanwhile, in 1886 and 1887, two more of the small states of the Negri Sembilan, Jelebu and Rembau, had asked for British officials, and in 1895 all nine of the small states united to elect a single ruler, the Yang di-pertuan, and accepted a single British Resident. In the following year all four states then under British protection—Perak, Selangor, Pahang, and Negri Sembilan—united to form the Federated Malay States, and Federal departments of finance, public works, police, health and agriculture were set up under the first Resident-General, Frank Swettenham.

In 1909, Siam transferred to Britain her rights over the northern Malay states of Kedah, Perlis, Kelantan and Trengganu, in return for the cancellation of British extra-territorial rights in Siam, and for a loan from the Federated Malay States for railway construction.

Each of these states, by separate agreements, gradually accepted a measure of British advice, although none was willing to join the Federation and accept the loss of administrative independence that this would entail. Finally, in 1914, Johore (which Britain had guaranteed against external attack by a treaty of 1885) found that the rapid development of the rubber industry had introduced financial and administrative problems beyond the capacity of its Malay officials to handle, and the Sultan signed a treaty by which he accepted a British "General Adviser," whose advice must be asked for and acted upon on all questions other than those of Malay religion and custom.

British Malaya had now achieved the political structure which was to last, almost unchanged, until the Japanese invasion of 1941. The four northern states and Johore (which were known as the "unfederated" states), had British advisers, British protection and a small number of British officials, but maintained a large measure of real independence. In the centre were the four Federated Malay States where British control, through the Federal administration based in Kuala Lumpur, had largely superseded the old State Councils although attempts were made to revive these in the 1930s. South and west lay Penang, Malacca and Singapore, the three parts of a British colony subject to

Colonial Office control. The Governor of Singapore was the unifying factor in this arrangement, for he was also High Commissioner to the Malay States.

Relations between the races in Malaya were generally good, perhaps better than in any other part of the Empire. There was little sign of the development of a nationalist movement before the Second World War. Indeed, the Malays welcomed the protecting presence of the British, for the growing Chinese element in the population was causing them increasing anxiety. Malaya's two chief industries, tin-mining and rubber-planting, were largely British owned, but since the Malays themselves showed little inclination to abandon their traditional agricultural way of life, most of the labour had for over a century been performed by Chinese and Indian immigrants, and the commercial activities of the peninsula were conducted almost entirely by Chinese businessmen. By 1939, approximately half of the population was of Chinese or Indian origin, and it was clear that post-war Malaya would have very serious racial problems to solve.

While Britain consolidated her vast—and initially unwanted— gains in India, Burma and Malaya; while Holland colonised the Dutch East Indies, and France made Saigon—the capital of French Indo-China (now Vietnam)—the Paris of the East, Germany cast about desperately for some colonies she could call her own.

Forestalled in Malaya by Lord Kimberley, Germany decided to annex New Guinea. New South Wales had already urged the British Government to do this, and New Zealand wanted to take over Samoa, Tonga and the Fiji Islands. The British Government at first rejected both these proposals. They already had enough territories to administer. There were, however, strong British protests at the first German moves in the area, and in April 1885, the two countries came to an agreement about their respective spheres of influence.

In 1889, Britain, Germany and the United States signed the Berlin Act affirming Samoa's independence, except for American rights at Pago Pago. The Islands were to be administered as a joint Protectorate of the three powers. Germany did more business in Samoa than either Britain or the United States, who tended to gang up against her, two against one. At the same time Britain was eager not to offend Germany, and the United States did not want to appear to be siding with Great Britain.

The United States made a treaty in 1875 with the King of Hawaii giving both parties to the agreement exclusive trading rights. America began pouring money into the sugar industry, and leased Pearl Harbor as a naval base in 1887. When Queen Liliuokalani came to the throne in 1891, she tried to shake off the American influence, and was at once deposed by a provisional "government of public safety" which began to negotiate for annexation by America. President Cleveland was a staunch anti-imperialist, and refused to have Hawaii annexed, but he was forced to recognise the pro-American provisional government as permanent. Annexation followed seven years later.

By this time, United States interest in the Far East was growing rapidly. During the Spanish-American War the Americans destroyed a Spanish fleet in Manila Bay, on May 1, 1898, and the defeat of Spain raised the question of what was to be done with her colonies. Germany wanted them, but Britain, fearing German expansion in the area, urged America to take over the Philippines.

A German fleet was sent to Manila, and the Americans reacted by taking over the Philippine Islands, although at first they had thought only of annexing Luzon. Germany made a secret treaty with Spain and received the tiny islands known as the Caroline, Marianas and Pelew islands to use as naval and coaling stations.

The Samoan King died in that year and civil war broke out in his islands. Germany suggested that the three-power Protectorate was unwieldy and that the islands should be divided between the three powers. At first, Britain rejected this idea, but then agreed to it, largely because with her difficulties with the Boers in South Africa, she did not wish to have trouble farther afield. As a result, the Germans took over two of the Samoan islands, the United States the other two, and Britain received Tonga.

❂ ❂ ❂

In China, the Dowager Empress held undisputed sway. In 1873 the boy Emperor T'ung Chih became, in theory, old enough to rule, but the old lady remained in power, the leader of all reaction. The young Emperor was largely brought up by eunuchs, became a homosexual and died at the age of nineteen, leaving his mother as China's unchallenged ruler.

Relations with Britain, never very good, had deteriorated even further after the murder of a British subject, A. R. Margary, in February 1875. The British minister at Peking, Sir Thomas Wade, demanded an investigation into the circumstances of Margary's death. He had apparently been killed by bandits in the jungles near the Burmese frontier. Wade did not believe this convenient explanation and insisted that the Governor of Yunnan province, Ts'en Yu-ying, be held responsible. Rather than dismiss Ts'en Yu-ying, who was competent and well liked, the Chinese Government bought off the British by opening more treaty ports and granting further trade concessions at the Chefoo Conference in 1876. This further surrender inflamed anti-foreign reaction.

China was also in dispute with France over French activities in Indo-China. China felt bound to assist Vietnam in her struggle with the French, in much the same way as she supported the Viet Minh movement seventy years later in the fight to regain independence. By 1883, China and France were at war and the following year a French fleet threatened the Chinese coast. China put up a fair resistance, and with the help of the British, peace talks were begun and a peace treaty signed in April 1885. China evacuated Tongking and renounced her suzerainty over Vietnam. Chinese troops in Vietnam had inflicted two heavy defeats on the French, at Hanoi and at Bac Lé, but the Vietnamese King was doubtful about continued Chinese help and accepted the protectorate the French had determined to impose on him.

"To establish ourselves," wrote the French Admiral Dupré, "in the rich country bordering on China is a question of life and death for the future of our rule in the Far East."

The reforms undertaken by the Emperor Meiji were not popular with everybody in Japan, and especially not with the samurai or warrior class, who felt that various new measures, such as conscription, would be fatal for the old order. Eventually, in 1877, an armed rising broke out in Kyusha, led by one Saigo Takamori. This rebellion was quite easily put down by the Government, who discovered, as a result, that the working class conscript could fight just as well as the professional knight. The consequences of this discovery were to be momentous for the whole of Asia.

Japanese leaders now confidently believed that an army trained and equipped on modern lines could challenge, first, China and then even Russia with every chance of success. Saigo's rebellion, as Richard Storry[2] points out, was not only the last stand of the feudal system; it was inspired also by ultra-nationalist ideals of exactly the type which were to lead Japan, within seventy years, to disaster.

Meanwhile, compulsory education had been introduced in 1872, and as education spread, so did the idea of Japanese expansion. On February 11, 1889, Meiji adopted a written constitution. This was largely prepared by a conservative, Ito Hirobumi, and it was based on the Prussian Constitution. Ito had gone to Germany and been impressed by Bismarck—just as forty-one years later, another Japanese conservative, Tomoyuki Yamashita, was to lead a mission to Nazi Germany and be impressed by their technological achievements. Consequently, although the Constitution included an impressive declaration of human rights, and although it provided for an elected assembly, the real reins of power remained in the hands of a few men, the Emperor's personal advisers, who were responsible not to the assembly, but to the Emperor.

The Meiji Constitution was nevertheless a definite step in a democratic direction, and it was not until some time after the granting of the Constitution that a new rule was added to the effect that the Ministers of War and the Navy must be serving generals and admirals. This proposal eventually led to the under-

[2] In *A History of Modern Japan.*

mining of the Diet's prestige by service ministers in the months before the Pacific War in 1941.

The last ten years of the nineteenth century saw the spread of Japan's industrial revolution. At first, the state took the lead in starting up new industries. The Government was wisely careful about borrowing money for expansion from abroad, for this would have invited European interference with what results the Japanese could see about them. Nevertheless four huge business empires were soon founded: Mitsubishi, Mitsui, Sumitomo and Yasuda. The tremendous organisational drive and efficiency of these great concerns, and the hard work of a labour force indoctrinated to believe that work was a patriotic duty, enabled Japan to attain the status of a great power within fifteen years, starting more or less from scratch. At the same time, to prove that Japan was now a modern, civilised state, considerable judicial reforms were carried out, and, for the same reason, the Government commissioned a British architect to put up a handsome building known as the Hall of the Baying Stag, where lavish receptions were held for foreign envoys. Here Japanese ladies in Western dress—which at that time meant bustles—learned about European cookery and music.

For centuries before all this, China had claimed suzerainty over Korea, and indeed over all her neighbours. The Japanese also coveted this peninsula. In the summer of 1894 a revolt broke out in Korea, and Chinese troops were sent to assist the Korean King. This gave Japan an excuse for armed intervention.

As in 1904 and 1914 the Japanese Navy struck the first blow before war had actually been declared, sinking a Chinese troopship. During the next nine months the Japanese threw the Chinese Army out of Korea, bombarded a Chinese fleet off the mouth of the Yalu River, captured Port Arthur and the Liaotung peninsula in south Manchuria, and seized the port of Wei-hai-wei on the Shantung coast.

China asked for peace, and Japan was able to dictate her terms, in which she received Formosa, Port Arthur and the Liaotung peninsula, a huge indemnity, and the abandonment of the Chinese claim to suzerainty in Korea. The Japanese triumph seemed complete, but only a week after the treaty had been signed Russia, France and Germany intervened. They advised Japan to surrender Port Arthur and the Liaotung area, because Japanese possession of this territory would threaten Peking and disturb the peace of Asia. This "Triple Intervention" as it was called was, understandably, resented in Japan, but since a strong Russian fleet lay at Vladivostock, and Japan had no allies, she had to follow the advice she had been given. The Emperor Meiji told his people that they must bear the unbearable—words which were to be repeated by his grandson Hirohito in 1945.

China had been shown up as a sick, decadent state. Agreed, she had built a few railways and a military academy had been set up, but the Dowager Empress had managed to divert funds intended for the building of a navy in order to repair the Summer Palace destroyed by the British and French in 1860. The outside world assumed that China was falling apart, and they fought for the pieces.

In 1898, while the Western powers were thinking about possible concessions, a new Emperor really did try to instigate a number of administrative and military reforms. This alarmed the Dowager Empress and the forces of reaction, and it was decided that the Emperor's reforms must be halted. The only way to do this was to seize the Emperor. The Emperor learned of this intention and planned to forestall it by sending troops to the Summer Palace to murder the Dowager Empress. This plan was betrayed, however, and the Emperor was imprisoned on an island in the Lake Palace adjoining the Forbidden City. The reformers were hunted down and put to death. It was assumed the Emperor would suffer the same fate, but foreign envoys protested, the South threatened to revolt, and the Emperor survived. At about this time, in the province of Shantung, where foreign pressure was most acute, sympathy with the "Boxers"—the Society of the Harmonious Fist I Ho Tuan—spread among the starving peasants. They resented foreign intervention, the vast and organised corruption in their country; and when the Yellow River burst its banks in Shantung with disastrous floods, it seemed that even nature was against them.

German forces stationed at Tsingtao had already caused a lot of bad feeling. The Germans had previously been dependent on the British base at Hong Kong for supplies and coal and wanted a base of their own. When two German missionaries were murdered by bandits in Shantung this excuse was seized on to send a German squadron to occupy the Kiaochow area. Russia protested, but Britain was not displeased to see Germany and Russia quarrelling in the North, as this left the South more open to her.

In March 1898, Germany obtained a ninety-nine-year lease of Kiaochow Bay and proceeded to build a big military and naval base at Tsingtao. She also managed to acquire extensive rights which made the whole of Shantung virtually part of the Prussian Empire.

Russia now demanded Port Arthur. This time, Britain protested and sent a few warships which made an Anglo-Russian clash seem possible, but when China leased Port Arthur to the Russians, Britain decided that a war was not justified and instead asked for a lease of Wei-hai-wei, which was just opposite Port Arthur, and which had been occupied by the Japanese since the Korean war of 1894.

Japan was willing to hand over the base so long as the British promised not to use it against her. France now demanded a coaling station and was ceded Kuangchow Bay in the South. Italy then asked for Sanmen Bay in Chekiang, but this time China refused. Italy threatened war and recalled her ambassador, but the Chinese stood firm and nothing more was heard of the affair. In general, Western rivalry over China was caused by the fear that others would exploit the country. As Lord Salisbury, the British Foreign Secretary, had said earlier in that year: "The living nations will gradually encroach on the territory of the dying, and the seed and causes of conflict among civilised nations will speedily appear," which they speedily did.

In the foreign enclaves in China at that time, Europeans regarded themselves, and were regarded, as first-class citizens. The indigenous Chinese were second- or third-class citizens, not permitted inside the best hotels or restaurants, although, in

some cases, special rooms were set aside for Chinese guests.
They were not allowed to enter local European clubs, and, in
the shops, Chinese people, even in the middle of giving their
orders, would have to stand aside patiently and wait until an
American or a European, who might have come in after them,
was served.

While the Dowager Empress lived her remote life behind the
high walls of her summer palace, her empire was in decline
and decay, eroded by inefficiency and lack of rule. As the late
Aga Khan wrote in his memoirs: "The power and prestige of
the foreigner was so great, and the authority of the Manchu
Government so feeble, that the real rulers of China in those
days were the consuls of the European Powers, chief among
them the British Consul-General in Shanghai.

"In the disintegration from which China's administration was
suffering, wealthy Chinese brought their money and their in-
vestments into the foreign settlements for safety and protection
—just as today many Europeans send their capital to the United
States and Canada . . ."

He recalls travelling in a P. & O. liner from Hong Kong to
Shanghai with the imperial Viceroy of Yunnan province, a man,
as he says, of "some consequence in his own country."

When the ship docked at Shanghai, however, although the
Aga Khan and his Indian servants, and all British passengers
were treated with courtesy, the Chinese Imperial Maritime Customs ("nominally the servants of the Chinese Government")
dealt with the Chinese Viceroy "brusquely and rudely, all his
baggage was opened up, and the customs officials ruffled busily
through his robes and his mandarin orders . . ."

This was the background of insult and discontent against
which the Boxer Sect grew rapidly. The Boxers were not immediately suppressed, as they might have been, by the Court,
which was now in the hands of extreme reactionaries. This led
them to think themselves in high favour at Peking. Many of the
Dowager Empress' advisers thought that the Boxers should be
officially recognised and enrolled into a militia, where they
would doubtless perform valuable services to the discomfort

of foreigners. The foreign legations at Peking, on the other hand, were not at all happy at the approach of the Boxers, and when the railway station at Fengt'ai Junction, just ten miles south of the capital, was burned down they alerted their warships then in the China seas and asked for detachments to come and guard the embassies.

In June the Court invited the rebels to march on Peking. The British minister, Sir Claud Macdonald, asked Admiral Seymour, commanding the China squadron, to land troops at Tientsin to protect foreign property there, and to send more troops up to Peking. Seymour was unable to reach Peking, however, being driven back by imperial forces. The Boxers arrived instead, and began to massacre Chinese Christians and to molest foreigners.

At Tientsin, the naval commanders decided it would be prudent to seize the forts at Taku, guarding the mouth of the river. When the Dowager Empress heard of this she ordered all foreigners at Peking to leave, under close guard. They very wisely refused and the German ambassador, the Baron von Ketteler, was dragged out of his sedan chair and murdered. The rebels now laid siege to the embassies.

They also attacked at Tientsin but enough foreign sailors were there to repulse them. At Peking, Boxer attacks on the legations were also driven off. The commander of the imperial forces, Jung Lu, had artillery and could easily have wiped out the legations had he so wished, but, strangely, he refrained. The southern provinces of China remained neutral, and saved the country from the worst possible consequences of the Boxer rising, which would have meant complete annexation and partition. In July, the allies were in full command at Tientsin, and the American Minister at Peking, Conger, managed to send the news that the legations were still holding out.

In August, allied forces marched from Tientsin towards Peking, which was now in a state of advanced anarchy with bandits roaming the streets. Peking was relieved on August 14, 1900, and the Dowager Empress fled. In the autumn, Russia occupied

Manchuria. Pro-Boxer ministers were ordered to commit suicide or be decapitated. Fifty years were to pass before China, under Mao Tse-tung, recovered her prestige and, more significant, her sense of purpose.

Chapter Three

In 1902, the year before Curzon's Great Durbar in India, Britain concluded an alliance with Japan, which was to have totally unexpected and, indeed, unimagined consequences. In signing the treaty, Britain underestimated—not for the last time—Japan's vast ambitions and miscalculated the relative strength of Japan and Russia.

Britain was at the height of her power; Victoria's long reign had ended, the imperial dream had still a thousand years to run. Britain, therefore, hoped that the alliance would deter Russia from attacking Japan and so stabilise the Far East generally. It was not realised that Japan, still smarting under the humiliation of the Triple Intervention of 1895,[1] intended simply to clear the field for an attack on the Russians in Korea and Manchuria; nor that this war would end in a resounding victory for Japan, which would make her the leader of the "Asia for the Asiatics" movement and eventually bring about the end of Western domination throughout Asia. Also, Britain did not foresee that Japanese aggression would sour her relations with China and the United States, or that the alliance would ever come to be regarded as being directed against America, which, of course, it was not.

Fear of Russian expansion and the desire not to be left behind in the international scramble for the spoils of China were the basic reasons for the alliance on both sides. In spite of the Triple Intervention, which had deprived Japan of Port Arthur, the Japanese had already done well enough at China's expense.

[1] Russia had persuaded Germany and France to join her in ordering Japan out of Manchuria. Japan, exhausted by her war with China, had no alternative but to agree. The reasons given for making Japan leave were that her presence there "menaced the Chinese capital, made a nonsense of Korean independence and thus constituted a threat to peace in the East."

The Sino-Japanese War left her in possession of Formosa and the Pescadores, and she shared in the huge indemnity that China had been made to pay after the abortive Boxer Rebellion, when Japanese troops had played a major part in the relief of the foreign legations at Peking. But Russian attempts to establish a protectorate over Manchuria, Russian interference in Korea, and the increase in Russian strength in the area resulting from the acquisition of Port Arthur and the completion of the Trans-Siberian Railway, convinced many in Japan that war with Russia was inevitable.

British interests were also threatened by Russian expansion, and the Russian battle fleet based at Port Arthur was at that time the largest concentration of naval power in the Far East. By 1900, Lord Lansdowne, the British Foreign Secretary, had so lost confidence in Britain's ability to defend her interests alone that he abandoned the policy of "splendid isolation" and began to look for a Far Eastern alliance which would leave the British fleet free to operate in home waters and the Mediterranean in the event of war with the Dual Alliance of Russia and France. A Japanese alliance, however, was at first regarded as too open a provocation to Russia, and Lansdowne's original intention was to form an alliance with Germany. It was only after the Germans had decisively rejected his proposals that he turned to Japan.

Negotiations, conducted on the Japanese side by the very able Japanese Minister Hayashi Tadasu, opened in London in April 1901. Progress was slow because Lansdowne was still hoping for an agreement with the Germans and because the Genro, Japan's ruling oligarchy of "elder statesmen," were by no means unanimously in favour of the alliance. Indeed, the Prime Minister Ito strongly opposed it, and was himself working for a peaceable settlement with Russia.

In May, however, Ito resigned, and he was succeeded by Katsura Taora, a nominee of Field Marshal Yamagata, the leader of the "war party." Both Yamagata and Katsura regarded the British alliance as essential, although Ito continued in his private capacity to urge a settlement with Russia, and aroused some suspicion about Japanese intentions when he visited St. Petersburg, ostensibly for his health, later in the year.

Lansdowne was also negotiating with Russia, in the hope of settling outstanding disagreements about Russian expansion both in Persia and Manchuria. But the Russians refused even to discuss these questions, and the British Admiralty pointed out that the British fleet would shortly be outnumbered by the combined Russian and French fleets in the Far East by nine battleships to four. The Admiralty seem to have been dazzled by statistics as statistics, for, in the event, the Russian fleet turned out to be an ineffectual fighting force. Nevertheless, this argument of numbers proved alarming and eventually decisive, and on November 5, 1901, the British Cabinet approved Lansdowne's proposals for a Japanese alliance.

The main point of the alliance was this: if either Britain or Japan became involved in war with Russia in the Far East, the other would maintain a benevolent neutrality. If, however, France joined Russia, then Britain and Japan would fight together. Discussions about the details continued for a further two months. Each side wanted to limit its own commitment, but not that of its partner. The British, for instance, did not wish to allow Japan a free hand in provoking war in Korea, and tried to limit their obligations to cases in which Japan was clearly the injured party. They also wished to extend the scope of the treaty to India and Siam, while the Japanese wanted to confine it to conflicts in China and Korea. Ultimately, the Japanese won both points, and the rather unequal bargain concluded with the signing of the treaty on January 30, 1902.

The preamble stated that the purpose of the treaty was "to maintain the *status quo* and general peace in the extreme East," and that the two governments were "entirely uninfluenced by any aggressive tendencies"—both falsehoods, at least so far as the Japanese were concerned. Nor need it be supposed that the British Government was entirely unaware of Japanese intentions: Satow, the British minister in Tokyo, had kept them very well informed.

The alliance gave great prestige to the military party in Japan, was confirmed by subsequent success in war, and may have done much to encourage the Japanese ambition to found an empire of their own in the Far East.

On the other hand, when war did break out, France dared not risk a conflict with Britain by going to the aid of Russia, and the war remained strictly localised. Whether France would, in fact, have intervened had the alliance not existed is, of course, another matter entirely.

One positive result of the alliance was a surge of pro-British feeling in Japan, and a good deal of enthusiasm for Japan in Britain, where the Japanese came to be regarded, rather patronisingly, as the British of the East.

Japan now devoted her energies to a massive armaments programme, and by 1904 she felt herself strong enough to try conclusions with Russia. Negotiations to effect the withdrawal of Russian troops from Manchuria had failed, and the Russians demanded a guarantee of territorial integrity for Korea (although not for Manchuria), a neutral zone in North Korea, and recognition that Manchuria was outside the Japanese sphere of influence.

On February 6, 1904, the Japanese broke off diplomatic relations, and on the same day a Russian force crossed into Korea. Two days later, a Japanese convoy disembarked troops, who proceeded to occupy Seoul, and that night Japanese destroyers made a surprise torpedo attack on the Russian eastern fleet anchored outside Port Arthur. Although the situation between the two countries was known to be critical, the Russian fleet was in an astonishing state of unpreparedness: its lights were undimmed, and torpedo nets had not been put out. Two battleships and a cruiser were severely damaged by torpedoes, and the rest of the fleet was forced to retire to the shelter of the port defences.

Japan, with a capital ship strength at the start of the action of six to the Russian seven, had gained a temporary naval supremacy, but it was now essential to reduce Port Arthur and destroy or capture the rest of the fleet before the arrival of the Russian Baltic fleet, which contained another seven battleships.

Accordingly, preparations for a siege were instantly made by the Japanese Third Army under General Nogi.

It was not until February 10 that Japan declared war, and the Russians, not unnaturally, felt justifiably aggrieved. In Britain and America, at least, where the growth of Russian power was regarded then, as now, with fear and loathing, they received little sympathy.

"The Japanese Navy," declared *The Times* in London, "has opened the war by an act of daring which is destined to take a place of honour in naval annals. . . . The cases in which a formal declaration of war precedes an outbreak of hostilities have been comparatively rare in modern history."[2]

The incompetence of the Russian naval command delayed the departure of the Baltic fleet for the East until October, but Port Arthur, which had been heavily fortified on the landward, as well as the seaward, side,[3] still held out. The fighting was bitter, and Japanese casualties amounted to about sixty thousand men. Further inland, Japanese troops captured Mukden, the capital of Manchuria, at the cost of forty thousand casualties. At last, on December 31, Port Arthur fell; the remnants of the eastern fleet had already been sunk at anchor in the harbour by artillery fire. General Nogi and the naval commander Admiral Togo duly took their place in the pantheon of Japanese national heroes, while the victorious Navy, now somewhat reduced since two battleships had been lost to Russian mines, retired to base.

Meanwhile, the Russian Baltic fleet, a total of some forty vessels, was making its way slowly east. Its officers proved to be almost more comically inefficient than their fellows at Port Arthur. They had heard of the daring and ingenuity of the wily Oriental, and such was their nervousness that they fired on some British fishing trawlers in the North Sea under the extraordinary impression that they were heavily disguised Japanese torpedo boats.

[2] A similar "act of daring" by the Japanese Navy had signalled the start of the Sino-Japanese War in 1894; and another, of course, was to take place in 1941.
[3] A precaution which was unfortunately neglected in designing the defences of Singapore, thirty years later.

In late May the fleet reached the Straits of Tsushima, between Japan and Korea, and here it was intercepted by Admiral Togo and his largely British-built and British-trained Navy. When the smoke cleared two days later, thirty-eight of the Russian vessels had been captured or sent to the bottom. Togo had won one of the most decisive naval victories in the history of war at sea.

Peace terms were arranged soon afterwards, through the mediation of the United States: under these, Russia recognised Japanese rights in Korea, ceded to Japan half the island of Sakhalin, and transferred to Japan her lease of Port Arthur and the Liaotung peninsula. Manchuria itself was divided two years later into Russian and Japanese spheres of interest. Thus Russia's ambitions in Asia had been checked for a generation.

Almost as important in its implications for the peace of the world was the fact that for the first time in modern history a European nation had suffered defeat at the hands of an Asiatic one. The point was not lost on nationalists, from India to the Middle East, and Japan began to see herself as the leader of a resurgent Asia.

No idealistic considerations, however, prevented her, in her new-found status as a great power, from joining enthusiastically in the exploitation of prostrate China, and the assassination of Ito in 1909 by a Korean provided the excuse for the forcible annexation of Korea, which remained virtually a Japanese colony until 1945. Britain, Japan's ally, was already too preoccupied with the growing menace of Germany to protest at this act of international brigandage. In 1907, the Anglo-Japanese Alliance was renewed for a further five years, and in 1911 for ten more years. Thus, at the outbreak of the World War in 1914, British possessions in the Far East were largely safeguarded by the promise of Japanese protection.

The European war was a tremendous stimulus to the Japanese economy, since it brought large orders for ships and armaments from Britain and France, and for consumer goods from countries such as India, which Britain was temporarily unable to supply. At the same time, by distracting the attention of other world powers from the Far East, it gave Japan unparalleled opportunities for extending her influence in China. The Anglo-Japanese Alliance did not apply to Europe, but in August 1914, shortly after the outbreak of war, Britain asked for Japanese naval assistance against German raiders in the Pacific. Japan went further than this request and declared war on Germany, seized the German islands in the Pacific and attacked the German naval base at Tsingtao. The Kaiser ordered the defenders to hold out to the last, but the fortress fell in little more than a month. Japan had previously assured China that she had no designs on Chinese territory: nevertheless, she kept Tsingtao, and with it all the economic privileges that the Germans had enjoyed in the province of Shantung, for a further eight years.

The reasons for Japanese interest in China were primarily commercial. China was the nearest source of certain raw materials, notably coal and iron, that were vital to the Japanese economy, and a prosperous China could provide an almost limitless market for the products of Japanese industry. On the other hand, China was still weak enough to constitute a standing temptation to aggression.

The Manchu dynasty, in the person of the infant Emperor P'u Yi, had been overthrown in 1912, four years after the death of the Dowager Empress, by a republican rebellion led by Dr. Sun Yat-sen. Yuan Shih-k'ai, the Commander-in-Chief of the imperial army, had defected to the rebels and was in return appointed first President of the new republic. But the new regime showed itself as incompetent and corrupt as the old, there were signs that other generals hoped to follow Yuan's example in seizing political power, and Yuan himself soon showed that, so far from holding genuinely republican ideals, he was instead planning to make himself the first Emperor of a new dynasty.

If he succeeded in establishing a strong central government, Japanese interests would be forced out of China. If he failed, there was a possibility that Russia or some other power would establish itself in China, constituting a serious threat to Japanese security.

For these reasons, Okuma, the Japanese Prime Minister, now decided to intervene, at the risk of forfeiting the goodwill of Britain and America. In January 1915, the Japanese minister in Peking presented Yuan with a secret list of twenty-one drastic concessions required by the Japanese Government. This list was typed on official Japanese War Office notepaper which bore the martial watermark of battleships and machine guns, a point not lost upon the recipients.

The list, which became known as the Twenty-one Demands, was designed to give Japan virtually complete control over the policy and administration of China. Not only was Japan to retain the German concessions in Shantung and receive additional mining and railway rights in Manchuria and Inner Mongolia, but China was to undertake not to cede coastal territory to any other power. Japanese military, financial and political advisers were to be appointed to key posts in the administration, and Japanese police forces were to be set up in certain areas.

Yuan allowed news of these demands to leak out, and there were protests from Britain and the United States. At this the Japanese claimed that the so-called Twenty-one Demands had not in fact been demands at all, but merely "wishes." Years later, the poet Ogden Nash summed up the Japanese attitude in this couplet:

> How courteous is the Japanese;
> He always says, "Excuse it, please!"

In fact, Japan dropped the last two demands, but the rest were presented in May 1915, in the form of an ultimatum, and Yuan was forced to submit. It meant the end of his plans to found a new dynasty, for the indignation of the Chinese people at this further humiliation at the hands of foreigners was such that within a year Yuan's authority collapsed and his empire broke up in a series of military revolts and civil wars.

This affair revealed for the first time the full extent of Japan's predatory intentions toward her neighbour, and it did much to sour relations between Japan and the English-speaking countries.

Furthermore, in the areas Japan controlled, she had discriminated harshly against the trade of other countries, and this was seen as a threat to the large British and American commercial interests in China.

In America, where Japanese immigration had already become a political issue, there was sympathy for China, resentment of Japanese commercial practices and a growing emotional (and quite unrealistic) fear of Japanese invasion. None the less, Japan, in 1917, managed to obtain British recognition of her position in Shantung in return for providing destroyer escorts for use in the Mediterranean. In the same year, America, on entering the war, recognised that "territorial propinquity creates special relations between nations and consequently Japan has special interests in China." France and Italy made similar statements, in return for Japanese help in "persuading" China to enter the war against Germany.

At the Peace Conference of 1919, where Japan, now the dominant power in the Far East, was one of the "Big Five," Japan's right to the former German concessions in Shantung was written into the treaty. Chinese protests were ignored and the Chinese delegation refused to sign the treaty; it was not until 1922 that the two countries came to terms, and Chinese sovereignty in the area was restored, while Japan retained her economic privileges.

Meanwhile, hostility between America and Japan continued to increase, largely as a result of constant disputes over Japanese immigration. Japan, anxious to find an outlet for her growing population, had tried to have a racial equality clause inserted in the Charter of the League of Nations, but this was prevented by Britain (prompted by Australia) and by America. There seemed to be a possibility of war between America and Japan: at the same time, with Russia still suffering from the effects of revolution, no other country was in a position to threaten Japan.

In all these circumstances, there was strong American opposition to the continuation of the Anglo-Japanese Alliance, and the British Government decided to allow it to lapse. At the Washington Conference in 1921 the alliance was replaced by a vague Four Power Pact of friendship between Britain, Japan, France and the United States.

This pathetic attempt to save Japanese face only served to increase Japanese paranoia. Japan had regarded the alliance in some sense as the symbol of her acceptance as one of the great powers of the civilised world; now she saw its termination as a humiliating sign of her rejection by those powers. Henceforward Japan would make her own way in the world, and Britain, having rejected Japan's friendship, had lost the chance of influencing her.

Although all the signatories to the Conference agreed "not to support any agreements by their respective nationals with each other designed to create sphere of influence or to provide for the enjoyment of mutually exclusive opportunities in designated parts of Chinese territories," the Japanese rulers only regarded these words as words and nothing more. As Professor Louis L. Snyder[4] wrote later: "To fiery Japanese militarists, any promises, treaties or agreements were so much dry rot, the impedimenta of decadent Western liberal democracy."

In a Europe darkened by fears of Russian Communism spreading after the Revolution, with millions unemployed, and the future grim and uncertain, what was happening in Japan, thousands of miles away, seemed of little importance. More pressing worries and dangers were far nearer at hand.

In 1919, Senator Henry Cabot Lodge had already warned the West of Japanese intentions.

"Japan is steeped in German ideas and regards war as an industry because from war she has secured all the extensions of the Empire," he said. "She means to exploit China and build herself up until she becomes a power formidable to all the world. . . .

"She will threaten the safety of the world. . . . But the country that she would menace most would be our own, and unless we carefully maintain a very superior navy in the Pacific, the day will come when the United States will take the place of France in another great war to preserve civilization."

[4] *The War: A Concise History 1939–1945.*

A further result of the 1921 Washington Conference was a naval treaty, limiting the size and numbers of capital ships that the major powers could maintain. With Germany eliminated as a naval power, at least for the time being, the United States wished to be equal with Britain in naval strength. The tonnage ratio they proposed was 5:5:3 for Britain, the United States and Japan respectively: France and Italy were to be allowed 1.75 each. It was made clear that if no agreement was reached at the Conference, then the United States would build a navy which neither Britain nor Japan could rival for size, and whether for this reason, or simply for the sake of American friendship, the British delegation under Balfour hastened to accept the proposals.

Japan at first held out for a ratio of 10:10:7, but was eventually persuaded to sign in return for a further agreement that no new bases or fortifications would be constructed anywhere nearer to Japan than Singapore or Hawaii.

Japan had protested at the ratios, no doubt because her government felt that to admit naval inferiority was to lose face at home.[5] But, in fact, Japan gained more from the treaty than anyone else. In an unrestricted naval building race, she could never have maintained 60 per cent of either the British or the American strength, and the restriction on bases assured her security from naval attack.

For Britain, on the other hand, the agreement represented a drastic change of policy, and the acceptance of a greatly weakened position in the Far East. Until the turn of the century, British naval policy had been based on the "two-power standard," under which Britain maintained a navy equal to the next two largest navies combined. In 1911, in the face of heavy German naval construction, Churchill, then First Lord of the Admiralty, had had to accept a superiority of only 60 per cent over the German fleet. Now, a British Government had agreed to, and indeed appeared to welcome, a one-power standard.

[5] Churchill wrote later that his Government "had to choose between Japanese and American friendship." He "had no doubt what our course should be" (Winston S. Churchill, *The Grand Alliance*).

The decision meant that a substantial number of British battleships had to be scrapped, and this undoubtedly would save
Britain a lot of money which would otherwise have been spent
on defence.

More important in the long march of history, the treaty also
meant that Britain could no longer guarantee to protect her
interests in the Far East, at a time when the ending of the
Japanese alliance had made war with Japan a distinct possibility.

In 1921, Britain still had by far the largest navy in the world.
She had 50 per cent more battleships than the United States,
and nearly three times as many as Japan. True, the United
States had a large building programme in hand and would
soon achieve parity: but no one in Britain contemplated a war
against the United States.

The position with regard to Japan was extremely serious.
Before the Washington Conference, a British fleet equal to the
entire Japanese fleet could have been detached and stationed
permanently at Singapore; after the Conference, no capital ships
at all could be spared for the Far East, for all were needed in
Europe. In the event of trouble in the Far East, the plan now
was for the main fleet to steam from Europe to Singapore, a
strategy that presupposed peace in Europe. Meanwhile, when
the largest British ships in the East were a few cruisers based
in Hong Kong, a potentially hostile Japan had become mistress
of the Western Pacific.

Until this Conference, Britain faced no potential enemies in
the East. India, Ceylon, Burma, Malaya and Borneo were, of
course, within her own Empire; Indo-China was part of the
French Empire; Siam, China and Japan were on terms of cor-
diality with her.

As a result of this Conference's decisions, the Japanese felt
that they had greatly lost face, not only before the Western
world, but, more important, close to home, among Asiatics.
Britain and America had thus created a potential enemy of
infinite cunning, resource and determination.

The British delegates returned from Washington realising this, and at once plans were put into operation to select a base in the East from which any future aggression by Japan in the East could be met and contained. The need was great, but the search, and the subsequent building and fortification of this base, was carried out against an extraordinary background of political myopia in Britain, and an ignorant indifference among British voters. It was all happening too far away, and they had far more serious problems—jobs, houses, strikes—close at hand.

After the Armistice, at the end of the First World War, Lloyd George's Liberal Government, understandably anxious to cut down on armament expenditure after four years of war—in which out of a total 65,000,000 men mobilised on both sides, there had been known military casualties of 10,000,000 dead, plus 3,000,000 presumed dead, another 20,000,000 wounded, and 9,000,000 war orphans and 5,000,000 war widows—issued an edict to the three service departments. In all future estimates for equipment and other defence expenditure, they were to assume —quite reasonably at that time—that, with all possible enemies defeated, it was unlikely that the British Empire would be involved in any other great war for at least ten years, i.e. not until 1929.

Each year, the Chiefs of Staff submitted to the Cabinet their annual reports on military, aerial and naval strength and requirements. These reports were drawn up against a Foreign Office memorandum which annually reviewed the international political scene, and listed any dangers in different countries that could conceivably lead to military action in which Britain might become involved.

With each year that passed, this "Ten Year Rule" was renewed, and with each renewal it had less and less relation to international events: the discord in Italy and Germany, which produced Mussolini and Hitler, and mounting anti-Western resentment in Japan.

Winston Churchill became Chancellor of the Exchequer in 1924, and he asked the Committee of Imperial Defence, which was concerned with the defence of the Empire, to review the rule, but without success. Four years later, the matter was discussed again, and it was agreed "that the basis of estimates for the service departments should rest upon the statement that there would be no major war for a period of ten years, and that this basis should advance from day to day, but that the assumption should be reviewed every year by the Committee of Imperial Defence."[6]

In theory, every service department and all Dominion governments could raise the issue should they so wish. But Lord Hankey,[7] as Sir Maurice Hankey, who combined in the mid '30s the position of Secretary to the Committee of Imperial Defence with being Secretary to the Cabinet and Clerk to the Privy Council, wrote later: "What made this unlimited extension so dangerous and demoralizing was that, during preceding years, including Mr. Churchill's term at the Treasury (1924–28), the rule had been used to cut the services to the bone, with the result that their efficiency was diminished and the arms industry was perishing for lack of orders, discharging skilled men and designers, and scrapping plant of importance to our national war potential."[8]

The comforting assurance, repeated parrot-like, that there would be no war for ten years, was the answer to every service request for modernisation. But there was what Lord Chatfield, the First Sea Lord, in 1932 called "an imperfection in the rule, since it implied a date . . . by which the services *were* to be ready for war."

The Admiralty used this as a lever, because capital ships took years to plan and build, and dockyards that had been closed for a decade could not possibly function efficiently simply when the gates were reopened. So until the "Ten Year Rule" was revoked, "the three services would always be at ten years' notice" for action.

"Protest was unavailing. Gagged and bound hand and foot,

[6] *The Gathering Storm* by Winston S. Churchill.
[7] Hankey, a former Royal Marine officer, had built up the organisation of the Cabinet Secretariat, which kept all records of Cabinet decisions. Some called him a soldier in peace and a secretary in war. He was a spare, slight figure, who frequently ate a two-shilling vegetarian lunch, and would as soon travel by bus as in a taxi.
[8] *The Times*, November 2, 1948.

they were handed over to the Treasury Gestapo. Never has there been such a successful attempt to hamstring the security of an empire. It was, of course, in those days, a secret instruction, not to be let out, so that a future enemy might not hear of it and lay his plans. Parliament must not be told, nor the public."[9]

Churchill left office in 1929, but there still seemed no positive reason to change what had been decided. In the event, war broke out ten years later in 1939, and as he wrote himself, "Ten years is a long time in this fugitive world."

It is indeed, but the ten years lost between the early '20s and the early '30s could never be regained. Ideas and inventions that could have shortened the war were prematurely adandoned or were still-born.

For instance, Britain produced a prototype flying bomb or missile as early as 1927—sixteen years before Hitler's V-1 and V-2 rockets from Peenemünde rained over London in 1943. This British missile, with the code name of "Larynx," looked like an ordinary aircraft and was powered by a 180-horsepower Armstrong-Siddeley Lynx aero-engine. The prototype could carry for a distance of 200 miles half the amount of explosive of the conventional daylight bomber of that time. Obviously, with further work on it, this range and bomb load could have been greatly extended. This missile, remarkably sophisticated for its day, had an automatic pilot, and a radio transmitter which sent out messages every ten miles so that its direction could be plotted as it flew on test above the English Channel off the south coast of England.

By the following year further tests had been so promising and the accuracy of the prototype was growing so great that the Chief of Air Staff asked for more money—less than £1,000,000—to develop it. The Cabinet refused this request on the grounds of economy.

It is not too fanciful to argue that this money spent then could have saved itself a million times over in terms of human life and human misery, and in terms of loss, destruction of property and the decline of British prestige in the years between then and now,

[9] *It Might Happen Again* by Lord Chatfield.

which are so depressingly marked by grey milestones to timidity and lack of decision.

As the historian Basil Collier put it[10]: "There was never a time between the Armistice and 1932 [when the Rule was finally adandoned] when any strategic proposal, no matter how necessary or how reasonable it might seem to its sponsors and even to the Government, could not be turned down on the pretext that it would take less than ten years to complete, and that therefore a start could safely be deferred. . . ."

The long-term aims of successive British governments—Liberal, Conservative, Labour and coalition alike—were roughly the same, if their means of achieving them differed, but, by clinging to this ridiculous thesis, they deliberately denied themselves the chance to achieve these aims.

Each government had inherited an empire supreme in arms, secure in liberty, uncalculably rich in terms of its potential. Together and separately they conducted it nearer to the edge of darkness and oblivion.

Two hundred years earlier, Frederick the Great had observed that diplomacy without arms to back it up was like playing music without instruments. During the 1920s and early 1930s, successive British governments imagined that they could implement their foreign policies and preserve peace and prosperity at home and within their Empire without either arms or armour. This was not only music without instruments; nobody even knew the score.

Economy was the overriding consideration, the yardstick by which all plans, all suggestions, were judged and usually found wanting. And, in addition, the pacifists, some sincere, others seeking a conventional and popular stepping-stone for their own self-advancement, raised shrill voices against the warning of war-serious minds. For, as the poet Cowper wrote on another occasion: "I know the warning song is sung in vain, That few will hear, and fewer heed the strain."

After the First War, possibly as a reply to Lord Roberts' pre-war campaign stressing the advantages to Britain of National Service, the pacifist element in the Labour party grew more

[10] *Barren Victories; Versailles to Suez 1918–1956.*

powerful than the industrial element, and asserted this new ascendency by adopting a policy in which a general strike would be called in order to check what the Labour party might consider to be warlike action by any British Government.

They attempted to have such a policy adopted internationally, since a general strike in every country of the world would, in their opinion, "oppose all wars that may threaten to break out in the future." The Socialists particularly resented the building up of the three services because they reasoned, quite illogically, that this would lead to war. This assumption, still with its vehement adherents, is as unreasonable as assuming that insuring one's property brings nearer the risk of fire or flood.

After the First World War, there were proposals to absorb the R.A.F. into the Army or Navy. Air Marshal Sir Hugh (later Lord) Trenchard vetoed this and won—fortunately for Britain in 1940—but one of the strongest planks in his platform of persuasion was that an air force independent of the other services would be a cheap alternative to a properly balanced strategy which no British Government of the twenties or thirties felt the country could afford.[11]

Lloyd George, anxious to save money on warships and troops and mechanised equipment, accepted the argument that it was essential for Britain at least to equal this performance, although it should have been clear that wars were not won simply by bombing civilians, and that an Air Force was only of value as an ancillary arm to a strong navy and an army equipped with modern, scientific devices of war, which other countries even then possessed.

The theory that Britain should have air parity with France, and later with Germany, was hotly disputed by the Labour

[11] In fact, Britain's aerial bombing during the First World War had not been notably successful. Owing to poor technical equipment it was associated in the public mind with throwing small bombs or grenades over the side of the cockpit in the general direction of the target beneath. The Germans had proved, in the summer of 1917, that aerial bombing could be more damaging. In two daylight raids over London, thirty-six German bombers had inflicted six hundred casualties without sustaining any damage themselves.

party. As late as 1933, the year in which Hitler seized power, the Socialists adopted as their slogan: "A Vote for the Tories Is a Vote for War." And, in the following year, Mr. Attlee (now Lord Attlee) told the House of Commons: "The Opposition do not think that disarmament and security could be separated. We stand for a system of collective security under the League of Nations, and are entirely opposed to separate alliances. The Labour party will oppose increase of armaments on the plea of either national defence or parity."

This was said two years after Japan had seized Manchuria, an act which will be discussed later at more length, when the League had shown itself to have all the virility of a eunuch.

Some time later Attlee expanded his view and added: "We deny the proposition that an increased British Air Force will make for the peace of the world and we reject altogether the claim to parity. We think that parity is an out-of-date conception of the balance of power . . ."

It was against this background of unrealism and muddled thinking that a suitable base was sought in the Far East from which British Far Eastern possessions, and possibly Australia and New Zealand, could be defended in the event of a Japanese attack.

Before the First World War, Britain's strength in the Far East pivoted on her naval base at Hong Kong, which was sufficient when the main challenge to Britain's maritime supremacy came from an occasional Chinese pirate junk. But for a base against more serious adversaries, it was realised that Hong Kong was no longer feasible as a main naval base. Its docking and repair facilities were inadequate. Worse, it was too much of an isolated outpost to be defended and was separated from China by a narrow spit of leased land.

Admiral Jellicoe toured the Far East in search of a better site, and in 1919 he recommended Sydney, Australia, with Singapore as an advanced outpost. In 1921, the Committee for Imperial Defence decided against the Admiral's advice, and on June 16 of that year, the Cabinet approved the decision to build up Singapore, where, at that time, there only existed weak defences.

Singapore was geographically the best place, it was felt, from which to guard Britain's trade routes and also it was strategically placed for the defence of Malaya, Burma, Australia and New Zealand. Geographically, at the southern tip of the Malay peninsula, it could dominate the eastern approaches.

Singapore is the name of the island, separated from the Malayan mainland by the Johore Strait, and also the city on the island. The island itself is diamond-shaped, and measures at its widest point twenty-seven miles from east to west, and thirteen miles across from north to south. There are mangrove swamps on the northern shore, and extensive rubber plantations further inland. The city of Singapore lies on the southern shore of the island, a humid, thriving trading centre with more than half a million people in those days, of whom the majority were Chinese.

The vital link between the island and the mainland is the Johore causeway, which is 1115 yards long and has its own road and railway line. It was to the east of this causeway that the naval base was built.

From the very start, the Singapore naval base was the subject of political and military controversy. In 1923, the Cabinet approved the Admiralty's recommendation of a site on the Johore Strait, on the north of the island, on the grounds that the existing commercial port, Keppel Harbour, on the south coast of the island, was more exposed. It was never visualised that the mainland of Malaya could be invaded; the War Office maps marked the jungle on either side of the road that ran north to south, like a spine, as unpenetrable.

The site of the proposed base having thus been decided, the next question was what defences should be employed.

Admiral Sir Percy Scott who in the Boer War had devised land mountings and mobile carriages for the naval guns that had made possible the release of Ladysmith wrote in *The Times:*

"Everyone ought to realise that our base at Singapore should be defended by submarines and aeroplanes, which would keep any battleships from coming within five hundred miles of the Island, as the Germans kept our battleships from coming near their coast." Unfortunately, very few people in 1923 possessed

Sir Percy Scott's prophetic understanding. These few did not include the generals or the admirals.

As early as 1914 Sir Percy had written, also in *The Times*, that "battleships are no use either for defensive or offensive purposes; submarines and aeroplanes have entirely revolutionised naval warfare."

The official view was that it was not even necessary to station a fleet permanently in the Far East, because, if attacked, Singapore could be relieved by the arrival of the main fleet within seventy days, which was the time it would take to steam from European waters. Aircraft were not held to offer a serious threat to naval vessels—except, as we shall see, by such forward-thinking men as Hugh Trenchard. The Navy, ever jealous of its premier position as Britain's senior service, ridiculed the new element of the air.

Towards the cost of constructing the base, the New Zealand Government made a grant of £1,000,000, and the Federated Malay States, on a motion put forward by the Sultan of Selangor, a grant of twice this sum. Australia, whose anxiety in 1941 contributed to the fatal decision to hold on to Singapore until the last, made no initial grant.

In 1924, work on the base was stopped altogether by the British Labour Government, ostensibly as a contribution to world disarmament, but largely as an economy, a decision which both Australia and New Zealand bitterly opposed. They were far nearer Japan geographically than Britain, and they entertained no illusions as to Japan's eventual intentions.

Work restarted again when the Conservatives returned to office, then stopped when Labour was re-elected. This stop-start attitude added nothing to the impetus that should have marked the entire undertaking.

Meanwhile, the battle as to the best means to defend this unfinished base raged more strongly than the battle to defend it nearly twenty years later. Admiral of the Fleet Lord Beatty, speaking in 1923 at a banquet given by the Lord Mayor of London, an accepted stage to air important opinions, said: "This project of putting Singapore in order so that it shall be of use to the Navy has been attacked by many as though it is something new. This is far from the case. For many years it was a naval base, a base recognised by many of the most astute as being the best strategical position in the Far East."

Lord Beatty mentioned Raffles and others as being among the most astute, and of course he was quite right. But he ignored the fact that they had lived in a world when sea power was paramount; now the power of the air was in the ascendency, and Trenchard, as head of the R.A.F., while not disagreeing with the outlay that was necessary for floating docks, arsenals and facilities for the repair of every type of naval vessel, had his own views on the means of defending it.

His biographer, Andrew Boyle, wrote: "What perplexed and vexed him was the contrast between these modern installations and the antedeluvian system proposed for their defence. Beatty seemed to be breathing the air of the nineteenth century, the tone of disregard for complete realities of the twentieth, which Trenchard could not condone."[12]

Trenchard, as Chief of the Air Staff, wanted torpedo bombers which could seek out an attacking naval vessel, perhaps 150 miles from shore, and attack it in a way that no 15-inch guns could ever do.

The old argument of the power of the battleship against the new bomber broke out again. Neither the Navy nor the Air Force would give way. The Prime Minister of the Labour Government, Ramsay MacDonald, agreed with Lord Haldane's proposal that these matters be put to one side and raised again at some future and unspecified date.

This turned out to be the following year, in 1925, when Stanley Baldwin, by then Conservative Prime Minister, decided that they should be discussed. Sir James Grigg, who was Joint Private Secretary to Winston Churchill, Chancellor of the Exchequer in that year, and who, seventeen years later, was Secretary of State for War when Singapore fell, wrote in his book *Prejudice and Judgement:* "I have always considered that the real tragedy of the Singapore decision was . . . that Lord Beatty's view pre-

12 *Trenchard: Man of Vision* by Andrew Boyle.

vailed over that of Lord Trenchard in regard to the methods to
be adopted for defending the base.

"The naval view meant fixed defences and big guns and forts,
and these turned out to be useless. But it might have been a
different story if Lord Trenchard's plans of entrusting the protection of the fortress predominantly to the air had carried the
day."

For "might," read "would."

Trenchard had in mind a chain of airfields from Calcutta
through Burma and to Malaya, from which planes could be
ferried to Singapore in the event of danger. Ferrying was necessary because there was no aircraft capable of flying to Malaya
from any base in India or in Ceylon—save the Catalina seaplane
which was slow and clumsy and thus of limited use—until the
Liberator bomber went into service in the East in 1944, the penul-
timate year of the war.

The naval plan for defending Singapore was totally different.
An enormous base would be built with underground stores to
contain food, ammunition, spares for naval vessels and supplies
of every kind for a minimum of seventy days. This, as we have
seen, was calculated as being the maximum time the British
main fleet would take to reach Singapore. Until their deliverance,
the defenders would live like moles behind their fortifications.

Of course, this plan visualised there being a fleet that could
be sent. It did not hint at the possibility—then quite un-
considered—that the fleet might have sustained heavy losses in
European, Mediterranean and Atlantic campaigns, and thus
enough vessels of the right size would not be available for a
relief voyage to Singapore.

Trenchard was against this traditional view. He argued that
if he could have enough airplanes in India and Burma, he could
fly them to Singapore within four days, as opposed to seventy.
The Admiralty stuck out for their six 15-inch guns. The Navy was
quite capable of defending itself *and* Singapore.

Trenchard pointed out that "it is when the fleet ventures
within radius of shore-based aircraft that the Air Staff have
serious misgivings as to its safety."

This was fair comment, for the Admiralty had earlier admitted that "co-operation of air forces would be essential" in a major sea battle, although paradoxically, they had been unimpressed by tests carried out in 1921 by the American airman General Billy Mitchell on two old German battleships to prove the vulnerability of warships to determined attack from the air.

In his attempts to prove this thesis, Mitchell had set off with four bombers from Langley Field, Virginia, to attack these two floating hulks before an audience of sceptical American service chiefs. Such was the climate of disbelief in his abilities to sink the ships, or even to damage them severely, that a former Secretary of the U. S. Navy had declared he would stand bare-headed on the bridge of either vessel throughout the exercise and be unharmed. This brave intention was not carried out—for-tunately for him—for the first battleship sank within eleven minutes after several direct hits, and the second a few minutes later.

The British Admiralty stubbornly maintained that in their own Navy-Air Force exercises the bombers had claimed many near misses; they could not accept that anything save a direct hit could put out of action a capital ship of thousands of tons' dis-placement, and equipped with watertight compartments. Some naval authorities even went so far as to doubt the need for having anti-aircraft guns aboard battleships. With existing weapons, surely the ships would be unsinkable?

"In relying on the high rate of fire of the multiple pom-pom," replied Trenchard, "the Admiralty have practically no experience of hitting an aeroplane in flight with these small-calibre weapons.

"The torpedo plane approaches at a rate of 120 miles per hour. Assuming it is sighted four miles away (a liberal assump-tion) the defenders have but two minutes in which to bring it down at a minimum range, for some few seconds, of some 400 yards. The time taken to launch a torpedo attack of twelve machines is about two minutes. Our experience is that the fleet have the greatest difficulty in avoiding complete surprise even when they are actually expecting attack. . . ."

The British Navy had been supreme for centuries, and her

admirals, steeped in the maritime glories of its past, could not, or would not, accept that the third arm of the air completely altered a sea strategy evolved through the centuries.[13]

Finally, with a tragic genius for compromise, the British Government appointed a committee to study the potential vulnerability of warships to attacks by torpedo bombers. The committee's deliberations produced nothing new, but possessed the specious advantage of postponing yet again the moment of decision.

They admitted that an aircraft, which in those days need cost only about £150,000, might indeed successfully bomb a capital ship which had cost £7,000,000. Also, for this sum, the country could have bought forty-three twin-engine medium bombers. But despite this obvious calculation in relative values, the committee concluded that the capital ship was the one remaining surface vessel which was not liable to be sunk, even if it were hit severely by a bomb from the air.

They added a rider which events later touched with irony. Regarding the views of the R.A.F., they admitted: "If their theory turns out well founded, we have wasted money; if ill founded, we would, in putting them to the test, have lost the Empire."[14]

Their theory turned out to be impeccably well founded. As a direct result of disbelieving it, successive governments lost not only millions in money, but also the Empire they were set to defend.[15]

---

[13] Naval conservatism had deep roots. In 1804, the Admiralty had turned down the offer of an American, Robert Fulton, to build a submarine for them, on the grounds that, if Britain indulged in such new experiments, other countries would follow, which could be "the greatest blow at our supremacy on the sea that can be imagined."

[14] Report Her Majesty's Stationery Office.

[15] Both Lord Ismay and General Sir Leslie Hollis later recalled a strange case of prophetic vision during one of these meetings.

Captain Tom Phillips, R.N., and Group Captain A. T. Harris (later Marshal of the Royal Air Force, Sir Arthur Harris) were arguing over the relative claims of aircraft versus ship.

"Bomber" Harris turned to Phillips and said: "I had the strangest dream last night, Tom. I saw your future so clearly. War was declared

Trenchard's own proposals to defend Singapore from the air were these: he would not need 15-inch guns, but he would keep the existing armaments, which included 9.2-inch guns, plus a squadron of torpedo-bombers which could intercept any hostile fleet miles out to sea far beyond the range of any shell. Should a serious emergency arise, this squadron would be reinforced from India, with an additional squadron of fighter aircraft.

Next, Trenchard advocated developing the air route from Calcutta to Singapore and using flights of reconnaissance planes. By 1930 the whole question could be reconsidered in the light of technical developments which were constantly taking place.

Beatty was ill when Trenchard presented this alternative plan. Two years earlier, in January 1924, Beatty had written despairingly to his wife about Singapore and the constant wrangling over its defences. "That infernal place's name will be engraved on my heart," he wrote. "The struggles I have had over it are to be repeated more bitterly than ever and with doubtful results."

Now, from his sickbed, Beatty wrote to Trenchard asking, "For the sake of the nation, not the Navy, could you not moderate your intransigent attitude to the present plan of defence?"

Trenchard felt that he had failed in not being able to convince his service colleagues of the value of his scheme. He decided to modify his proposals. That morning, he saw Baldwin, the Prime Minister, and said, as he explained to Beatty, "I agree, subject to certain remarks, that a start should be made on the [first] three 15-inch guns for Singapore."

Thus the stage was prepared for the humiliations of the future, when the only shots these great guns would fire in anger would be when they were traversed round as far as they could turn,

---

in the East and the Japanese had taken Siam. You'd been promoted Admiral, and you set off in your flagship up the east coast of Malaya to deal with the situation. Suddenly, down comes a raid of bombs and aerial torpedoes. You look down from your bridge and say, 'What a lot of mines we've hit.'"

Four years later, in 1941, Vice-Admiral Sir Tom Phillips, as he became, was in command of the 35,000-ton *Prince of Wales*, and the 32,000-ton battle-cruiser *Repulse*. Both were sunk by Japanese aircraft off the east coast of Malaya within minutes of being sighted.

to aim at targets on the Malayan mainland. And even then, their value was infinitesimal. They fired armour-piercing high-explosive shells, capable of puncturing the heaviest hull afloat. But the net result of firing them at Japanese concentrations on land was only to drill enormous holes in the earth. Unless they scored a direct hit, the side effects of these shells was small.

While the argument as to the relative potentials of Air Force and Navy burned on, the advocates of modernisation in the British Army, ever the Cinderella of Britain's fighting services, were arousing much opposition and registering little success. Efforts to secure mechanisation of cavalry units brought forth retorts from cavalry officers that they did not wish to become only mechanics in uniform.

This attitude towards the horse was typified by the views of Field Marshal Earl Haig, who wrote[16]:

Some enthusiasts today talk about the probability of horses becoming extinct, and prophesy that the aeroplane, the tank, and the motor car will supersede the horse. Personally, I always feel that these great inventions somehow or other cure themselves; what I mean is that they always produce an antidote.

In this connection, I hear of a tremendous discovery in the way of a bullet which gives much greater range and far greater accuracy than anything produced up to date. So it seems to me that the need for horses in the future is likely to grow. How can the infantryman with his full kit (and other things he has to carry) hope to take advantage of a decisive moment, created by fire from machine guns of a range of 5000–6000 yards?

Surely, it seems to me, it is by utilising the horse and equipping our light troops properly, mounted troops and mounted artillery, that we are likely to take advantage of these modern weapons. I am all for using the air-plane attacks, but they are only accessories to the man and the horse, and I feel sure that the time is at hand when we will find just as much use for the well-bred horse as we have done in the past.

Therefore, one must not be despondent when one hears that the day of the horse is over.

[16] In the *Canadian Defence Quarterly*, Vol. III, No. 4, July 1926.

Meanwhile, as controversy over the best means to defend Singapore waxed and waned in Whitehall, as work on the base itself stopped and started according to the political complexions of succeeding British governments, the Japanese, unhampered by the brakes of democratic processes and pacifist ignorance of hard, irrefutable international realities, moved ahead with their long-term plans for expansion.

Japan's economic difficulties, like her population, were growing rapidly. Britain and forty other countries, in order to protect their own manufacturers, had been forced to impose tariffs and import restrictions on Japanese goods which, because of the very low wages paid in Japan, were so much cheaper than they could make themselves. China thus became Japan's best customer for these goods and her main supplier of coal and iron ore for her factories. Japan, therefore, sought to gain political control over China so that China could not deny her these basic needs for her industries.

In 1929, what became known as the *Tanaka Memorial* was published, as useful and as detailed a declaration of Japanese intentions as *Mein Kampf* was of Hitler's, and to which the democracies paid even less attention.

In July 1929, Baron Tanaka, the Japanese Prime Minister, who was also leader of the Seiyukai (Liberal) party and a general of the Imperial Japanese Army, presented to the Emperor an original scheme for solving Japan's problems of space in which to expand, and for securing for their country the raw materials they needed so desperately.

In essence, the *Tanaka Memorial* laid down the Baron's solution for Japanese problems as follows:

"In Japan, her food supply and raw materials decrease in proportion to her population. If we merely hope to develop trade, we shall eventually be defeated by England and America, who possess unsurpassable capitalistic power. In the end, we shall get nothing. . . .

"Our best policy lies in the direction of taking positive steps to secure rights and privileges in Manchuria and Mongolia.

"Having China's entire resources at our disposal, we shall

proceed to conquer India, the Archipelago, Asia Minor, Central Asia, and even Europe.

"In order to conquer China, we must first conquer Manchuria and Mongolia. In order to win real rights in Manchuria and Mongolia, we must first use this district as a base, then penetrate into the rest of China under the pretence of developing our trade.

"Armed with already safeguarded rights, we shall seize the entire land. If we are able to conquer China, all the other Asiatic countries and the countries of the South Seas will fear us and will capitulate before us."

Manchuria would certainly be an immensely valuable acquisition; an area of half a million square miles rich with deposits of copper, lead, magnesium, gold, iron, coal, oil shale, and almost equally important, half a million square miles where the Japanese, increasing at an annual rate of 700,000, could have more room. Politically and strategically, too, Manchuria could be a useful buffer between Japan and Russia.

The *Tanaka Memorial* was understandably branded by the Japanese Government as a forgery; if a forgery, it proved remarkably true, and how it came to be discovered is an indication of the swift-moving undercurrents in world diplomacy.

An employee in the Japanese Naval Ministry in Tokyo sold photographs of each page of this report to a Russian secret agent for a sum of $3000. Leon Trotsky, the Communist leader whom Stalin pushed from power, claimed that this film was despatched by a circuitous route to Moscow. Copies were then made and sent by other roundabout means to various countries where they were conveniently "discovered." This secrecy was necessary so that no link between the Soviet and these diplomatic disclosures could be found. Nor was any even suspected until Trotsky broke silence.

The climate for expansion had been growing continually since the war. As early as 1919, the Kokuhonsha (National Foundation Society) was pouring out its niagara of xenophobic propaganda, plus lavish praise for the Japanese nation.

"From the fact of the divine descent of the Japanese people

proceeds their immeasurable superiority to the natives of other countries in courage and intelligence. . . ."

"Japan must no longer let the impudence of the white man go unpunished. . . ."

These were two of their assertions which found a wide and ready public, willing to believe, eager to act.

Another society, the Dai Nippon Kokusuikai (Greater Japan National Essence Society) with a million members, was doing much the same thing. And political assassinations, ruthless and well planned, provided in Japan, as in Germany, another lever to stir the uncommitted.

In November 1930, the Prime Minister of Japan was assassinated. In the following March, an attempted military coup d'état failed simply because some senior officers would not support it at its most crucial stage.

Two years later, other Army officers, all members of Kodo (The Imperial Way), an ultra-patriotic group, murdered the Finance Minister, and a month later the head of the enormous Mitsui commercial concern was also killed.

In 1930, the Japanese Government fell, the reason being given as "interference by the Army." Against this background of incipient revolt, inspired by feelings among the officer class that their country was being left behind in the technological march of the twentieth century, by the loss of their traditional privileges and rights, by an anger against profiteers, the Army became the real ruler of the country, the power behind political puppets. In that year, too, a fifty-year-old officer, Tomoyuki Yamashita, was appointed to a most influential post in the Japanese Army: Chief of Military Affairs. Eleven years later he was to lead the brilliantly successful attack on Singapore, the citadel of the white man's supremacy in the East.

As with Hitler, the military rulers of Japan needed some incident, either real or arranged, which they could parade as a legitimate excuse for their ambitions, and which the timid and the gullible in many lands would hail as reasonable.

What became known as one of the first "China Incidents" took place in September 1931, when hired Chinese bandits laid a small grenade on the tracks of the South Manchurian railway, which was controlled by the Japanese.

The total length of railway track destroyed by this explosive device amounted to thirty-one inches. This was little enough, but it was sufficient excuse for the Japanese Government, which immediately declared that this was "banditry" and must be revenged by force. In the same month, without even consulting the Cabinet, the Japanese Army captured Mukden and ten thousand Chinese soldiers who happened to be in the barracks at the time.

China appealed to the League of Nations which, unable to do anything positive, appointed Lord Lytton to lead a commission to investigate the incident and recommend what action should be taken. In fact, no action was taken; no one was prepared to do anything. Japan went on to conquer Manchuria by the following January.

Fearful atrocities—rape, the murder of children, the deliberate shooting of prisoners of war, indiscriminate bombing and looting —accompanied the conquest, as later they would follow the conquests by Mussolini in Ethiopia, by Hitler in Czechoslovakia and Poland and elsewhere. This was incidental. What mattered to the Japanese was that they had achieved their intention.

Professor Snyder records that the most popular tune of the day, "The Song of the Human Bomb," commemorated the action of three Japanese soldiers who blasted a way through a barbed wire entanglement by fastening grenades to their bodies and throwing themselves upon it, to perish in unending glory.

In October, the Lytton report was published. It proposed that Manchuria be declared autonomous; that it would still be a part of China, under the watchful eye of the League of Nations, while China and Japan came to an agreement about the extent of their interests in Manchuria.

America was not a member of the League; Britain did not support sanctions against Japan, and nothing was done. Two years later, in February 1933, the League of Nations refused to recognise what the Japanese called "the independent Republic of Manchukuo," which was their new name for Manchuria. Japan withdrew from the League in the following month.

As Churchill wrote later, "Germany and Japan had been on opposite sides in the war; they now looked toward each other in a different mood. The moral authority of the League was shown to be devoid of any physical support at a time when its activity and strength were most needed."

Thus, as Basil Collier has written, "The grandiose plans which stemmed from the Washington Conference collapsed at the first hint of danger, and the Japanese were confirmed in their opinion that the Anglo-Saxon peoples had lost the will to resist aggression and were no longer formidable."

In England, these events in Manchuria, 15,000 miles away, aroused little popular interest. Various pacifists propounded the suggestions of their kind, throwing up particles of print with their theories. One, Dr. Maude Royden, announced the formation of what she called a "peace army." Its members were expected to make their own way to Manchuria and there to intermingle, unarmed, of course, with the Chinese and the Japanese so that defenders and attackers would not be able to shoot at each other without risking the lives of the "peace army." That they might not care whether they shot the Europeans did not seem to occur to the doctor, or to others who put forward equally impossible suggestions.

Not for the last time, the moralists confused the moralities.

In Japan, what mattered was the success of their audacious scheme. The equation of violence and thirty-one inches of railway line had resulted in Japan acquiring half a million square miles of new territory, plus all the mineral riches that lay beneath it.

The Japanese had marched into Manchuria on September 18, 1931. Their timing was no accident. Exactly three days earlier, on September 15, units of the British fleet, anchored at Invergordon in Scotland, refused to take the ships to sea. This became known as the Invergordon Mutiny.

An agitator among the sailors, one Len Wincott, addressed the men in their canteen, and pointed out that in view of the

Government's economy measures—again this negative word—their pay was being cut from 4/7d a day (as able seaman) to 3/-. Wincott was a Communist. Others of the same outlook addressed sailors in different ships, and when the order "Prepare ship for sea" was given, the crews sat on the anchor cables to prevent them being lifted. The "mutiny" soon petered out, but the ominous fact was that it had happened at all.

Sir John Pratt, who from 1925 to 1928 was Adviser of Far Eastern Affairs at the Foreign Office, wrote later: "Few people remember, even if they ever realised, the effect produced in every foreign country by the news that the sailors of the fleet at Invergordon had refused to take the ships to sea and that the manoeuvres had been abandoned.

"Invergordon was the signal for which the Japanese Army in Manchuria had been waiting."[17]

A British businessman in the Far East put it even more plainly when he said: "It was as though the policemen of the world had gone on strike."

That same year, partly as a result of loss of confidence due to the "mutiny," Britain went off the gold standard.

"Nothing that had ever happened before in my lifetime was more wounding to British pride," wrote the Duke of Windsor in his memoirs.[18] "I could not bring myself to believe that it had happened.

"Then . . . the Government announced that Great Britain had gone off the gold standard, an event as shattering to the United Kingdom's position as the world's banker as the mutiny of the fleet had been to British prestige.

"For a dreadful moment one had the feeling that the foundations of British power were being swept away. . . ."

The Japanese also had this feeling. It encouraged them to believe that the British fleet could not now be relied on politically, quite regardless of the fact that its equipment was out-of-date, and also that Singapore was not in any state of preparation to receive the British fleet, even if it did sail. They

[17] *War and Politics in China* by Sir John Pratt.
[18] *A King's Story* by H.R.H. the Duke of Windsor.

also knew that, throughout the length and breadth of the British Empire in the East, there was not another naval harbour that possessed seaward guns which were not outranged by a contemporary cruiser's armaments.

Just how low British ability to defend herself had sunk can be gauged by this situation. In the summer of 1914, the Liberal Government of that time disposed an enormous fleet, and was able to send six infantry divisions and one cavalry division to France. In 1931, the Labour Government of the day had at its command a fleet that had technically mutinied, aboard ships so old-fashioned and of such outdated performance that the threat they presented was minimal. Instead of six infantry divisions and one cavalry, all they could have mustered (but did not) were one infantry division and a single cavalry brigade.

The fact that there was a cavalry brigade was again an instance of the antique thinking of those responsible for the national's defence. The tank, again a British invention, had not been modified and adapted as it should have been.[19]

By 1935 the Army had only 375, most of them ten or eleven years old; 300 were officially admitted to be obsolete.

Many of the R.A.F. aircraft—(the Home Force of which was ten squadrons below the minimum strength agreed ten years earlier) were out-of-date. Most were based on aircraft flying in the 1914 war. The Gloster "Gauntlet," which was the main so-called "new" fighter aircraft, could only reach 230 m.p.h. The "Hind" and the "Hendon," as the main daylight bombers, could carry only a 500-pound bomb load, and a 1500-pound bomb load respectively, for distances of 430 and 920 miles.

The bombs in use in 1939 were, incidentally, twenty years old. The largest ones were 500-pounders, because the Air Staff quaintly imagined that heavier bombs were no more effective. Worse, the bombers of that era had been designed to carry bombs

---

[19] As late as May 1940, the British Expeditionary Force in France did not possess a single armoured division. The 1st Army Tank Brigade at that time possessed seventeen light tanks and one hundred so-called "infantry" tanks—three-quarters of which were only armed with machine guns.

of this size—and bigger bombs would have needed larger planes to carry them.

The explosive most favoured contained amatol, less destructive than the explosive used in German bombs. A more powerful ingredient—RDX—was evolved, but its production ceased in 1937. Not until five years later was this in general use in British bombs.

And of the total 500-pound weight of each bomb, only about a quarter was explosive.

Of eleven firms which had been making Service equipment before the First World War only one was still capable of manufacturing heavy munitions, and these on an extremely small scale.

The Army, being as usual the most conservative service, had the most out-of-date equipment. Four years before the Second World War, the British Army's most modern field gun was one made in 1914. The Vickers gun, which dated from 1880, and the 1912 Lewis gun, were the Army's automatic machine guns.

In 1914 the British Army was the only one in the world that had field guns incapable of firing a high-explosive shell. As war grew nearer in 1939, it was probably the only European army without rimless cartridges, sub-machine guns and percussion grenades.

Delay and procrastination throttled all attempts to drag it into the twentieth century. On February 14, 1938, St. Valentine's Day, plans for the Valentine tank (of low performance even for that time, having a two-pounder gun) were submitted—and rejected.

In June 1939, the same plans were reviewed and some orders placed. But sixteen months had been lost, and in that time many modifications should have been adopted.

The very successful German "Tiger" tank, first seen in the North African campaign in 1943, was already a working prototype on St. Valentine's Day, 1938, when the British "Valentine" plan had not even been approved.

But, as General Sir Leslie Hollis, Assistant Secretary to the British War Cabinet and the Chiefs of Staff Committee, wrote

later: "It was never questioned . . . that the British Army's cavalry lances and swords, their saddles, horseshoes, picks, shovels
and tent mallets were the equal of any in the world."

An instance of the lack of urgency that clouded the British
nation in the 1930s is afforded by the experiences of Mr. Edward
Barford, M.C., chairman then, as now, of the powerful Aveling-
Barford concern, Britain's premier producers of road rollers and
heavy earth-moving equipment.

In 1936, Mr. Duff Cooper (later Lord Norwich) and at
that time Minister for War, explained to Barford that he wanted
a number of medium-sized industrial firms not previously connected in any way with armament manufacture to be prepared
"to educate themselves in these matters." Then, in an emergency,
their factories, which would already be tooled up for this type of
work, could speedily increase production.

It was essential that this should be done discreetly, without
publicity, and it was suggested that Aveling-Barford should
produce machine-gun carriers.

These were light tracked vehicles, known as Bren-gun carriers,
powered by a Ford V8 engine, and Barford—mindful of his
own painful experiences as an eighteen-year-old officer in the
First World War, when his battery had been rationed to two
shells a day, because Britain had failed to anticipate the demand
for armaments, while the Germans could mount a day and night
barrage—immediately agreed.

He was given a firm order for twenty-five Bren-gun carriers
on condition that they be ready for the Brigade of Guards
manoeuvres in the following summer. Barford pointed out that
in order to produce them within nine months they would have
to have the drawings immediately. He was assured that he would
have them within a matter of days. But no letter arrived confirming the order, and neither did any drawings.

Six weeks later, the drawings had still not arrived. He drove
to London, and saw a senior officer who had been present at
the meeting. This officer expressed surprise at the delay, but
assured Barford that he would immediately receive a letter of
authority confirming the deal.

Another six weeks passed, but still no letter and no drawings. Barford again approached the War Office, received the same shocked surprise, the same assurance, but again no letter and no drawings.

He assumed that the War Office must have found a firm able to produce these carriers more quickly, and so they were placing the order elsewhere.

Some months later, while he was in London on business, two cars arrived at his factory at Grantham, in Lincolnshire. One contained Guards officers in civilian clothes; the other, War Office officials. They explained that they had come to see the carriers on test. If they were not quite ready for testing, they would at least like to see how far they had progressed, for manoeuvres were now only three months distant.

There was, of course, nothing to see, and although Barford at once contacted Duff Cooper and the plans eventually arrived, the mass production of these carriers had been delayed by at least a year.

As soon as the first carrier had been completed, it was tested and photographed, and Barford drove to London with the prints still damp in his briefcase. The War Office gave a second verbal order for more carriers—although at that time they had still not confirmed the initial contract!

By now war was imminent. Barford knew that it would take months for official approval to construct a "shadow factory" to make the carriers, or for a financial grant to be made available, so he borrowed the money from his own bank, built his own extensions, and turned out carriers at the rate of sixty a week. As a result, roughly 40 per cent of the carriers in the use of the British Army in 1940 had been produced by his firm.

There is an ironic postscript to this tale of initiative and endeavour. Because Barford had refused to delay production while he awaited official permission to extend his factory in order to make the carriers, the Government refused to pay anything toward the cost of expanding his factory and purchasing all the additional machinery needed, which could only be used to produce these vehicles. The country's enormous gain by his initiative and patriotism proved to be his monetary loss.

Other firms acted with the same vision and resourcefulness, which were so sadly lacking in the Government of the day.

If the Armed Forces were in such feeble state, and so ill equipped for the defence of Britain, their homeland, how much more antique was the equipment at their disposal in the East? And there the danger to the West grew with each passing year, each missed opportunity to halt the march toward the battle between East and West that would change the world forever.

The Manchurian Incident (as it was called in Japan) had marked a new period in Japanese politics. From then on, by means varying from terrorism and assassination to threats of rebellion, actual mutiny and the politics of the *fait accompli*, a hard core of fanatically nationalist officers in the Army was able to dominate the government of Japan, dictate its policies and commit the country to a course of expansion and continental aggression which was to lead ultimately to war first with China, and then with the West.

Nor was the Army confined to these harsh and unconstitutional means of enforcing its will. An Imperial Ordinance of 1900 had provided that only officers on the active list could be appointed to the position of Minister of War or Navy Minister. One result of this rule was that the service ministers—unlike their democratically elected counterparts in Britain—always had expert knowledge of their subjects. Consequently, Japan's Army and Navy were never permitted to fall into the state of disgraceful unpreparedness that was accepted in Britain at this time.

This was counterbalanced by the immense disadvantage that no government could be formed in Japan without Army and Navy support, for professional solidarity in the services was such that no general or admiral would join a Cabinet of whose policies his professional colleagues disapproved. Thus Army and Navy were in a position to force the resignation of any government at any time, a threat which was no less powerful for being rarely carried out. In practice, the Navy had the reputation of being much more moderate than the Army, and one is tempted to see in this a reflection of the fact that in the early days the Army had been trained by German, the Navy by British, instructors.

It would probably be more accurate to say that the Navy, as a comparatively new service, had no long tradition of political power, while its officers were, by virtue of their profession, well travelled and better informed of conditions in the outside world. Army officers, on the other hand, were not only narrow-minded as a body, but regarded themselves as the legitimate successors of the samurai, the ruling warrior caste of Tokugawa Japan.

It is possible that, after Japan's invasion of Manchuria, concerted action by Britain and the United States might have checked further Japanese aggression. Certainly Britain, as the most powerful member, could have imposed her policy on the League. But although popular feeling in both countries was outraged, and although their commercial interests in China were threatened, the Washington Conference had left them in a poor position to fight the war which might have resulted from the imposition of sanctions on Japan. The bases at Pearl Harbor and Singapore were thousands of miles from Manchuria, and attacking or blockading forces would have had to pass through waters well guarded by the Japanese bases in the Pescadores and at Okinawa. The Singapore base itself, a bone of political contention since its inception, was still vulnerable and incomplete. Its defences were weak, and its repair facilities by no means finished.

In the circumstances, as we have seen, neither government was prepared to risk a war with Japan. Thus the League of Nations, following Britain's lead, met its first major crisis with a united front of paralysed indignation. "Collective security," the policy of disarmament policed by combined action through the League, had already broken down; but the increasingly academic discussions of the Geneva Disarmament Conference dragged on until October 1933, when it was learned that Hitler's rearmed Germany had withdrawn from both the Conference and the League.

This year was also marked by the passing by undergraduate

members of the Oxford Union of what Churchill called "their ever-shameful resolution," "That this House will in no circumstances fight for its King and Country."

"It was easy to laugh off such an episode in England," he wrote, "but in Germany, in Russia, in Italy, in Japan, the idea of a decadent, degenerate Britain took deep root and swayed many calculations."

In 1935, Italy successfully defied world opinion over Abyssinia, while Germany introduced conscription and announced the establishment of the Luftwaffe. In April, the Council of the League of Nations unanimously condemned Germany's repudiation of her obligations under the Treaty of Versailles; nevertheless, two months later, an Anglo-German Naval Agreement was announced, under which Germany was to be permitted to build a navy up to 35 per cent of the tonnage of that of the British Commonwealth, with the right to an equal submarine tonnage with the Commonwealth. Assurances were given, of course, that these submarines would never be used against merchant shipping, although in the First World War submarines had proved virtually useless against anything else.

"What a windfall this has been to Japan," said Churchill in Parliament. For if Britain had failed to act over Manchuria, it must have seemed obvious in Japan that the chances of the British fleet being sent to the East were now even more remote.

In November 1936, Mussolini announced the formation of the Rome-Berlin Axis; three weeks later, Japan and Germany concluded an Anti-Comintern Pact, which was joined by Italy in the following year.

Japan now felt confident that she could go ahead with her plans for China without fear of interference from the democracies. For some time, while in theory maintaining the "Open Door" policy of equal opportunities for all in the China trade, she had in practice been quietly squeezing out non-Japanese interests in Manchuria, and the process was quickened by the Japanese military occupation of North China in 1935.

A Japanese "Asiatic Monroe Doctrine," and the exclusive responsibility of Japan for the peace of East Asia (a term that was to replace the European description, "Far East"), had now been proclaimed. The London Naval Conference, which met in December 1935, was wrecked by the Japanese demand for an adjustment of the ratios to give Japan absolute parity with Britain and the United States; when she failed to get her way, Japan flounced out of the Conference and announced that she would accept no further limitation of naval armaments. Finally, in July 1937, Japan launched a full-scale invasion of China. By August, Peking and Tientsin were in Japanese hands, and with the fall of the capital Nanking in December, Japan hoped for a Chinese capitulation.

Chiang Kai-shek's Nationalist Government, which in 1926, a year after the death of Sun Yat-sen, finally succeeded in defeating the warlords and ending the ten years of anarchy which had been the legacy of Yuan Shih-kai, had at first set about reform with genuine revolutionary ardour.

Chiang had been trained in Moscow, and the Chinese Communists, on Russian orders, at first supported Chiang's Kuomintang party. But in 1927, Chiang suddenly broke with the Communists, murdered as many of their leaders as he could find, and set himself up as a right-wing dictator somewhat after the lines of Yuan Shih-kai. He failed in his attempt to destroy the Communists, and civil war between them and the Nationalists was the inevitable consequence.

The Generalissimo had ignored successive Japanese aggressions, preferring to concentrate on the internal war against the Communist forces of Mao Tse-tung. By this policy he had lost Manchuria, Jehol, Inner Mongolia and North China almost without resistance. But in December 1936, the situation suddenly changed. Chiang was kidnapped in Siam by his own rebellious Manchurian troops and forced under threat of his life to come to terms with the growing popular demand for a national resistance against Japan. After this, internal differences were shelved, and, outwardly united if inwardly divided, Chinese Communists and Nationalists fought together against the common enemy.

Convinced that the democracies would eventually be forced to enter the war against Japan to protect their own interests,

the Government "sold space for time," conducting a courageous
and orderly retreat into the interior, while the Communists established a guerilla organisation, by which they were eventually
to gain control of all China, behind the Japanese lines. Japan
was in for a longer and more arduous campaign than she had
envisaged.

Meanwhile, the democracies were characteristically slow to
protect their interests. Public opinion in both Britain and America
was sympathetic to China. In London, the Archbishop of Canter-
bury presided over a public meeting in the Albert Hall in
protest against the indiscriminate bombing of Chinese cities.
The League of Nations, of course, roundly condemned Japan;
so did the United States, although she continued to provide
Japan with most of her essential war materials. Little else was
done, while British nationals were stripped naked and slapped
by Japanese troops in the streets of Tientsin, non-Japanese trade
with China was disrupted, and an American gunboat was sunk
on the Yangtze River.

The Americans were as unready as the British, and equally
unwilling to provoke any incident that could lead to war.

They withdrew more and more into their comfortable cocoon
of isolationism. The British, meanwhile, like a once-strong man
now grown old and weak who looks back on the vanished years
of strength and youth, confused the illusion of strength and
technological achievement—the Aldershot Tattoo, the Hendon Air
Display, winning the Schneider trophy—with the sad reality of
their country's actual position in the world. It was more comfortable to dwell on the past, when the glory had been great,
than to accept the bleak fact that Britain was a small island
kingdom, off the coast of Europe, unable now to defend the
vast commercial interests, the enormous legacies of trade and
overseas possessions, that her ancestors had built up around the
world.

Turning in on themselves, the British mused on handed-down
glories, dreaming of an imagined strength, while all around them
their real wealth withered, their reputation was in decline, their
Empire was approaching sunset.

Chapter Four

SINGAPORE base was infinitely slower to build than it was to fall.

The Defence Resolutions passed at the Imperial Conference of 1923, recognising that Britain was no longer able to shoulder alone the entire burden of imperial defence, emphasised the primary responsibility of each part of the Empire for its own local defence, but noted the deep interest of Australia, New Zealand and India in the provision of a British naval base at Singapore.

Nevertheless, because of the Conservative Government's economy campaign, and because of the implacable opposition of the Labour party, for whom the very word "battleship" symbolised aggressive imperialism, progress on the base was at first extremely slow.

A site of about four square miles of marshy ground in the northeast of Singapore Island was selected in 1922, and the land was bought and donated by the Straits Government. The base was to be constructed over a period of ten years, of which the first two would be needed for surveying, draining and clearing the ground. This preliminary work started in 1923, and had not got very far when at the beginning of 1924 the Conservatives fell from office, to be succeeded by the first Labour Government.

Labour had opposed the base from the start, and the new Prime Minister, Ramsay MacDonald, lost no time in announcing that he had decided to abandon it.

In an emotional speech in the House of Commons on March 18, he admitted that the construction of the base was not contrary to the Treaty of Washington, and that if Great Britain were to become involved in a naval war in the Pacific, then the strategic position of Singapore was unique. But his Government had come to the conclusion that to proceed with the scheme would be to exercise a most detrimental effect "on general foreign policy, and we should almost inevitably drift into suspicion and competition of armaments in the Far East."

In short, he felt that the moral value of cancellation outweighed the strategic considerations, and he claimed to have obtained a large measure of dominion support for his policy.

This boiled down to support from General Smuts of South Africa, who described the new plan as a bold move towards enduring peace. Canada and the Irish Free State offered no advice at all, while the two dominions most directly concerned, Australia and New Zealand, strongly—and understandably—opposed cancellation.

The Australian Government sympathised with the policy of international conciliation, but felt that the policy proposed would have the opposite effect to that intended by MacDonald—as indeed events proved—while New Zealand approved of the Singapore base on strategic grounds and considered that the time had not yet come to rely solely on the influence for peace of the League of Nations.

Nevertheless, the cancellation went through, and steps were taken to dispose of the equipment and disperse the teams of experts and technicians gathered on the site.

Soon, however, there was a new reversal of policy. In November 1924, the Labour Government resigned, and at the ensuing general election the Conservatives were returned with a large majority. The new Government immediately announced its intention of resuming work on the base, and in the Estimates Debate of March 1925 the First Lord of the Admiralty provided details of the expenditure proposed. The sum of £11,000,000 was to be spent on the provision of docking facilities for the largest battleships, and £800,000 on fortifications to be constructed on land provided by the Government of the Straits Settlements. Large contributions from Australia, New Zealand and Malaya ultimately offset some of this expense, and it was still thought that the base could be completed by 1932.

At this point a further delaying factor appears, in the surprising shape of Winston Churchill with the "ten-year no war" rule.

In 1928, when the first ten years had almost expired, Churchill, then Chancellor of the Exchequer, proposed that the ten-year rule be extended for a further ten years, "and that this basis should advance from day to day." In other words, no war was to be expected for ten years, *but the end of the ten years was never to get any nearer.* It is difficult to see what was the logical meaning, if any, of this extraordinary suggestion, but it was nevertheless adopted in July 1928 by the Cabinet and the Committee of Imperial Defence. Its practical effect was, of course, to relegate all Defence projects to the very bottom of the list of priorities, and it was not only the Singapore base that languished in consequence.

The ten-year rule, with what Churchill called "its ambulatory baseline," survived the fall of the Conservative Government in 1929 and was only officially abandoned by Ramsay MacDonald's National Government in 1932.

In 1929, a Labour Government took office, and it was announced that work on the Singapore base was to be drastically slowed down. The Government wanted to spend as little as possible on the base before the naval conference which was to be held the following year, in case the resolutions there adopted should make the base unnecessary.

This hope was not entirely fulfilled, and at the Imperial Conference of November 1930, New Zealand, Australia and the United Kingdom once again discussed the future of Singapore. It was decided that, for the moment, the original plan of establishing a defended naval base there should be maintained—or at least kept in mind.

The air base was to be completed as planned, but completion of the docks and defence works was to be postponed until 1935, and then reconsidered in the light of the conditions then prevailing. This "truncated scheme" lasted another year, but was abandoned by the National Government in 1931, and in the Estimates Debate of March 1932 the First Lord of the Admiralty announced that changes were being made which would actually result in a 50 per cent increase in accommodation for capital ships at the base.

In July 1933, the British public was informed that the Singapore base would be ready in 1935.

"It was the determined attitude taken by the dominions, especially Australia, that finally defeated the plots to sabotage the work," declared the *Daily Express*,[1] a trifle prematurely.

Now that the base was actually being built, the next problem was how best to conduct its defence with the weapons agreed by the chiefs of the services in London.

Lord Ismay, later Military Secretary to the War Cabinet in the Second World War, wrote in his memoirs:

"The defence of Singapore soon became one of the stock exercises at all military academies, and I was first introduced to it as a student at Quetta Staff College in 1922.

"We were required to put ourselves in the place of the Japanese General Staff, and to make recommendations as to how Singapore was to be captured.

"My solution was to land a force of several divisions in the north of Malaya or the south of Siam, in order to attack the fortress from the north, while the fleet maintained a sea blockade."[2]

Although this method of attack seemed feasible enough, Ismay added that so long as there was a British fleet "in being" that could sail to the Far East, then, in his view, it would be "an unwarrantable risk" to attempt such an invasion from Japan, which was 3000 miles away.

He could not then conceive two factors quite outside all the calculations of planners until the outbreak of war. The first was that there would not be a British fleet that could be sent. The two most important vessels in the "fleet" that was sent—two capital ships, *Prince of Wales* and *Repulse*—was at the bottom of the sea within minutes of being seen by Japanese torpedo-bombers.

The second unknown factor then was that, when France capitulated in 1940, French Indo-China would be marked by the Japanese for occupation when they wished, and thus the enemy

[1] July 23, 1933.
[2] *The Memoirs of Lord Ismay.*

suddenly possessed a huge naval base 750 miles from Singapore and airfields within 300 miles of the Malayan coast at its nearest point, Kota Bharu.

Thus two essentials to the success of the defence of Singapore as originally visualised were removed. Singapore was, therefore, doomed as early as June 17, 1940, when France sued for an armistice.

In 1928, a Staff College exercise had been held in India which simulated as closely as possible a landward attack by the Japanese on Singapore. This took place on the island of Salsette, north of Bombay, specially chosen for its geographical likeness to Singapore. The object of this exercise was to devise a satisfactory defence against such an attack. The exercise was regarded as a success, but no notice whatever was taken of its lessons. There thus seems to have been no point in conducting it in the first place.[3]

Indeed, every year until the outbreak of war, the defence of Singapore was a regular exercise set both at the Staff College in Quetta, and at the Imperial Defence College at Camberley in Surrey. More important, it was also an annual exercise at the War College in Tokyo.

The Japanese students of war reached the same conclusion as their British counterparts. The only difference was that they put what they had learned into practice when, in 1941, twenty years after the Washington Conference that had, in their own opinion, so humiliated the Japanese, they attacked Malaya, not

[3] The Japanese acquired some experience in successfully attacking the naval bases of European powers. They had captured Port Arthur from the Russians in 1904, and Tsingtao from the Germans ten years later. In both cases, the main assault had come from the rear, while naval activity was confined to ferrying troops and equipment, and a blockade to prevent the arrival of reinforcements.

In view of these two successful Japanese attacks, it came as a shock to many people, including Churchill, to learn on the eve of the Japanese invasion of Singapore in 1942, that this was the one type of attack the island's defences were not designed to meet. It was equally disturbing to learn, too late, that defences in Johore, on the mainland, facing Singapore, were so rudimentary that they could be (and were) completely discounted.

in miniature, on a sand-table, but in reality—with twenty years of rehearsals to help them.

In January 1936, what the *Daily Express* correspondent in Singapore colourfully described as "Britain's £20,000,000[4] fortress carved out of jungle and swamp, at the foot of the Malay peninsula, with sea roads to Australia, New Zealand, China, Hong Kong and all Empire possessions East of Suez," was the subject of mass British manoeuvres.

In the previous year, the British fleet air arm had attempted to "attack" Singapore. The exercise, so it was claimed, had proved "to the satisfaction of the authorities that no hostile aircraft-carrier could approach within 100 miles of the fortress before being blown out of the water."

What it had not proved was that hostile aircraft could be kept that distance away—especially if they were carrier-based.

These manoeuvres had been held to dispel the view that without greatly increased armaments, and especially more aero-planes, Singapore would prove indefensible in emergency. But the manoeuvres proved nothing, for they were based on the false, but convenient and traditional, notion of an attack from the sea.

It was also stated publicly that "without greatly increased armaments, and especially more planes, Singapore would prove a white elephant in an emergency."[5] Singapore's plan of defence still involved the passage of the main British fleet to the East, although in the light of German rearmament, the Japanese denunciation of the Washington Treaty, the Anglo-German Naval Treaty and the establishment of the Rome-Berlin Axis, this plan was beginning to appear increasingly unrealistic to all but those most closely involved in it.

In the manoeuvres, a hundred-odd aircraft took part—the maximum that could be assembled, from Singapore, India and even as far away as bases in Iraq. An anti-aircraft battery had set up its one gun outside the Raffles Hotel, but, as Reuter's correspondent reported, "Europeans entering the hotel gave the

[4] Actually, the final cost, by 1938, was in excess of £60,000,000.
[5] *Daily Express*, December 19, 1936.

'defences' only a casual glance; they appeared to be more interested in the cabaret."

However, great interest was shown in Japan in these manoeuvres, to such an extent that the Japanese newspaper correspondents, who had attended in surprising numbers—what was, after all, supposed to be a domestic exercise—complained that they could not follow them. To help them in this difficulty, the Japanese were issued outline drawings of the naval base and its defences. In that spring a British officer was posted with the rank of Chief Staff Officer (First Grade) to the headquarters of Malaya Command. He was Lieutenant-Colonel Arthur Ernest Percival. At forty-nine, Percival was old for the post, but then he had never intended to be a soldier. He was the son of a Hertfordshire land agent, had been educated at Rugby, an English public school, and then joined a firm in the City of London, Naylor, Benson & Company, as a clerk.

When the First World War broke out, Percival was twenty-seven, but despite his age he immediately enlisted in the Bedfordshire Regiment as a private soldier. Within a month, he was given a temporary commission in the Essex Regiment, and three years later he was commanding a battalion in action.

He was wounded, was awarded the Distinguished Service Order, the Military Cross, the French Croix de Guerre, and twice mentioned in despatches.

After the war Percival decided he would stay on in the Army as a professional soldier. In 1921 he was posted to Ireland and later wrote a report on the situation there. Its clarity so impressed Lloyd George, then Prime Minister, that Percival was invited to elaborate his views at a conference on the Irish situation being held in Inverness. Also present at this conference were Winston Churchill and Lord Birkenhead.

They were equally impressed by Percival's grasp of events— Churchill to such a degree that he recommended Percival for a course at the Staff College, although he was rather older than the usual run of officers who were selected.

In appearance, Percival was tall and thin, with a moustache and protruding front teeth. He was a keen sportsman; he played cricket for the Gentlemen of Essex. He was also an admirable staff officer; he could prepare a report or a memorandum that contained all the salient points of importance and still was easy to read.

As had been proved in action, he was an officer of exceptional bravery, but he lacked one essential for leadership when the chips were down: the inbuilt assurance that all successful military leaders need; panache and audacity and that unknown, invaluable quality that makes other men follow them.

Percival had been selected for the post in Malaya at the suggestion of the then Director of Military Operations and Intelligence at the War Office, Sir John Dill. Later, Dill was to be Vice-Chief and then a wartime Chief of the Imperial General Staff at the War Office, the supreme post in the British Army.

Percival had served as an instructor at the Camberley Staff College under Dill, and as he wrote later: "I had studied the attack and defence of Singapore on more than one occasion at the Staff College and at the Imperial Staff College, and was anxious to see what the place was really like."[6]

History was to provide Percival with ample and tragic opportunity for this, because, through no fault of his own, he was destined only five years later to command the land forces in the defence of Singapore against the Japanese in what *The Times* later described, without exaggeration, as "perhaps the most disastrous campaign in the history of British arms."

The General Officer Commanding in Malaya in 1936 was Major-General W. G. S. Dobbie, a deeply religious man, due to be knighted in 1942 for his gallant defence of wartime Malta, where he became Governor. Fighting, as he said, with "a sword in one hand and a Bible in the other," Dobbie attributed Malta's survival against Luftwaffe attacks largely to the power of prayer.

Percival, who had come to Singapore from a posting in Malta, where the services were predominant on the social scene, felt surprise that an officer of his rank meant very little in Malaya.

It was, as he wrote, "a rich commercial country whose people lived mainly on the production of rubber and tin. Before the

[6] *War in Malaya* by Lieutenant-General A. E. Percival.

arrival of the British more than a hundred years before, its people had been of a warlike disposition, but under British rule they had gradually learned ways of peace and for many years they had been left alone to develop their industries and enjoy the benefits of civilisation.

"They had not been touched even by the First World War, which had brought them great riches. . . .

"It was not to be wondered at that the people as a whole were not interested in defence. War had not come to Malaya for over a hundred years, so why should it come in the future? If the British Government liked to build a great naval base at Singapore—well, that was their business."

The social life in Malaya was altogether delightful for Europeans. Many employed several servants, including a chauffeur, a cook and a gardener; others ran two cars at a time when in Britain an employee of similar rank and standing could not afford a motor car of any description.

The climate was warm but very humid, and therefore enervating to Europeans, who needed regular and frequent leave to a cooler climate, either in Australia or in Britain.

Before the war, and before the advent of air travel, tours of duty for Europeans in Malaya lasted for four or five years, and then they might take six months' leave of absence.

From September 1939, when the war in Europe began, home leave to Britain had been impossible. Consequently, by 1941, many Europeans had served in Malaya for six or seven years without a break.

Children either were sent home to schools in Britain or else to the cooler atmosphere of the Cameron Highlands in the north of Malaya.

Salaries were high and living conditions, compared with similar jobs in Britain, were extremely good, for Malaya has an open-air climate. There were opportunities for nearly all forms of outdoor sport; for rugger, football, hockey, sailing and golf. In addition, wives spent a great deal of time playing mah-jongg and bridge. Hospitality ran at a very generous level.

Against this relaxed, confident background of good living, the peacetime activities of the Army counted for little. They seemed little better than Boy Scout manoeuvres by grown-up men. Inevitably, the underpaid privates—the enlisted men—in the British Army were not accepted socially by the affluent British civilians; and although in England many may well have sprung from the same social class, in peacetime Malaya and Singapore it is not too much to say that they were regarded in peacetime as almost second-class, poor-white citizens.

During the war very considerable efforts were made by the European, Australian and Asiatic communities to help the newly arrived British soldiers. They organised dances and concerts and games for them; cinema prices were reduced for troops, and entry fees either cut or waived altogether in clubs.

Singapore had an Anzac Club, built and financed by Australians and New Zealanders in Malaya, which opened in May 1941, and the Salvation Army Red Shield Club, which opened in August, plus clubs organised by the Y.M.C.A. and the Presbyterian Church. Penang had a Rotary Club and a leave hostel, and Kuala Lumpur a service canteen at the station and an Anzac Club.

But before the outbreak of war, things were very different. General Percival later quoted the pre-war editorial comment of one newspaper when it was suggested that barracks could be built, with other fortifications, on Penang Island, in the northwest of Malaya, to guard the western approaches to Singapore.

As regards the military barracks to be established at Tanjong Bungah on the rubber land on the other side of the road facing the Penang Swimming Club, the authorities are to be congratulated in the decision to place them thus well away from the town. A military population in the close vicinity of the town would not have been a pleasant experience for, without meaning any offence, we all know what soldiers are. . . .

In Penang, they were going to find out the hard way. One of the first places for British settlers in the days of Raffles, it was also the site of some disgraceful scenes during the exodus in 1942, because, while British families were evacuated, to travel south to Singapore, Asiatic families were left behind. No arrangements whatever were made for their evacuation.

It was no wonder, in view of this attitude, that when the Japanese seized the radio station in Penang, which, most unwisely, had been left in good working order and ready for them to operate, one of the chief anti-British broadcasters should be a former Indian civil servant.

The fortifications, incidentally, were useless. No anti-aircraft guns had reached Penang by the time the Japanese attacked and the island was quite indefensible. The pre-war swimmers in the Penang Swimming Club had been unnecessarily disturbed.

During his stay as a staff officer in Malaya, Percival was an observer at Japanese combined operations on the China coast. They used equipment "far in advance of anything which we had at the time." This, as we have seen, would not be difficult. They disposed innumerable landing craft for their purpose, while, as Percival noted, "ours at home had been limited by financial restrictions to what could be counted on the fingers of one hand."

❋   ❋   ❋

Nineteen thirty-six and 1937 were climactic years in Japan, when the struggle between the Army and those who favoured more constitutional government reached its peak.

In 1936, after the assassinations by soldiers of a number of prominent politicians and private citizens, Field Marshal Count Juichi Terauchi, later to become Japanese Commander-in-Chief in the Southwest Pacific, was appointed War Minister. In 1937, war broke out between China and Japan, and the Japanese intensified their attempts to discover how strong British defences were in Malaya and Singapore.

One Japanese businessman in Singapore, a Mr. Nishimura, arrested on a charge of espionage, swallowed a lethal pill on the steps of the police station and died, rather than face the ignominy of questioning on such an indictment. Another killed himself by jumping from a high window of the C.I.D. headquarters.

Successful intelligence, like genius, is a product of taking pains; or piecing together a jigsaw of seemingly unrelated happenings to produce a picture of events to come, the trend of future directions. Whereas, with one expection,[7] the British had an indifferent Intelligence system in Malaya and Singapore—again, because of cost and lack of application[8]—the Japanese were brilliant. Most towns and villages had at least one shop run by a Japanese; many had more. In general, these shops sold cameras and film,

[7] In September 1941, three months before the Japanese invaded Malaya from Siam, a British businessman, Mr. J. N. Becker (who later joined the Army, and as Captain Becker was attached to the British Intelligence Corps, on the Siamese-Malayan border) warned that Siam had already decided to side with Japan in any future conflict.

No notice was taken of this warning. Becker was, in his own words, "rapped over the knuckles" for interfering, and recalled to England "without any reason."

His prophecy proved correct. After the war, he wished to return to the Far East, but the Foreign Office at first refused him permission to leave Britain. Eventually, it issued him a passport marked "not valid for Siam." In August 1948, Becker was shot dead in his office in Singapore by a Chinese assassin. Becker, it was said, had claimed to have special knowledge of the Communist plot to seize power in Malaya. The Singapore C.I.D. announced that his murder had "no political significance."

[8] British Intelligence offices had access to certain police files on individuals, Chinese secret societies and political parties. Too much effort was expended on watching the movements of local Communists, whose influence then was not strong.

The Security Branch knew about a Japanese-sponsored organisation, the Fujiwara Heikan, which was designed to function throughout Malaya. On Singapore Island one hundred members were arrested shortly before the Japanese attack.

Earlier on, the Security Branch had submitted to the Government a list of five hundred Japanese and suspected Japanese co-travellers. These men were believed to be interested in sabotage, and it was suggested that dormant detention warrants be issued which could be executed on the declaration of war with Japan.

This was agreed, but the warrants were in fact never issued because there was no formal declaration of war. These five hundred suspects were rounded up, and with others, arrested up-country, they were interned at Port Swettenham and then sent to India.

In addition, sixty power boats with crews and their shore establishments, belonging to the Japanese fishing fleet in Singapore, were seized on news of the invasion.

did printing and developing, and were for general goods, groceries, cigarettes and candy.

These were deliberately selected because the Japanese correctly calculated that they were shops most likely to be patronised by British troops. Indeed, many photographic dealers offered extremely cheap rates for developing the films of troops who had been on leave. When the Japanese reached Singapore, many residents were surprised when a colonel in the Kempetai, the Japanese secret police, turned out to be a man well known in pre-war Singapore as a photographer.

North of Kuala Lumpur in January 1942, a Japanese tank was stopped on the main road by a British sergeant who, with a crew of three, manhandled a 4.5 Howitzer into position against it. They only had four rounds of ammunition, and their first shot went wide. So did the second.

The tank's machine guns meanwhile killed the three British soldiers, but the sergeant, still alive, fired for the third time at seventy-five yards distant—and still missed the tank. He reloaded with the last round, crouched down behind the shield of the gun, and waited until the tank came forward and was actually on the muzzle of his gun. Then he pulled the lanyard and destroyed it.

Among the belongings of the tank commander, a Japanese major, was a photograph of himself and his wife. This was sent to the local divisional headquarters. There Intelligence officers compared it with photographs of pre-war Japanese civilians. The wartime major had been a pre-war cycle repairer.[9]

[9] An equally elaborate spy ring of Japanese servants, barbers, masseurs and other apparently humble citizens existed in Pearl Harbor. The natural Japanese obsequiousness, plus their small stature, made this "cover" perfect for spying activities. Nor was this anything new; it had been tried with success at least since the end of the nineteenth century. In 1898, a group of six English diplomats in China were holidaying in the western hills. They sent back to Peking for a Japanese barber, who agreed to cut their hair for a total fee of three dollars.

On his journey to them he fell from his donkey and ripped his clothes, and so asked for an extra twenty cents to repair the damage. The British disputed this sum, but eventually paid. They next saw him two years later during the Boxer Rising. But then he wore the uniform and badges of rank of a colonel in the Japanese Legation.

Other Japanese shopkeepers managed to make long journeys into the interior, ostensibly to photograph big game, or for hunting trips.

These agents gathered information on tracks and jungle paths; on clearings and other topographical matters.

The Japanese also blackmailed Chinese in Singapore who had come from Hainan, where they had left many relations to whom many sent back much of their earnings. In the fashion since copied by Communist countries, the Japanese threatened the Chinese dependents left on Hainan unless their relations in Malaya and Singapore "co-operated" with information.

In addition, the Japanese owned extensive tin mines and rubber estates in such strategic areas as Johore—facing Singapore's virtually undefended north shore—and Trengganu, on the east coast, later a site for Japanese landings. Many of the fishermen along the coast were Japanese.

In the autumn of 1941 these fishermen quietly folded up their nets and went home to Japan. Many returned, with colleagues from the mines and the rubber estates, and acted as guides for the Japanese Army in December.

Some Japanese businessmen had carefully constructed fortified cellars beneath their houses in Singapore. When war broke out they descended to these cellars, expecting the Japanese to take the city even more quickly than they did. They were discovered and sent to India to be interned.

A remarkable number of Japanese students found it necessary shortly before the war to fly regularly from Singapore to Bandoeng in Java and back again. Passengers with them noticed how they always occupied window seats, and would photograph or sketch harbour installations and the Shell oil storage tanks at Pulau Bukom.

At weekends, too, in Singapore in the late 1930s many families would enjoy a fishing picnic at Ponggol Fishing Pond. The Japanese owner was always obliging with hooks and bait for anyone who wanted to catch *ikan merah*—local turbot—which could be cooked by Japanese cooks and served by Japanese waitresses.

In point of fact, this little enclave provided a useful cover for timing the arrivals and departures of British Catalina reconnaissance aircraft.

Other Japanese, on the innocent pretext of gathering material to repair service roads on the Japanese-owned estates, collected stocks of girders and tree trunks and piles of bricks and hid them near strategic bridges. This accounts for the fact that although the retreating defending forces blew many bridges to deny them to the Japanese, they were invariably open to traffic again within a matter of hours.

In old Singapore, the Japanese had maintained several hundreds of small hotels, little better than brothels. In the early years of the century, indeed, almost all prostitutes were Japanese, and because the law required that they should be medically examined from time to time, they were confined to certain areas, such as Malay Street and Malabar Street off Middle Road.

In the early 1920s, the Governor had set up what was known as the Venereal Commission, which discovered the illuminating information that something like 66 per cent of the population of Singapore at that time suffered from venereal disease, and these brothels were closed.

In the late twenties more pretentious Japanese hotels opened in their place, and although many people protested that they were still virtually brothels, and letters were written to local newspapers complaining of the situation, nothing was done because these hotels meant revenues from taxes and drinks.

A local doctor who lived in Singapore throughout the war wrote later:

Every Jap concern in this colony had its Fifth Column, as we learned to our cost after war broke out. The Jap salesman, the Jap barber, the Jap photographer, the Jap waitress, the prosperous Jap merchant —all these looked to the day when the Rising Sun . . . would be hoisted over Government House and Fort Canning. Yet nobody, in this chase-the-dollar island, seemed to care: why, the Japs were either cockeyed or—how could they fly with their oblique eyes? Those slits of eyes could not possibly help the Jap to be a first-class airman! We knew later, to our terrible cost, what complacency meant . . . !

The Japanese had their own clubs and restaurants. One was on Selegie Road. Another meeting place was the Japanese Golf Club on the hill adjoining Tanglin Road and Alexandra Road, now partly built on and known as Phoenix Park.

This clubhouse afforded excellent views of the fortifications built on the long ridge of the Pasir Panjang hills. Once, Japanese were seen watching this work in progress through a huge telescope from a clubhouse window. The person who reported this was greeted with amusement. Afterwards, the joke did not seem so funny.

The Singapore silk merchants were Japanese, so were the owners of toy shops, whose toys were so much cheaper than European toys.

On Saturday, December 6, 1941, the biggest silk shop in Southeast Asia, Echigoya & Company, announced on posters: "Cheap Sale Tomorrow." At four o'clock on the following morning, the first Japanese bombs fell on Singapore. It was not only silk that was being sold cheaply; it was the British Empire.

Japanese doctors, dentists, bakers, builders, barbers, shopkeepers, all played their part in gathering tiny pieces for the Intelligence mosaic, and gradually a picture of Singapore's true strength emerged in Tokyo.

As Colonel Masanobu Tsuji, who was in charge of the small group of Japanese officers who worked out the details of the Japanese campaign against Malaya, wrote later: "The absence of rear defences of the fortress constituted a very grave defect. The strength of its position was purposely and extravagantly propagandized without regard for the complacency which would be promoted among the public, and even among those responsible for its defence. . . ."

The British had repeated so often that Singapore was impregnable that the city became a victim of its own myth. Few appreciated what Churchill was later to call "the hideous efficiency of the Japanese war machine," or realised how two-edged propaganda can be.

The legend of Singapore's impregnability, created to fool the Japanese, fooled only the British, civilian and military, by lulling them into a sense of false and quite illusory security.

"Our work consisted chiefly in developing the defences of Singapore in accordance with a War Office plan," wrote Percival later. "Approval had to be obtained for all major expenditure and, owing to the shortage of available funds, demands were often heavily cut. It will be readily understood, therefore, that the G.O.C. was strictly limited as to what he could do on his own initiative, while delays were occasioned by the necessity to get War Office approval, first for a project, then for an estimate, and finally for a contract." Thus, the cost of defending the British Empire's greatest outpost in the East was, in the last analysis, decided by some anonymous civil servant in Whitehall, who may never have been farther east than Southend pier. Days lengthened into weeks and the weeks melted into months while requests for permission to proceed poured ponderously across the world.

Percival also claims: "I think we were the first to start actual training in the jungles and plantations of Malaya and to discover that they were not quite so impassable as had been thought."

This may well have been so, but making this rather obvious discovery and implementing it effectively were two entirely different things. The fact remains that most staff officers, viewing the jungle, green and thick and unwelcoming, on either side of the Singapore to Kuala Lumpur road, from the comfort of their cars as they sped north or south on business or pleasure, considered it sufficiently impenetrable not to warrant any attempt to march through it, let alone to live in it or off it. Maps were marked to this effect.

Too many senior officers were too confident with too little knowledge of the country or its conditions.

The daughter of a former member of the Legislative Assembly married an officer in an Indian regiment shortly before war broke out, and his colonel attended the wedding. When some guests, fearing a possible Japanese invasion, asked what was being done in the way of defence, the colonel replied: "Malaya is the easiest country in the world to defend. There's one main road running roughly from north to south and a railway line. So long as we can hold these, the country stays ours."

Someone asked what was being done about the beaches. The reply was that they were unimportant. The military maps showed complete blanks from the beaches to the main road. Two-thirds of the country had been scored out as being impenetrable jungle.

Because these officers had never penetrated the jungle, they assumed that no one else could. They did not realise, or seemed incapable of understanding, that the jungle was riddled with animal tracks, with tracks made by locals going to and from villages, local market places, rivers and wells.

One young officer who suggested that it would be an excellent idea to take a patrol through this jungle to see how impenetrable it was, found himself called before his C.O.

The C.O. agreed that this was an excellent idea, but he made it a condition that the young lieutenant bring back one or two local girls who could possibly do cabaret turns at the club. He had heard that they were excellent belly dancers. The lieutenant could not promise to do this; the patrol never left.

By mid-1941, when Spencer Chapman, later to be awarded the D.S.O. and to fight for most of the war behind the Japanese lines as a guerilla leader, arrived in Singapore, he reported, "The High Command in Malaya were not in the least interested in guerilla warfare in any of its forms.

"At that time, the war in Europe had set no example of a successful resistance movement, and there were too many at Far Eastern Headquarters who still thought in terms of the last war. . . . The defence of Malaya was considered to be purely a military undertaking and to be already well under control through the proper channels."[10]

Because Malaya had enjoyed such a long period of peace and prosperity, it was difficult to attune civilian thinking to the possibility that these easy, gracious years could ever end. In fact, little attempt was made to do so. Although Singapore was British, the overwhelming majority of its inhabitants were British only in the fact that they were British subjects.

They were Chinese, Malays, Indians and some Arabs, and their initial loyalty was to their own race, rather than to the British flag. This was to prove a fatal weakness.

[10] *The Jungle Is Neutral* by F. Spencer Chapman.

Many senior members of the British Civil Service had enjoyed a classical education, but they had not learned an invaluable lesson on imperial history from the old Roman Empire. The Romans, like the British later on, raised many of their legions from foreign races. But every inhabitant of each country within the Roman Empire became a Roman citizen with full rights and privileges—Paul, the Jew, was proud to claim that he was a citizen of Rome by birth, and had not bought this advantage.

The races within the British Empire, although owing technical allegiance to the British Crown, did not think of themselves as Britons—although they might hold British passports. They regarded themselves as Indians, Africans or Malays, or whatever other nationality they might have been born.

The Malays were easy-going, pleasant, good-natured people, lacking political or national aspirations, content that their country should be run for them. The Chinese, although a numerical minority, controlled many of the commercial firms, they were extremely hard-working, and grew rich, gradually extending their commercial control to the extent that such Malays who considered the matter at all were worried.

The Indians were there, like the Europeans, to make money.

As one British staff officer wrote bitterly: "There was no common bond of love of country, or pride of race, but the whole four communities gave the impression of being loosely knit together by the ties of business interest.

"Money was the god. Nothing else mattered but money, and the ways in which money was acquired were, as often as not, scarcely in keeping with the accepted standards of honesty.

"On top of these business communities, a military force of fair size was superimposed and this military structure sat very uneasily on its foundations. There was no unity of purpose embracing the whole resources of the States and colonies and including the military forces. There was neither strength nor power, nor greatness in the Government. There was never any serious effort to prepare the country mentally or materially for totalitarian war."[11]

[11] *Who Dies Fighting* by Angus Rose.

Although this view was held by numerous British officers who had recently arrived in Malaya, it was, in fact not entirely accurate.

At the outbreak of war with Germany in 1939, the Malayan Government, on instructions from Britain, had refused all exit permits from Malaya for European nationals, except in exceptional circumstances. They were ordered to remain in their jobs because of the importance of the tin and rubber production for the British war effort.

"But for this," the Governor wrote later, "the majority of British males would have gone home long before the Japanese invasion. It is only fair to the men to say this, because rightly or wrongly, I had gained the impression during my service in Malaya that the military authorities regarded the European community as chiefly interested in making money. They disliked intensely the thought that a trained man, speaking Malay or Tamil, might be more usefully employed in tin and rubber production whole time than in joining the volunteers."[12]

Also, most Europeans were liable for compulsory service in the defence of Malaya. As proof of this, Sir Shenton Thomas later pointed out that, despite the fact that civilian internment camps contained young men who had come ashore from sunken merchant ships, their average age at the beginning of their internment in 1942 was forty-six—which underlined the fact that most of the younger male Europeans were interned with the Armed Forces, as members of the Volunteers or other service units.

Giles Playfair, who worked for the Malayan Broadcasting Corporation, described Singapore's civilian population bluntly as: "Asiatics—Chinese, Malays, Indians, Arabs—who mostly dislike the whites and, what is more alarming, dislike each other. There is no spirit of one for all and all for one here. There is no national feeling. The Chinese don't show the least inclination to fight for the Malays, nor the Malays for the Chinese, nor the Arabs for anyone."[13]

The results of these clashes in temperament, psychology and

[12] The private papers of Sir Shenton Thomas.
[13] *Singapore Goes Off the Air* by Giles Playfair.

outlook, the lack of a common bond, a common denominator of patriotism and nationality meant that the military encountered numerous difficulties and a widespread apathy which would have been hard to overcome had they themselves been men of resource, drive and initiative.

In the event, these difficulties proved impossible to overcome. As Percival himself admitted: "When I had been at the Imperial Defence College, everything had seemed so easy. When difficulties arose between the representatives of military and civil interests they were almost invariably settled by a compromise.

"But it is one thing to compromise on paper and quite another thing to compromise when you have real interests to consider. This was the root of most of the difficulties which arose in Malaya. Never before had we attempted to build a fortress on the top of a rich and prosperous commercial centre. There were clashes of interests, and important ones, too, at every turn."

On February 15, 1938, Sir Shenton Thomas, Governor of the Straits Settlements of Malaya, formally opened the new £1,000,000 graving dock, large enough to take the greatest battleship afloat, at Singapore. The ceremony was attended by about 11,000 people, including the Duke and Duchess of Sutherland, Viscount Monsell the First Lord of the Admiralty, Sir Charles Vyner Brooke, the "white rajah" of Sarawak, and hundreds of Indian and Chinese labourers who had helped to build the dock.

Twenty-five British warships from the China and East Indies stations and from the Royal Indian Navy stood by, while planes from the aircraft carrier *Eagle* roared overhead.

The three American cruisers *Trenton, Milwaukee* and *Memphis* were the only foreign ships invited to witness the ceremony. This event, declared the *Daily Express*,[14] "will announce to the world that Britain's £20,000,000 naval base (Gibraltar of the East) is ready."

Four years and one day later, this Eastern Gibraltar surrendered.

No one in sufficiently high authority had appreciated that it

[14] February 14, 1938.

was, as the *Express* correspondent so accurately described it, a *base* and not a defensive or even defensible position with the weapons agreed for its use.

Actually, as subsequent events were to show, very painfully, Singapore as a base might be ready, but its defences were not, and this fact was no doubt fully reported to his superiors by Mr. Okamoto, the Japanese Consul-General, whom the *Express* correspondent described as "the loneliest figure at the ceremony."

The naval base at Singapore, the hub on which the big wheel of British imperial Far Eastern strategy now revolved, however creakily, was of enormous size and impressive complexity. Iron gates and high walls ringed in what was virtually a self-contained town, covering several square miles, latticed with wide streets on which stood estates of bungalows and houses which, from their architecture, might have been transported from any suburb around London.

Millions of tons of earth had been moved to build vast catacombs, all with special ventilation systems for stores and underground headquarters, immune from the explosion of any known bomb. The course of a major river had been diverted; thirty-four miles of concrete and iron piles had been driven down through the swamps to meet solid bedrock beneath, some to a depth of one hundred feet, to secure the foundations.

For the off-duty needs of those who would serve in this expensive tombstone to the white man's supremacy in the East, there were churches, canteens, cinemas, seventeen football pitches. The graving dock was second in size only to that of Southampton, and could take the *Queen Mary* with room to spare.

The floating dock, built to accommodate a 45,000-ton battleship, had cost £250,000 simply to transport it by sea from England. This included one single charge of £10,000 for Suez Canal dues.

There were cranes that could lift 500 tons—a complete gun turret from a battleship—and underground, far beneath the surface of the sea, lay rows of bombs, shells, spares of every kind and all available sizes. The oil tanks contained enough oil to refuel every ship in the British Navy on its longest cruising range. The stocks of food could victual the entire British Navy for three months—which was calculated to give a safety margin of two to three weeks over the original siege limit of seventy days.

Such was the significance of this base that early Short flying boats were named "Short Singapores" in its honour. Over twenty years, at a cost of more than £60,000,000, it represented by the late thirties nothing more than a gift of vast warlike treasure stores prepared and stocked for any enemy. It was completely indefensible. It stood as a monument to a strategy, even then departed, soon to be defeated and denigrated.

It had been designed for war at sea, conceived in nineteenth-century terms of shot and shell, of gunboats and smoke screens, the besiegers and the besieged. It had been designed for an out-of-date battle that would never be fought. Its design was as remote from twentieth-century reality as the pathetic plan for its defence.

All its statistics of size and cost and complication, so proudly catalogued, all its vast dimensions so frequently photographed in the illustrated periodicals of the day, only emphasised its elephantine uselessness. As a correspondent of *The Times* was to cable sadly before the collapse of this fortress that never was: "It had been tucked away at the back of the island as if an attack on the base from the mainland was a possibility that had never occurred to its builders.

"Indeed, it had been built on the premise that our Navy and Air Force would never permit an enemy to come within one hundred miles of Singapore. But Singapore's back door had become its front door. One machine gun firing across the Strait was worth all the 500-ton cranes in the world. . . ."

＊　　＊　　＊

In a conversation with the writer, General Percival pointed out that "the strategy of the defence of our Eastern empire [outposts] in pre-war years was that they would be defended by a skeleton garrison on the understanding that, if any danger in that part of the world blew up, part of the British fleet would go there and prevent any enemy fleet from attacking the localities or landing troops there.

"This referred not only to Singapore, but to all other outlying parts of our Empire.

"Most military bases in the Empire thus had nucleus garrisons. The reason for this was that we had not got the troops at that time to maintain them at full strength at these different places. It would have been very uneconomical to do so, and, in fact, we did not have the number of troops necessary. There is a limit to the number of troops you can raise in Britain in peacetime. . . .

"When the war in the West looked fairly imminent, it became obvious to us (I was Chief of Staff in Singapore at that time) that the time might come when we would not be in the position to send the necessary naval force to Malaya, because they would have to be retained in the West, and we represented that very strongly in 1937.

"I personally wrote an appreciation of that situation at the request of Sir William Dobbie, which was sent to the War Office. We pointed out that the time might well come in these conditions when a fleet would not be able to go out there. In those conditions the existing garrison, as it was in Malaya, would be quite inadequate."

No notice was taken of this report for two years when, as Percival further explained, "the Committee of Imperial Defence agreed if this was a fair picture, that situation *might* arise.

"It was then that they started building up the defences so far as forces that were available. Of course, they were all heavily committed in the worst way, and it became a question of priorities for the available forces and equipment. That was another major problem."

The whole question bristled with problems like a porcupine with quills. They were left to bristle. The defence of Malaya and Singapore against a sea-borne invasion had certain similarities with any plan of defence for England and Wales from a similar enemy. The peninsula of Malaya is roughly nine hundred miles from north to south, sixty miles across at its narrowest portion and about three times as wide at its thickest. It is bounded on three sides—again like England and Wales—by sea. Where Scotland stands in relation to England, Malaya shares a border with Siam. Down the centre of the country a range of hills extends like a spine: at their highest they are 7000 feet and these effectively divide the country into two parts.

The west side is the more heavily populated, with Penang Island, Ipoh and Kuala Lumpur. Down this west side of the hills the main road runs north to south with the railway line. The east coast had few roads; one was only a fine-weather track which followed the coast from Trengganu to Kuantan. There was an east coast railway, like the west coast one, of metre gauge, but the towns were small and spaced apart.

Rice was the predominant crop in the north of Malaya, with miles of flat paddy fields criss-crossed by ridges about eighteen inches high to contain the heavy rain. In the tin-mining areas of the states of Perak and Selangor the country was open. In the rubber plantations, the largest in the world—more than 35,-000,000 rubber trees by 1940—there was no difficulty about transporting either men or materials, but there was a psychological drawback to camps being established under the rubber trees. They produced a strange, curious sense of depression among troops, otherwise cheerful and in good heart.

This may be due in part to the strange sensation felt by seeing, on all sides, as far as the eye could reach, rows of rubber trees completely in line. When the watcher moved it seemed, by an optical illusion, that the distant trees also moved—or were they concealing human enemies who were moving? This phenomenon was to be of some importance later in the campaign, when the nerves of the defenders, fighting thousands of miles from home beneath these dripping trees, were taut with apprehension; when the enemy had only to wear local Malay costume, and, to inexperienced European eyes, it was impossible to distinguish Asiatic friend from foe.

In relation to Malaya, Singapore Island is like the Isle of Wight in relation to England, separated from the mainland by a causeway 1100 feet long that carries both a road and a railway.

To conceive of defending Singapore against an attack from an enemy who already holds all Malaya is thus even more impractical than imagining that the Isle of Wight could be held for seventy days against an invader who controlled all England and Wales.

Before Percival returned to London for reposting in 1937, he felt sure that if, through war in Europe, which by then seemed extremely likely, the British fleet was unable to sail to the Far East, the real danger to Singapore would come not from the sea, but from the mainland.

Putting himself in the position of a Japanese commander, Percival visualised seizing airfields in Siam and Kelantan, and the island of Penang and then ruthlessly driving south. It was, therefore, essential that Singapore should have far more aircraft, more troops, and also fast, small naval craft that could operate in shallow water near the coast and along rivers and inlets.

General Dobbie agreed with this entirely and wrote his own memorandum, in which he said:

"It is an attack from the northward that I regard as the greatest potential danger to the fortress. Such attack could be carried out during the period of the northeast monsoon. The jungle is not in most places impassable for infantry."

Percival wrote afterwards with remarkable restraint: "It was, to say the least, unfortunate that this appreciation did not . . . bring home to the authorities in England the change in the whole problem of the defence of the Singapore naval base.

"The existing policy that the British main fleet must sail for Singapore in the event of war, whatever the circumstances might be in European waters, was reaffirmed. What a short-sighted policy . . .

"National interests should come before any party or private considerations."

General Dobbie started to organise defences on the southern part of Johore but work stopped because there was not enough money to carry it out. The British Government, however, authorised an extension of supplies in the base from withstanding a siege of seventy days to withstand one of one hundred eighty days. In the event, this simply meant that the Japanese were able to seize not seventy days' supplies when they took Singapore in 1942, but, rather, more than twice this amount.

Back in England, Percival was appointed Brigadier, on the General Staff of Aldershot Command. The G.O.C. at that time was General John Dill.

"When I joined his staff he asked me if Singapore was impregnable. . . . I told him that, in my opinion, far from being impregnable, it would be in imminent danger if war broke out in the Far East unless there was an early realization in high places of the complete change in the problem of its defence which was then taking place. . . .

"Dill was in general agreement. . . . He never had any doubts as to the great importance to us of Singapore."

But still nothing was done. The men who would have to defend Singapore were not to be allowed even the basic weapons they knew were necessary, let alone the superiority of weapons, in quality and quantity, that could have persuaded the Japanese of the folly of attempting any attack.

Meanwhile, in Europe the threat of war grew nearer. It broke out in September 1939. With the retreat of the British from Dunkirk in the following June, the collapse of France and the Battle of Britain above the skies of southeast England in the autumn of 1940, it was understandable that, with the dearth of warlike equipment to stave off what appeared to be an imminent German invasion, there was nothing much to spare for a possible—and at that time still hypothetical—attack on Singapore, 11,780 miles away.

In Singapore, Lieutenant-General L.V. (later Sir Lionel) Bond had succeeded Dobbie as G.O.C. He was equally aware of the pathetic state of Singapore's defences and asked the Governor of the Straits Settlements, Sir Shenton Thomas, for a coolie labour force to construct more defences.

On January 27, 1940, Thomas reported to the Colonial Office that, in his talks with Bond, he had raised the question of the conflicting priorities of defence and industry. There was a general shortage of European manpower due to enlistment, and the

Malayan Government's orders were to maintain at a maximum the output of the tin (half the world's output) and the rubber (one-third), essential to the war effort.

Sir Shenton added: "I conceive it to be our duty to give absolute priority to the claims of industry," and thought that the conscription of a labour force, as requested by Bond, was undesirable.

Sir Shenton, the son of a Cambridge vicar, had spent twenty-five years in the colonial service in Africa. He had been appointed to Malaya in 1934 and should have been relieved in 1940, but his period of office had been extended. He was then in his sixties, a man of considerable personal courage, but in no sense a commanding personality; and his years in Malaya had been, as Percival tactfully noted, "a long time in a trying climate."

Thomas frequently described Malaya as "the dollar arsenal"— which, of course, it was ($135,000,000 in 1940–41 compared with $98,000,000 in the first year of the war). So the Malays, Indians and Chinese worked on in the tin mines and rubber plantations. And they went on working there, even when war in the East was imminent, instead of building pillboxes, gun sites and anti-tank barriers that could have preserved the dollar arsenal from attack and capture.[15] It was argued that rubber was of the highest priority for war in other theatres; synthetic rubber was not yet well developed and lacked the wearing qualities of real rubber.

This role of rubber and tin producer was not, in fact, of Sir Shenton Thomas' own choosing, but had been imposed on him by the British Government in London. As he wrote later: "The primary role allotted to Malaya . . . [was] the maximum possible production of tin and rubber and the conservation of foreign exchange. She sold more to the U.S.A. than any unit

[15] Percival told the writer that the British Government laid down "very definitely that the production of rubber and tin from Malaya must be continued at all costs and must have priority to everything else. The majority of rubber and tin being used for our war effort came from that part of the world, and one could not use the labour force there for military purposes or defences because they were all fully occupied in producing rubber and tin."

of the British Empire save Canada and, whereas Canada bought much from the U.S.A., Malaya bought little.

"In 1939, her sales to the U.S.A. exceeded her purchases by more than twelve million American dollars a month, and in some years the U.S.A. bought from Malaya twenty-five times as much as they sold to her. In 1937 they bought to the value of 235 million Straits dollars, while the colonies which most nearly approached this figure, i.e. Ceylon and the Gold Coast, sold to the value of twenty-one million dollars. (A Straits dollar is worth 2s/4d).

"The maximum unrestricted production of tin with the existing plant was estimated by the industry to be rather less than 90,000 tons a year. In 1940, the production was 84,751 tons, and in 1941 to the end of September it was 61,645 tons, equivalent to 82,198 tons in a full year. In that year European supervision had been reduced owing to the demands on manpower.

"There were some 3,250,000 acres under rubber. There is normally a large acreage of immature or seedling rubber. In 1941, the tappable acreage was 1,747,101 of which 1,640,931 acres, or 94.5 per cent, was tapped. The production in 1940 was 505,749 tons, and in 1941, to 31st October, 500,932 tons. Nearly half of the acreage is in the form of Asiatic small holdings of one hundred acres or less.

"During the quarter ended the 30th of November 1940, no fewer than 137,331 tons of rubber were shipped to the U.S.A. alone."

Sir Shenton, in cables to London, stressed the necessity of increasing the number of aircraft in Malaya, as this would greatly reduce the threat of war.

Air Vice-Marshal J. T. Babington, Air Officer Commanding, Far East (later Air Marshal Sir John; in 1945 he changed his name to Sir John Tremayne) agreed with the Governor's views. In a memo to the Air Ministry in London he pointed out that the arrival of the main fleet, on which the defence of Singapore rested, was no longer a viable proposition and that the Air Force must therefore be increased.

Babington was taking the air force view that aircraft were a better insurance against attack than fixed guns. On April 13, 1940, Bond sent to the War Office a detailed appreciation of the problems involved in the defence of Malaya, prepared in consultation with Babington. In this they stressed that it was vital to defend the whole of Malaya, not just Singapore. They demanded considerable military reinforcements, and emphasised that since this demand was probably impossible, then the Air Force would have to be utilised to its fullest possible extent.

On May 16, the Overseas Defence Committee met to consider the memoranda sent by Sir Shenton Thomas and General Bond, agreed that reinforcements were necessary, but said that there were none available. By this time the whirlwind had broken with all its force in Europe; the Nazi hordes swept through the Low countries and France, causing the British to evacuate at Dunkirk and prepare to fight desperately for survival over the skies of Britain.

On September 10, with the Battle of Britain at its height, Churchill told his Chief of Staff, General Ismay, "The Prime defence of Singapore is the fleet. The protective effect of the fleet is exercised to a large extent whether it is on the spot or not. The fact that the Japanese had made landings in Malaya and had even begun the siege of the fortress would not deprive a superior relieving fleet of its power.

"On the contrary, the plight of the besiegers, cut off from home while installing themselves in the swamps and jungle, would be all the more forlorn. The defence of Singapore must therefore be based on a strong local garrison and the general potentialities of sea power. The idea of trying to defend the whole of the Malay peninsula cannot be entertained."

This was Churchill's answer to the request for reinforcements.

But in September 1940, with Nazi invasion threatening Britain, what forces could he be expected to send? After all, there was no war in the Far East; the war was raging around southeast England. Nonetheless, his comments looked ill for the future, for he was repeating the old fallacy about the supremacy of sea power, and adding another to it by contending that Singapore could be held without defending Malaya.

The Chiefs of Staff were concerned at the lack of a comprehensive scheme of defence to cover Malaya, Burma and the Bay of Bengal. So, to satisfy this want, Sir Robert Brooke-Popham was appointed Commander-in-Chief, Far East, on October 17, 1940.

Known to flying men as "Brookham," he was a tall, gangling man with a straggly, reddish moustache; he had a somewhat high-pitched voice and a shy, abashed manner. He had led a distinguished career in the Air Force (a First World War veteran, and the first man to fire a gun from an aeroplane in 1913) before retiring in 1937 to become the Governor of Kenya.

Recalled to the active list on the outbreak of war, he was sixty-two years old when he took up his Far East appointment, and without recent war experience. However, as the first R.A.F. officer to be appointed a C-in-C, he naturally enough realised the crucial role of air power in the defence of Singapore. He also realised, whatever Churchill might say, that it was essential to hold the whole of the Malay peninsula.

Besides stressing the grave shortage of land forces he pointed out to the Chiefs of Staff "in picturesque language"[16] that the position in the air was even worse. Against their estimate of 336 aircraft as the necessary minimum, there were only forty-eight planes—and none of these were fighters.

The Chiefs of Staff thought that their figure of 336 should be achieved by the end of 1941. But it never was. In any case, Churchill was reluctant to sanction the diversion of forces promised by the Chiefs of Staff from actual theatres of war. On January 13, 1941, he sent a memo to the Chiefs of Staff that stated, among other points: "The political situation in the Far East does not seem to require, and the strength of our Air Force by no means permits, the maintenance of such large forces in the Far East at this time."

Thus, whatever arrived for Brooke-Popham was to prove too little and too late. He had neither the means nor the time to succeed. He was, despite this, a party to much of the facile optimism which proved so damaging. As he later admitted:

[16] *Official History of the War in the Far East*, Vol. II, by Professor J. R. M. Butler.

"One of the steps taken to discourage the Japanese from starting war was to emphasise the growing strength of our defences in Malaya."

In February 1941, the 8th Australian Division, under Major-General H. Gordon Bennett, arrived in Singapore. Air Vice-Marshal Conway Pulford relieved Babington as A.O.C., Far East; and in May, Percival replaced Bond.

Percival's war until then had been varied but lacked the action he would have liked. He had served with Dill in France as Brigadier, General Staff, of the 1st Corps, and returned in February 1940 to command a training division in Wiltshire. He was then posted to the War Office, where he rejoined Dill, who had been appointed Vice-Chief of the Imperial General Staff.

Percival was one of three Assistant Chiefs of the I.G.S., co-ordinating the day-to-day work of the Operations and Intelligence Directorates. He has noted that it was "a time of great interest and great activity and [he] sometimes attended meetings of the War Cabinet," but he yearned for more active work, and requested to be returned to a field formation. He was appointed Commander of the 44th (Home Counties) Division. In March 1941, he was ordered by telegram to report at the War Office on the next day with all tropical kit.

Here he was informed that he had been appointed General Officer Commanding Malaya, following Lieutenant-General Lionel Bond, and must set off within three days for Singapore by flying boat, then the only aerial means for such a long and important trip.

He settled his personal affairs as quickly as possible, and was then informed that the flying boat was undergoing repairs. There would thus be a delay of a further three days. In fact, Percival waited for five more weeks until the aircraft was ready, for, as he wrote later, "if one flying boat broke down, there was apparently no replacement."

The air journey from London to Singapore occupied another fortnight—he was delayed for a week on the way—and he only covered the distance so quickly because he managed to change planes at Rangoon and fly on in an R.A.F. aircraft.

Although Percival was the General Officer Commanding, the structure of command was not as simple as the layman might suppose from Sir Percival's official designation. As he wrote, with some understatement, "Considerable changes had taken place in the defence organisation." To the lay eye these changes seemed to have brought with them at least a plurality of command. Brooke-Popham was Commander-in-Chief, Far East, with his headquarters in the naval base. His duties dealt with the "operational control and general direction of training" of British land and air services, not only in Malaya, but also in Burma and Hong Kong. Brooke-Popham was also responsible for co-ordinating plans to defend these places, but was not concerned with administrative or financial matters, which were supposed to be the duties of the General Officers Commanding Malaya, Burma and Hong Kong. Nor had he any jurisdiction over the Air Officer Commanding, Far East, and neither command nor control over any part of the British Navy.

All these senior officers dealt direct with their ministries in London—the War Office, the Air Ministry, the Colonial Office and the Burma Office, on matters that concerned them and their areas.

On the civilian side was the Governor, Sir Shenton Thomas. Later, Mr. Duff Cooper was to be appointed British Resident Cabinet Minister in the Far East. So many men, so many services, had their hands on the controls—but who was in ultimate command, who had the power of decision? As the *Straits Budget*, the weekly issue of the *Straits Times*, asked pointedly in an article published on January 1, 1942, "Who *are* our leaders?"

Later, after Singapore fell, when the British were retreating in Burma, the *Rangoon Gazette* echoed this question with two headlines of its own:

OUR FINEST FIGHTING EFFICIENCY WILL BE WHEN THE
BUREAUCRATS HAVE GONE

FAITH IN OUR FIGHTING MEN: BUT SAVE US FROM
NON-BELLIGERENT DOPES!

With so many commanders, the paper work did not decline. Some remembered wryly the reply of the Duke of Wellington to his Secretary of State for War in 1810: "My Lord, if I attempted to answer the mass of futile correspondence that surrounds me, I should be debarred from all serious business of campaigning. I must remind your Lordship—for the last time —that so long as I retain an independent position, I shall see to it that no officer under my command is debarred, by attending to the futile drivelling of mere quill-driving in your Lordship's office, from attending to his first duty—which is, as always, to train the private men under his command that they may without question beat any force opposed to them in the field."

Initiative was further dulled by the inertia of the humid climate, and the necessity for even the simplest orders and instructions to be passed around the various bases, and up through the echelons of seniority to the officers concerned. Urgent matters, such as the erection of defences, the siting of weapon pits, had often to be referred to the Sultans of the states concerned; and days lengthened into weeks and weeks into months, and the tide ebbed out for the West.

These delays occurred in spite of the fact that the Civilian Secretary for Defence in Singapore dealt with all war preparations for the whole of Malaya, and so was in close contact with each individual state and settlement as well as with Sir Shenton Thomas.

The latter wrote later: "Each ruler had authorised his British Resident or Adviser to deal immediately and direct with the Secretary for Defence on behalf of his state government. Thus, any war matter in any state which required any consideration went straight to the Secretary for Defence and from him to me. Similarly, any instruction or request from me or the War Council was sent direct by him to the state or states or departments concerned.

"In pan-Malayan matters the Secretary for Defence issued circular letters and received replies for me to consider. On defence matters it was rarely necessary to consult the various governments: the War Committee or War Council decided, and instructions went out. . . .

"There were other safeguards. There was the War Council, of which the Service heads were members. They could always bring up any matter and get a quick decision. There was also the Executive Council of the colony, of which the G.O.C. was a member, and to which he could refer any question and get a quick decision. And there was the power vested in the High Commissioner for Malay States (who was also the Governor of the colony) whereby he could, if he thought fit, *require* action to be taken if any state proved obdurate.

"This power was called 'advice' in the treaties with the states. I had never to use it. Lastly, it was always possible for any service commander to see me officially and informally. This happened frequently. Some were very kind in keeping me informed or in asking my advice. We were all the best of friends. . . ."

Percival found that he did not have one single military aircraft of any kind to aid the Army. So slender were other R.A.F. resources that the Air Officer Commanding asked him specifically not to use aircraft for communication purposes "except on special occasions." Thus Percival either travelled across Malaya in the ordinary civil airlines of the day, or in single-engine Moth planes with Volunteer Air Force pilots. But if the defence of the West's bastion in the East was not "a special occasion," a definition of what constituted one should have been supplied.

The airstrips had been built to R.A.F. specifications and instructions without proper regard to the fact that they might be in completely indefensible positions. In the event, many were never used by the R.A.F. because there were not enough aircraft to fly from them. They were, however, appreciated by the Japanese who refuelled their own planes from the stocks of gasolene which they found on arrival.

Labourers, apart from the coolies in the tin mines and on rubber plantations, could have been found, but the pay and conditions the armed services offered were totally inadequate to attract them.

The labourers were Chinese and Tamils. In January 1941, eleven months before Japan attacked, the wage rate for an adult male Tamil (excluding payments in kind) was fifty cents a day, and between eighty and eighty-five cents a day for a Chinese contract tapper on a rubber plantation.

A year later, the local rates were stated, in the War Council minutes of January 23, 1942, as being one hundred cents a day, plus food and quarters, with increases for more senior men. Even so, the best that the War Office offered in April 1941 was forty-five cents a day, and forty for a Tamil woman worker.

Sir Shenton Thomas wrote later: "No Tamil male had been rated so low since September 1938, and for a Chinese I have no figure less than sixty-five cents. I should be very interested to know on what advice the War Office fixed forty-five cents, and why Bond [General Bond] did not immediately protest. The civil government would surely have backed him. . . .

"The Services were . . . offering less than half the proper rate, with no food, no protection, no compensation for casualties. These are the reasons why Service labour was difficult to obtain during the campaign.

"In the end, I had to wire home for the grant of carte blanche to the Services in such matters, and pending a reply I authorised them to draw on civil government funds for what they needed and to refund in due course. . . ."

But events overwhelmed the negotiations and so the defences which Percival and Dobbie had said should be dug as a matter of urgency in 1937 were, by 1941, at best still only vestigial, and at worst existed only on a paper in some planner's office. The relationship between the Indian coolies and the European managers had worsened, for one side—and apparently unanticipated—result of the influx of British, Indian and Australian troops to defend Malaya was that the cost of living soared.

This meant little to most Europeans, but for coolies working for wages equivalent to £1 or less a week, it meant disaster. Indian labourers on rubber estates in Selangor demanded an increase, and it was pointed out, on their behalf, that, while rubber prices had increased three times since the outbreak of war, their wages had not increased at all. The employers retorted that their wages were still higher than those being paid in India, and if they did not like the jobs they could leave, and be replaced by Javanese and Chinese labourers.

Early in 1941, this situation had reached a crisis. Indian labourers on estates in Selangor appealed to their employers, and to the Government Controller of Labour in Kuala Lumpur. They asked for a wage increase to meet the higher cost of living; the replacement of clerks or under-managers whom they accused of ill-treating them; education for labourers' children; medical aid; protection for their womenfolk from unwanted attentions by unscrupulous clerks and managers; permission to entertain friends and relatives in their quarters; eight hours' work a day, and an end to arbitrary dismissals of labourers on what they called "baseless charges."

Regarded now, these requests seem reasonable enough, but then they were thought to be only the first of possible future demands, which could cripple the economy.

They were not met, and the coolies went on strike. To try and break this strike, the managers cut off the water supply and rations to the labourers who lived in "lines"—long, single-storey blocks of hutments.

Local Indians who sympathised with them were forbidden to help them, under an emergency ordinance. Fights broke out between European managers on one side and Indian strike-leaders and agitators on the other. The police were called.

Finally, the government intervened because the need for rubber in the war was vital. Troops were given emergency powers and the trouble simmered down.

But, in fact, only the surface was serene. These labour troubles, springing from genuine grievances, but assiduously fomented by the enormously strong Japanese Fifth Column, financed through the Japanese Embassy poisoned relations between Europeans and Asiatics at a time when it had never been more important that these relations be good.

One Indian later wrote that this "resulted in a feeling of

aversion among the Indian community toward British Imperialism and in a longing for freedom from foreign domination."[17]

Thus, when the Japanese arrived with such attractive slogans as "New Order," "Greater East Asia Co-prosperity Sphere" and "Asia for the Asiatics," their words had unusually receptive audiences.

After all, what Indian labourer, with real or imagined injustice rankling in his mind, was going to fight for a European manager whom he felt was responsible for his humiliation?

And to some British troops, already inclined to socialism by their own experience of unemployment and poverty in Britain in the hungry thirties, it seemed that the Indian labourers had a strong case, and they sympathised with them. These views also had their bearing on the trend of events.

Of these troops under his command, General Percival wrote later: "It was hardly to be expected that inexperienced troops would withstand [the trials of the campaign] as steadfastly as would regular seasoned troops."

The British troops in Malaya and Singapore were 11,748 miles away from their homes, measured in distance, and immeasurably farther away in terms of outlook. Many could see no reason for being there at all. Their home towns and cities in Britain were under heavy German bombardment from the air, plus the threat of German invasion by sea. They had left a world of blackout, strict food rationing, petrol and clothes rationing and severe austerity, for one of warmth and light and plenty.

Despite all the efforts of local people to make them feel welcome, there is no doubt some felt that they were not accepted in the homes of British civilians; possibly they might not have been accepted into their homes back in Britain, but so far away, this great gulf, both socially and financially, between the fighters and those for whom they had come to fight brought its own resentment.

Training often seemed futile, because while Nazi Germany had overrun Europe to the Channel ports in one direction, and

[17] *Chalo Delhi* by K. B. Subbaiah and S. A. Das.

was even then preparing to drive east through the snows to the heart of Russia in the other, British troops in India, Burma, Malaya and Singapore could see no reason for being sent so far from home against a purely hypothetical enemy, to counter what appeared to them to be a totally illusory threat.

Japanese troops, on the other hand, knew exactly what their task would be. All were issued with the manual, *Read This Alone and the War Can Be Won*. This dealt with the history of the East—heavily slanted toward Asiatic brotherhood; descriptions of the countries where they would be fighting, hazards of weather, sun, monsoon, snakes; how to live off the land, how to avoid malaria, how to move through jungle and bamboo groves.

The defenders, meanwhile, had little except a diminishing faith in themselves.

Centuries before, Cromwell's Ironsides had been successful because they knew what they were fighting for, and they loved what they knew. Percival's army was not sure what it was fighting for. It had never been told convincingly; it could not love what it did not know.

Men might have been resigned or even prepared to die for their homes in Glasgow or Manchester or in London. No one wanted to die for Singapore.

Chapter Five

D URING the early part of the European war, Japan maintained an uneasy neutrality, although she continued to fight in China without achieving any decisive result.[1] There had been a strong pro-German party in pre-war Japan, but its influence was temporarily diminished after the Russo-German Non-Aggression Pact of 1939, which was signed in violation of the Anti-Comintern Pact and at a time when Japanese troops were engaged in open warfare against Soviet forces on the Manchurian-Outer Mongolian border. The Prime Minister, Hiranuma, who had been associated with negotiations for an alliance with Germany, was forced to resign. His successor announced that Japan would not be involved in the European war, but would "concentrate her efforts on a settlement of the China Affair."

The "China Affair" could not be dealt with in isolation, for it was gradually affecting Japan's relations with all the other powers. British, French and American trade was being systematically squeezed out of China in favour of Japanese monopolies. In 1938 the U. S. State Department forbade the sale of more American aircraft to Japan. In the following year, the British and American governments each lodged hundreds of claims for reparations for property destroyed by the Japanese military operations in China. Some of this damage arose out of the accident of war, but much of it had clearly been deliberate.

Neither Britain nor the United States felt ready to provoke a possible war with Japan by direct retaliation, but both were

[1] This poor showing by Japan proved as misleading to the West as the indifferent equipment used by the Russians in Finland in 1940. In both cases the deduction that Japanese and Russian troops and weapons could be discounted proved entirely false. Maybe both these countries wished this comforting illusion to be believed; whether they did or did not, it was.

sending supplies and giving economic assistance to Chiang Kai-shek. This support naturally aroused much hostility in Japan, where it was felt that without it the Chinese resistance could not have continued.

In July 1939, too, the American Government gave six months notice of its intention to abrogate the Japanese-American Commercial Treaty of 1911. This was the first hint that the United States was contemplating sanctions against Japan, and it came as a severe shock in Tokyo. Its effect was to intensify the Japanese desire to obtain control of alternative sources of raw materials which would free Japan from dependence on the United States. The most important of these raw materials was oil, and the nearest alternative source was the Dutch East Indies. Accordingly, the Dutch East Indies now became one of the chief targets of Japanese expansion.

It soon became obvious that the temporary coolness between Germany and Japan concealed basic similarities, both in their situations as dissatisfied powers, and in their attitudes to third parties. Both saw Britain and the United States as the obstacles to a desired expansion of territory, and both, in spite of the Russo-German pact, feared and hated Communism. Hitler, hoping that an alliance with Japan might discourage the United States from entering the war, continued to work for an agreement with Japan. Pro-Axis opinion in Japan was much strengthened by the German victories of 1940, and preparations began to be made for a southward move against the British, French and Dutch possessions in Southeast Asia, which would be seized in the event of the Allied defeat which now seemed imminent.

In July 1940, a month after the fall of France, President Roosevelt froze all Japanese assets in North America. A further Export Control Act gave Roosevelt power to regulate or to stop directly the export to Japan of material likely to be of use in war, such as chemicals and machine tools. On top of this, a blockade maintained by America, Britain, China and the Dutch East Indies—known as the A.B.C.D. powers—denied Japan 75 per cent of her imports.

By the following month, Japan had managed to force the

withdrawal of the British garrison at Shanghai and the temporary closure of the Burma Road over which supplies were still being sent to the Chinese Nationalists. In September, the Vichy Government was compelled to agree to the establishment of Japanese bases in northern Indo-China, ostensibly for the purposes of the Chinese war. At the same time, Thailand (as Siam now preferred to be called) made demands for the restoration of former Thai territories now under French control.

The Thais, as it later appeared, were also nursing a secret desire for the return to Thai control of the four northern Malay States of Kedah, Perlis, Kelantan and Trengganu, over which they had once exercised an uncertain suzerainty. They were now assured that these states would be the reward for Thai co-operation in the establishment of Japan's proposed (and as yet undefined) Greater East Asia Co-Prosperity Sphere.

Although Thailand maintained an appearance of neutrality to the last, this consideration, coupled with the obvious superiority of Japanese to British forces in the region, was sufficient to win Thai support for Japan, which proved extremely valuable in the subsequent Malayan campaign.

The Netherlands Government, however, showed no inclination to accord special privileges to Japan in Indonesia, and it became clear that these would have to be extorted by force.

Two treaties completed Japan's diplomatic preparations for war. The first, signed in September 1940, was a tripartite pact with Germany and Italy. It was intended as a warning to America, and it provided that if any of the signatories became involved in a war with the United States, the other two would immediately give assistance. Thus Japan at last formally aligned herself with the Axis powers.

Finally, in April 1941, she signed a neutrality agreement with Russia, which relieved her of anxiety about her northern frontiers. But Japan was still not anxious to enter the war until she could be certain that she was joining the winning side. In February 1941, Ribbentrop had urged the Japanese Government, through its ambassador in Berlin, to attack Singapore. This, he said, would cripple Great Britain and deter the United States from entering the war. The reply was polite but unenthusiastic. He was informed that preparations for an attack on Singapore were in hand, but that Japan had to consider the danger that this might also involve war with the United States. She did not therefore intend to attack before the promised German invasion of England had begun.

But even without the German invasion, matters were slowly coming to a crisis. Negotiations between the United States and Japan for a general settlement in the Pacific had already been going on for some months. So far, they had only proved that no reconciliation was possible between the basic American demand that Japan withdraw from China and check her advance in Southeast Asia, and a basic Japanese unwillingness to comply. They were now reopened with a new sense of urgency by the Japanese Government.

The drastic economic sanctions had apparently been quite unexpected, and Japan had as yet no alternative source of oil. She must, therefore, either submit or fight; and her ability to fight would depend from now on upon her rapidly dwindling stockpiles of oil. The Army decided that, in view of the state of oil stocks and the weather conditions anticipated, warlike operations would have to begin, if at all, not later than December 1941; which in turn meant that a final decision for war or peace must be taken at the beginning of October. Tojo told his Prime Minister, Prince Konoye, that they would have to fight or it would be too late: "To carry on negotiations for which there is no possibility of fruition, and in the end to let slip the time for fighting, would be a matter of the greatest consequence," he said.

Konoye got the message. He proposed a personal meeting with President Roosevelt[2] in Honolulu, in a last attempt to find a solution. Roosevelt was unwilling to agree unless preliminary talks showed some success. There seemed little hope of this,

[2] It has been suggested that this invitation would have led to an attempt to kidnap him, possibly to hold him to ransom, by no means an unheard-of procedure in Far Eastern politics at that time. Disaffected Chinese had kidnapped Chiang Kai-shek only five years earlier. They released him after he agreed to their terms.

since the Japanese Navy, previously for peace, had now joined
the Army in preferring war rather than agreeing to withdrawal
from China. In October, Konoye resigned, and was succeeded
by his War Minister, General Tojo, who now took the combined offices of War Minister, Prime Minister and Home Minister.

Tojo, who was on record as saying that the European war
was Japan's opportunity of a thousand years, was a rigid militarist of the old type, and his appointment represented the
triumph of the Army and the war party. Negotiations with the
United States were renewed, but this time it was understood
that unless agreement was rapidly achieved, Japan would go to
war.

On November 20, Japan made her final proposals. She would
evacuate southern Indo-China, pending a general settlement with
China, when she would withdraw altogether from Indo-China; in
return, the United States was to leave Japan a free hand in
China proper and restore normal commercial relations. The offer
to withdraw from southern Indo-China was a substantial concession, and Roosevelt was prepared to propose a three-month
"modus vivendi" on the general lines of the Japanese note,
pending further discussions of a general settlement for the
whole Pacific area.

Churchill, it should be noted, had no fear of a Japanese war.
Any temporary setbacks which might occur at the outset of
such a conflict would be more than balanced by the advantage
of full American assistance—military, economic, political—against
Germany. In a speech, he promised America that, should war
break out between her and Japan, "a British declaration would
follow within the hour."

Both Churchill and Chiang Kai-shek, for different reasons,
protested at the weakness of the American proposals, and their
combined indignation was enough to make Roosevelt change
his mind. The proposals were never put to the Japanese envoys.

Instead, they were given a much firmer "ten-point note," demanding a total Japanese withdrawal from both China and
Indo-China. Submission to these demands would have involved

the abandonment of everything Japan had fought for in a long and bloody war, and the acceptance of a position of subservience to the whims of American foreign policy in the future.

At an Imperial Conference on December 1, Japan's leaders decided that this humiliation was too great to be borne. They chose the only other alternative: war.

Of the sanctions which produced this situation, Winston Churchill admitted later: "It had not perhaps been realised by any of us how powerful they were."

Perhaps a better clue to the motives of Roosevelt, at least, is provided by his confession to Churchill that "I may never declare war; I may make war. If I were to ask Congress to declare war they might argue about it for three months."

The Japanese attack on Pearl Harbor involved America in the war against Germany whether Congress liked it or not.

＊　＊　＊

A year before this point of no return—when Tojo was still only Japan's War Minister and not the Prime Minister—anxious to build up close technical ties with the two other Axis countries, he had persuaded Konoye that a Japanese military mission should go to Europe to study what Germany and Italy had learned in the art of making modern war. It was proposed—although not by Tojo, who feared and envied his influence—that General Tomoyuki Yamashita should be its leader.

Yamashita—unlike Percival—had always intended to become a soldier. He lived like one and, in the end, he died like one. He was the son of a doctor, born in the village of Osugi Mura in Shikoku, the smallest of the four islands that constitute Japan. The name of the village means "Great Cedar"; it was surrounded by giant cedar trees two hundred feet tall and jealously preserved.

These trees made such an impression on young Yamashita that when he wrote small poems—a habit that stayed with him all his life; he actually wrote a verse on the day he set sail for Malaya—he would sign them with the pseudonym "Great Cedar."

His older brother studied to become a doctor like his father, but Yamashita, not being apparently clever enough to attempt this career, was sent to a military institution, The School of the Southern Sea, where boys could be educated, later to play their parts as officers in the modernised Army and Navy that the Emperor Meiji was endeavouring to build in the late nineteenth century.

From this school, Yamashita went on to the Central Military Academy in Tokyo. He was commissioned shortly after the Russian-Japanese war, when the Japanese seized Mukden, and sat the examinations for the War College, the Japanese equivalent of the British Staff College. He failed the first time he took the entrance paper, but persevered until he passed, because this was an essential hurdle on the road to high command.

He married the daughter of a Japanese general on the day before his graduation, and was posted to Switzerland as an assistant military attaché at the Japanese Embassy in Berne. A colleague there was Captain Hideki Tojo, later to be both Yamashita's Minister of War and then his Prime Minister during the Second World War.

In the traumatic days of the thirties, when the Japanese Army became increasingly and alarmingly active in Japan's domestic affairs, Yamashita held the position of Chief of Military Affairs. His appointment gave him wide authority over mobilisation, the modernisation of the Army, expenditure and general problems of national defence. He was then in his fifties, and something of an eccentric. In his office, for example, he deliberately placed his desk so that it faced the Emperor's palace. Also, he had a habit of sleeping in his chair if pressure of work was slight, and would snore openly if faced with men or matters he considered undemanding of his interest and attention.

This sleep was something of a mask. Only his eyes slept; not his mind.

It was as Chief of Military Affairs that he mediated between the young officers who felt that the politicians were not modernising and expanding the Army as speedily as they should, and the old-style generals who, cushioned by authority and tradition, resented what they considered was upstart authority.

Tokyo feared war between these military rivals, but Yamashita, as a go-between, persuaded the Emperor to issue an edict
directing both parties to return to their barracks. This was a
remarkable achievement, and owed its success to the high regard in which the Army held Yamashita, as a man above politics,
not dedicated to place-seeking.

Yamashita's capabilities during the military troubles in Tokyo,
however, made him some enemies on both sides, who felt that
they had lost the advantage in agreeing to sink their differences.
It was, therefore, suggested that, until those tempers cooled, he
should be posted to Japanese-occupied Korea as a major-general.
From here he was promoted lieutenant-general—in rank equal
to Percival—and became a Divisional Commander at the front
in China. It was from China that he returned to Tokyo with a
new appointment—Inspector General of the Air Force—to go, on
Tojo's orders, to Berlin with a group of forty service leaders
and scientific advisers.

They travelled by rail. Hitler greeted their arrival with full
military honours. After a private interview in the Chancellery,
Yamashita gave his opinion of the Führer, which received world-
wide publicity: "I feel that Hitler's mind is spiritual, transcending material plans. The Führer told me that he has been attracted to Japan since boyhood and has promised to instruct
Germans 'to bind themselves eternally to the Japanese spirit.'"[3]

But Yamashita, like all Japanese, had his public and private
viewpoints. Privately, he commented on Hitler in less adulatory
terms: "He may be a great orator on a platform, with his gestures
and flamboyant way of speaking, but standing behind his desk,
listening, he seems much more like a clerk."

Yamashita's visit was not completely successful. He was extremely anxious to know more about radar, which the Germans
were then developing, but they would not release any radar
secrets to him.

"His promise to show all his equipment was meaningless,"
Yamashita later complained. "There were several secret pieces
of information which he did not want us to know about. When-

[3] *The Life and Death of a Japanese General* by John Deane Potter.

ever I tried to persuade Hitler or the German General Staff to show us certain things, like radar, about which we had a rudimentary knowledge, the conversation always turned tactfully to something else."

Nevertheless, Yamashita's contacts had discovered the whereabouts of an experimental radar station. He ordered his air expert, General Harada, to investigate it. Harada arrived at the gates of this secret laboratory as though on an official visit. Mindful of the publicity that had surrounded the arrival of the Japanese delegation in Berlin, the technicians did not like to refuse. They opened their gates to the wily Harada. He took detailed notes and reported back to Yamashita. The secret of German radar was a secret no longer.

Yamashita learned much about co-ordination between infantry and tanks on his trip; about the advantages of a quick campaign, a *Blitzkrieg;* and he took back to Japan details of new armour-piercing shells, and 900-rounds-a-minute machine guns. In return, Yamashita promised to Germany full details of a diesel-engined tank and a prototype. This was, in fact, never delivered, because when Germany attacked Russia, the trans-Siberian railway through Manchuria was cut.

Hitler was anxious that Tokyo declare war on Britain and America, in the hope that this would prevent growing U.S. aid to the Allies in Europe. Yamashita pointed out that Japan was still heavily engaged in China. He also felt that Russia might still attack them through Manchuria. He said, "This is no time for us to declare war on other countries."

That time was coming, and coming quickly. Yamashita's party returned to Japan, having visited forward German stations in France—which were, at the time, actually under an attack by the R.A.F.—and then gone on to meet Mussolini in Rome.

Yamashita had, by then, formed his own assessment of events, one not entirely favourable to the Axis, but he realised that the Germans and Italians were so far advanced in their equipment and techniques of war that it would take Japan at least two more years to draw level.

Tojo disagreed. He wanted to strike as soon as possible at

the West, and if Yamashita's policy prevailed, this might be delayed in theory for two years but, in the event, forever.

In fact, Germany attacked Russia before Yamashita reached Tokyo, but Yamashita still feared an attack from Russia, Japan's age-long enemy. He stressed to his officers as they drew up their report: "I must ask you not to express opinions in favour of expanding the alliance between Japan, Germany and Italy. Never suggest in your report that Japan should declare war on Great Britain and the United States.

"We must not and cannot rely upon the power of other nations. Japan needs more time, particularly as there may be aggression against us from Russia. We must have time totally to rebuild our defence system and adjust the whole Japanese war machine. I cannot repeat this to you often enough."

Relations between the United States and Japan were steadily worsening, and there now began an elaborate and sophisticated plan to allow Japanese naval units at sea time to draw within range of their proposed targets, Singapore and Pearl Harbor. Tojo sent a special envoy, Saburo Kurusu, to Washington to assist the Japanese ambassador, Admiral Kichisaburo Nomura, in negotiations to keep peace between the two countries.

The British and the Americans had both "cracked" the Japanese cipher codes, and from the radio messages being passed between the diplomats in Washington and Tokyo, it was clear that little hope was held for the success of the talks. However, for what they were worth, the talks began on November 17, 1941. The Japanese demanded an end to the American military and other aid to China; an end to American embargo on imports to Japan; American recognition of Manchukuo, and an acknowledgment of Japan's Greater East Asia Co-Prosperity Sphere.

Eight days later, on November 25, the United States issued its counter terms for an agreement. Japanese troops would withdraw from China and Indo-China, and acknowledge the territorial integrity of China; they would also recognise the Chinese Nationalist Government under Chiang Kai-shek, withdraw from the Axis alliance and sign a non-aggression pact with the other powers in the Pacific.

In effect, this was a proposal that Japan completely reverse her entire policy. The conditions of each side were, equally and obviously, intolerable to the other. Two days later, Henry L. Stimson, the American Secretary of War, warned General Douglas MacArthur, Commander of U. S. Armed Forces in the Far East, that so far as he was concerned "for all practical purposes" negotiations seemed finished.

In fact, they had never begun in good faith, for against this front of diplomatic negotiations, the Japanese militarists were beavering away at their own plans like mice behind a wainscot.

Eleven months earlier, on January 1, 1941, groundwork began for the attack on Singapore. As the staff officer principally responsible for these plans, Colonel Masanobu Tsuji wrote later, "Success or failure of the attempt to capture it would completely decide the fate of our campaign in the southern areas."[4]

On Formosa, in a single wooden barracks behind an innocuous signboard, "Taiwan Army No. 82 Unit," a cover name for the research department into tropical warfare, all was frenetic activity. Here all the isolated items of information filtered from hundreds of secret agents, from Japanese sympathisers, from Japanese embassies and legations, were fused together in a mosaic of Intelligence. Here the whole strategy and outlook of the Japanese Army, for generations trained to fight a possible war against Russia in the frozen snows of Manchuria and Siberia, were now directed to a new war in the humid jungles of Malaya, the Philippines, in Burma and Java against new enemies: the British, the Americans, the Dutch.

Here in this building, the air sharp with the scent of new wood, ringing with hammer blows as other rooms were added, were studied such matters as marching in unaccustomed heat; living off the land; sanitation; preservation of weapons and vehicles against sea water and atmospheric moisture; even the final administration of occupied territories, and, but least important, the psychological approach essential for victory.

These Japanese troops were to know exactly what they were

[4] *Singapore: The Japanese Version* by Colonel Masanobu Tsuji.

fighting for. Their invasion, undertaken on the crudest grounds of greed and envy, an entirely unprovoked aggression, appeared, to the men taking part, with the trappings and glory of an almost holy war, East against West, Asiatic against white man, underdog against overlord.

In the booklet already mentioned, *Read This Alone and the War Can Be Won*, the situation was summarized thus:

We Japanese have been born in a country of no mean blessings, and thanks to the august power and influence of His Majesty the Emperor our land has never once, to this day, experienced invasion and occupation by a foreign power. The other peoples of the Far East look with envy upon Japan; they trust and honour the Japanese; and deep in their hearts they are hoping that, with the help of the Japanese people, they may themselves achieve national independence and happiness. . . .

A hundred million Asians tyrannized by three hundred thousand whites . . .

Three hundred and fifty million Indians are ruled by five hundred thousand British, sixty million Southeast Asians by two hundred thousand Dutch, twenty-three million Indo-Chinese by twenty thousand Frenchmen, six million Malayans by a few ten thousand British, and thirteen million Filipinos by a few ten thousand Americans.

In short, four hundred and fifty million natives of the Far East live under the domination of less than eight hundred thousand whites. If we exclude India, one hundred million are oppressed by less than three hundred thousand.

Once you set foot on the enemy's territories you will see for yourselves, only too clearly, just what this oppression by the white man means. Imposing, splendid buildings look down from the summits of mountains or hills on to the tiny thatched huts of the natives. Money squeezed from the blood of Asians maintains these small white minorities in their luxurious mode of life—or disappears to the respective home countries.

These white people may expect, from the moment they issue from their mothers' wombs, to be allotted a score or so of natives as their personal slaves. Is this really God's will?

The reason why so many peoples of the Far East have been so

completely crushed by so few white men is, fundamentally, that they have exhausted their strength in private quarrels, and that they are lacking in any awareness of themselves as a group, as peoples of Asia.[5]

Now, Japan was making them aware—and themselves the leader of this group.

Manoeuvres were carried out on Hainan Island to test schemes for sea-borne landings; bridges were blown and repaired hastily; horses abandoned in favour of bicycles, which the Japanese made and exported to Malaya by the hundred thousand. Every fact and factor, good or bad, large and small, was noted with the tireless precision of the Japanese mind; nothing would be left to chance. They would, in the Russian saying, "work for their luck."

Yet, despite the essential nature of this research, the total budget allowed was only 20,000 yen—and even this was cut by one-tenth.

In September 1941, the Japanese leaders for the projected campaign were chosen. Yamashita would be Commander-in-Chief of the Twenty-fifth Army in Malaya, and Colonel Masanobu Tsuji, in his own words unofficial "Officer in Charge" of operations, drew up the plans. The best troops would be used for Malaya because it was essential for the whole plan that Singapore fall.

First, they realized that it was the corner-stone of the British Empire in the East. If the West could not only be defeated militarily, but also humiliated before the millions of people it had ruled for so long, then all the "oppressed peoples of Asia" would be emancipated. After that, nothing in the balance of power between East and West could ever be the same.

Second, the Japanese recognised the significance of Singapore as the pivot for mastery of the East. It stood at the eastern approaches to the riches of India; at the northern approach to the empty vastness of Australia; and all the rice and oil of the Dutch East Indies lay to its south and east. Also, it controlled the sea routes, and through them the way to the Pacific Ocean.

All else could be gathered in easily enough once Singapore fell.

[5] Quoted in *Singapore: The Japanese Version* by Colonel Masanobu Tsuji.

The order of priority after Malaya and Singapore was Burma, the Philippines and the Dutch East Indies.

On September 25, Tsuji moved to Indo-China to supervise the siting and construction of airfields from which to attack Malaya. After months of intensive work on the projected attack, when he drove his subordinates so hard that several suffered physical collapse, he was surprised at the air of ease among the Japanese troops in Indo-China when he arrived.

In Hanoi, he found troops "enjoying their siesta under the shade of trees in a peaceful village in a land of everlasting summer." In Saigon, other Japanese soldiers lolled in the "cool, after-sunset air . . . the whole staff had retired to their quarters—a palatial country villa taken over from the French. They were all in bathrobes, drinking their fill of cold beer, and each with the exclusive use of a motor car. There were constant goings and comings to and from the gay quarters."

When the army commander heard the reason for Masanobu Tsuji's arrival, he speedily left his own commandeered country mansion and spread out his rush mat on his office floor. The time for pleasure was over; the time for war was about to begin.

Similar scenes of Eastern indolence were, of course, common in Singapore, for, as one staff officer recorded, "Sunday morning was either spent playing golf or sailing, and these sports would culminate in a curry tiffin, which was quite the most vicious social pastime that it has ever been my lot to encounter.

"The prelude to tiffin consisted of anything from one to three hours' drinking and this, on top of the meal itself, was guaranteed to prostrate the toughest constitution.

"When the tiffin was finished, everyone took to the privacy of his own bedroom and this well-established tradition was known as 'lying-off.' I used to make it a point of honour to play a round of golf after these orgies but it was frequently a most painful experience."

Colonel Tsuji was worried because work was proceeding far too slowly, and when his superior officer was unexpectedly recalled to Tokyo, Colonel Tsuji took over. He flew over Phuquok Island, off the coast, and found two far better sites than those on the mainland. Without bothering to secure permission from the French officials, without even consulting Tokyo—for, as he admitted later, "If we waited for permission through diplomatic channels it would be several months before we got a decision, and it was also certain that the financial authorities in Tokyo would regard this work with hostility and quibble about finding the funds necessary for its completion, which might quite possibly be the deciding factor in the successful invasion of Malaya"—he put two thousand coolies on the island and built the airfields there. These two new airfields assured complete protection for Japanese troops landing in Siam and Malaya.

Meanwhile, Japanese spies reported that the Siamese airports at Singora and Patani were crude compared with the British airfields at Kota Bharu in north Malaya. Also, Siamese troops seemed few in number; no pillboxes of defensive positions had been built near the proposed landing places—and there was one factor which could work both for and against them. This was the northeastern monsoon, which, after the middle of November, would produce extremely rough waves, nine or ten feet high. These waves kept local fishing boats in harbour, and it would be extremely difficult to land troops in such seas without casualties.

On the other hand, the very size of the waves would lull the defenders into a false sense of security. If the fishermen who had lived by or on the sea all their working lives did not dare to challenge such waves, they would argue, that surely no invader would take this risk. The attack could not be delayed after December or the monsoon would bog down both the invaders and the invaded.

There was, by now, no intention of delaying it. In Tokyo, Emperor Hirohito, the Son of Heaven, received General Tojo and the leaders of the Japanese Army, Navy and Air Force in the Imperial Palace for a special cabinet meeting. It lasted for only two hours, but, in terms of his country's destiny, it was probably the most momentous meeting he ever held.

The meeting agreed that war would begin in December against Britain and the United States. No declaration of war would be made, but before it began, Japan would conclude a secret military agreement with Siam that would allow her troops into the country. As a cover, the Washington negotiations with the United States would continue. There was the very slender chance that the United States would agree to all their conditions. If they did so by midnight, December 1, then the war preparations would be abandoned.

* * *

Professional Japanese agents, planted in Siam and Malaya, now reported back with the results of their missions. Staff Officer Asaeda, from Siam, and Major Nakasoni, from Malaya, had dealt with the topography of Singora and Patani, fifty miles north of the Siamese border, and Kota Bharu, ten miles south of the border, and Malaya's most northern port on that coast. All had airfields, but Nakasoni warned that landings could be difficult at Kota Bharu because it stood at the mouth of the Kelantan River, which was both tidal and muddy. Singora was the best place for a main landing. The beach there was flat and shelved gently; its harbour could provide anchorage and shelter for vessels able to come in close enough. And behind the beach stretched wide rice fields, flat enough to enable Japanese tanks and motor transport to disperse quickly into the countryside, and not stay as a target on the beaches.

In the third week of October, Masanobu Tsuji flew over the Siamese-Malayan border to see for himself what the land looked like from the air, to reassure himself that the choice was right.

He flew in a twin-engined reconnaissance plane with a fuel range of five hours' flying time. He calculated that he could leave Saigon, fly over the area and be back before the fuel ran out. The plane carried no weapons, and relied entirely on its superior speed to lose any pursuit. Before he set off, he changed into an air force uniform in case he should be forced down. He could then appear as an aviator who had lost his way. He carried no identity papers, only a flask of water, some white bread and his camera. As a precaution against ground observers, he ordered that the Hi-no-Maru, the familiar Japanese emblem, be painted out on the fuselage and wings.

He saw that the British had torpedo-bombers at Kota Bharu, which could ruin any convoy attempting to land troops at either Singora or Patani. This meant that the Japanese would have to capture Kota Bharu as well, as an essential to the success of the exercise—a fact he had not realised before.

The flight was bitterly cold. As he opened the window in the base of the plane through which the camera peered down at the glittering sea and the green jungle, his eyebrows froze with icicles.

They skimmed over Malaya, recognised the R.A.F. airfield at Alor Star, but no one saw them, and no planes came up to challenge them. They flew back to Saigon, over the limit of their range, ran out of fuel and had to glide down onto the landing strip.

The information Colonel Tsuji had gathered on this trip when, for five hours he flew unperceived, unintercepted and unseen by any of the British defenders, turned the campaign before it had begun.

Chapter Six

Against this meticulously planned Japanese campaign, in which almost every contingency and combination of events had been provided for, what was happening in Malaya and Singapore?

General Sir Lewis Heath, who had led the 5th Indian Division in the Eritrean campaign, was given command of the III Indian Corps, and made responsible for Malayan defence north of Johore and Malacca. The Corps consisted of two Indian divisions, the 9th and 11th. The first, under Major-General Barstow, was to garrison Kota Bharu and Kuantan on the east coast; the 11th, under Major-General Murray-Lyon, was in Kuala Lumpur, ready to drive north to defend the Siamese frontier.

Gordon Bennett's 8th Australian Division consisted of the 22nd Brigade, which had sailed from Sydney for a secret destination aboard the *Queen Mary,* and which was able to do some jungle training before the Japanese finally attacked, and the 27th Brigade, which was sent after the occupation of Indo-China by Japanese troops. The Australian brigades dug themselves in at Mersing on the southeast coast of Malaya with the intention of preventing a possible Japanese landing in Johore. None of these divisions was well equipped.

On July 17, Gordon Bennett wrote in his diary, "Barstow has no anti-aircraft or anti-tank defence and is expected to hold forty miles of front with two battalions. Sounds like another Crete."

While the Japanese had been drawing up their plans on Formosa and rehearsing them on Hainan, the defenders had also been pondering on the problems of a Japanese attack. But whereas the Japanese staff officers were, generally speaking, in their thirties and forties—and some younger—the British staff officers were much older. Percival was fifty-four; Heath was fifty. Their ideas lacked aggression and novelty. They were aging men cast, for the most part, in moulds too large for them. They were personally brave, but products of their class and their upbringing, believing in a traditional approach to a novel situation for which there had been no precedent in their lifetime. Their deliberations, like their plans, lacked conclusion and decision.

In April 1941, an inter-service conference was held in Singapore under Brooke-Popham's chairmanship; although, of course, America was then not at war with the Axis, U.S. officers were present with Dutch and British commanders. It was accepted that in the event of a Japanese attack, until the arrival of the main fleet, British policy would have to be purely defensive. In these circumstances, it was proposed that the United States Asiatic fleet act from the flank against any Japanese movement south by sea, using Hong Kong as an advance base, but falling back on Singapore if necessary. This would mean entrusting the defence of the Philippines to the Air Force. The Dutch Navy and Air Force could reinforce the British.

The report of the commanders attending this first American-Dutch-British conference was not accepted by the American authorities. The conference thus failed to produce a joint (i.e. Allied) plan for the defence of Southeast Asia in the event of war. The next attempt as a joint command was not made until America entered the war. In January 1942, American-British-Dutch-Australian—A.B.D.A.—Command was set up, under General Wavell. But was far too late, and Wavell, one of the war's most brilliant leaders, was, as a result, able to do little more than preside over the Allied collapse.

On April 25, at a Chiefs of Staff meeting in London, the Vice-Chief of Naval Staff, Admiral Phillips, recommended the despatch of Hurricane fighters to Malaya, but the Vice-Chief of Air Staff remarked that the Buffalo fighters already stationed there would be more than a match for the Japanese aircraft, which were not of the latest type.

In July 1941, the Japanese moved into south Indo-China, which provided them with a first-class naval base 750 miles off Singapore, and airfields just 300 miles from Kota Bharu, the nearest point in Malaya. Now their invasion force could be mounted at short and deadly range. No longer was there any question of a long sea-haul from Japan or Formosa on which all the original British plans for the defence of Singapore had been based in the 1920s. Only Thailand lay between the Japanese and Malaya, and Japanese pressure on Thailand increased. In that same month the Japanese Navy was mobilised.

In August, the British ambassador to Japan, Sir Robert Craigie, warned the British Government that another move south was impending. But apparently—and it was symptomatic of the complacency and chaos that prevailed—no word of this reached Air Chief Marshal Sir Robert Brooke-Popham,[1] the Commander-in-Chief, Far East.

At the end of September, Brooke-Popham delivered his expert assessment that "it is highly improbable Japan can be contemplating war for some months."[2]

Then, in October, he visited Melbourne and, suffering from the popular delusion about the strength of the Japanese Air Force, he told the Australian Advisory War Council that while the Japanese had superior numbers in the air, they did not have superior quality.

Brooke-Popham, with the intention of bolstering morale, declared on his return to Singapore: "We can get on all right with Buffaloes out here, but they haven't got the speed for England. Let England have the Super-Spitfires and Hyper-Hurricanes. Buffaloes are quite good enough for Malaya."

The facts were otherwise, as Sir Robert would have known had he possessed an efficient air Intelligence organisation. But until June of that year he had none at all. Then a makeshift Intelligence

[1] In October, a part Russian-part German journalist, Richard Sorge, ostensibly in Tokyo as correspondent for the *Frankfurter Zeitung*, but in fact a Soviet spy, learned of Japan's plans to drive south toward Singapore and the Pacific instead of north against Russia. This information meant that Stalin could withdraw most of the standing army of two million men he kept in Siberia against a possible attack. They reached eastern Russia in time to fight for Moscow in early December when Marshal Zhukov held the German drive—and saved the Soviet capital, and, possibly, the Soviet Union too.

[2] *The War Against Japan*, Vol. I, by Major-General S. Woodburn Kirby and others.

group was thrown together, but it was still incomplete when war broke out. This was unfortunate, for, in May, a Japanese Zero fighter was shot down in China. On September 29, the Combined Intelligence Bureau in Singapore, an organization under Admiralty control but supplying what was loosely referred to as "Intelligence" to all three services, passed on data about its performance figures and armaments to Air Command, where, "Faulty organization at Headquarters, Air Command, whose establishment did not include an Intelligence staff, resulted in this valuable report remaining unsifted from the general mass of Intelligence information, and in no action being taken on it."

In other words, nobody read the reports.

So, although the information was received at headquarters, the people who really mattered—the air crews—were never told.

As a result, the Zero fighter came as a surprise; so did the fast Nakajima torpedo-bombers which were to help sink the main fleet off Kuantan on December 10; so did the oxygen-powered torpedoes that these planes carried. The general impression in Malaya was that Japanese aircraft were made of rice paper and bamboo shoots; and, except for the Zero incident, Combined Intelligence Bureau supplied no information to the contrary.

In Hong Kong, Major-General Christopher Maltby, who received his information from the same source, was told that the Japanese did not like night fighting, preferred to advance along main roads, had been grossly flattered as to their fighting efficiency by the feeble opposition available in China, and that the Japanese Air Force would not operate at night and was no good at bombing. Japanese Intelligence, however, was such that the Air Ministry in London, having set as its target 336 front-line aircraft for Malaya, learned from Singapore a year later that a document captured from a crashed Japanese plane in China showed an estimate of British air strength in the Far East by the end of 1941 as being 336 front-line aircraft.

In August 1941, Percival asked for a minimum of forty-eight infantry battalions and two tank regiments. By December, he had thirty-three infantry battalions, little heavy artillery, few anti-aircraft guns and no tanks at all, for Whitehall did not consider that tanks would be suitable in jungle warfare.

Again, nobody told the Japanese, and when the Indian divisions were attacked at Jitra, in north Malaya, at the beginning of the campaign it was the first time that many of them had ever seen a tank.

None of the 336 aircraft promised by the Chiefs of Staff arrived, although airfields to house them were being hurriedly constructed in 1941, and throughout the Malay peninsula, with, as we have seen, little regard to the problem of defending them, which, of course, fell to the already overtaxed Army.

By December, the Royal Air Force possessed, in Malaya, 141 serviceable aircraft instead of the 336 front-line planes stipulated as a necessary minimum by the Chiefs of Staff and the 566 asked for by the men on the spot. Of these 141 machines, half were decisively inferior to the enemy counterpart. There were: 15 Hudsons for general reconnaissance, 34 Blenheim bombers, 27 Vildebeeste torpedo bombers, 43 Brewster Buffalo fighters, 10 Blenheim night fighters, 3 Catalina flying boats, 4 Swordfish and 5 Sharks. The pilots were mostly Australians or New Zealanders, with plenty of spirit but no combat experience. The Japanese had over 700 modern machines; their pilots were veterans of several years' fighting in China.

A comparison of performance figures reveals how badly the Allied airmen were served. The twin-engined Bristol Blenheim, with a maximum speed of 266 m.p.h., was a tolerably efficient medium-light bomber, although hardly adequate as a night fighter, and the American-built Lockheed Hudson, with a maximum speed of 225 m.p.h. but a range of over 1500 miles, was well suited for reconnaissance. But there were no modern torpedo bombers, the type most required for action against a sea-borne expedition. The Vildebeeste, declared obsolete in 1940, was so slow that it was called by its unhappy pilots "The Flying Coffin." Compared with its top speed of 99 m.p.h., the twin-engined Nakajima planes could fly and deliver torpedoes at speeds in excess of 270 m.p.h.

In August, the West took two crucial decisions. The first decision was to send the main fleet east to Singapore, according to the classical pattern of defence.

The second was to prepare a plan, known by the code name "Matador," by which a British force could advance into Thailand to deny the east coast ports to the Japanese. In the event, both decisions proved disastrous, but either could have altered the outcome of the war in the East.

Brooke-Popham devised Matador on the assumption that the best way to stop any Japanese invasion of Malaya from the north—apart from preventing them landing there at all—was to establish a firm line of defence on the narrowest point of the Malay peninsula, which was just north of the Thai border.

A British force was to be prepared, and when invasion appeared imminent, this would cross the border into Thailand and hold the two towns of Singora and Patani where, four years earlier, General Dobbie had correctly predicted that the Japanese would land.

The next step would be to move northward to a point known as The Ledge, where the main road was carved out of the cliff, and which provided the best defensive position in the whole area.

Brooke-Popham estimated that he needed thirty-six hours' notice to put the plan into operation. But while the Chiefs of Staff in London approved his plan, they would not give him permission to move north into Thailand, at his own choosing, without first referring back to London. They feared that premature occupation of Thailand could precipitate war with Japan.

In this view they were guided by a disturbing cable from the British minister in Thailand, Sir Josiah Crosby, a pleasant Pickwickian figure who had been in Thailand for thirty-seven years and loved the country, and who felt that the Thais reciprocated his feelings.

"For God's sake," the cable ran, "do not allow British forces to occupy one inch of Thai territory unless and until Japan has struck the first blow at Thailand."

Brooke-Popham, who believed that Crosby knew the feeling of that country, was therefore understandably reluctant to commit himself too soon. This indecision was fatal. The British troops who were to occupy Singora and Patani waited miserably in drenching rain south of the border, while north of it the Japanese made their landings virtually unopposed. The initiative thus passed to the attackers; it stayed with them for the next seventy days of the campaign.

British agents in Thailand (in fact, British service officers in civilian clothes) had already formed quite a different assessment of Thai intentions. They had stayed in hotels, like the German-run Zoo Hotel in Haad'yai, where sometimes the only other guests had been Japanese agents, and they felt confident that Thailand would side with Japan.

On December 5, Brooke-Popham received a change in orders from London. He could start Matador at once, and without further reference to London, provided he was certain that "a Japanese expedition was heading toward south Siam, or if the Japanese had violated any other parts of Siam."[3]

Next morning, R.A.F. reconnaissance planes reported that Japanese warships were steaming with other vessels from the East into the Gulf of Siam. It would seem that Brooke-Popham should have immediately put Matador into action. He did not. Instead, he ordered a state of "First Degree of Readiness."

As Percival wrote later in his "Despatches": "The Command was at the fullest degree of readiness, but there was no undue alarm, owing to the view that the Japanese expedition was directed against Siam."

There should have been the greatest and most necessary alarm.

At 6:30 the following evening, December 7, another reconnaissance aircraft reported a Japanese cruiser sailing west, then four destroyers, and a merchant ship packed with troops on the deck going south. Still nothing was done. Apparently, no alarm was felt.

"At 11:00 that same morning, the Japanese Ambassador in Siam had delivered an ultimatum, demanding free passage through that country for Japanese troops, planes, etc. Neither

[3] "Despatches" of Air Chief Marshal Sir Robert Brooke-Popham.

the British Legation nor British Intelligence appeared to have heard of it."[4]

Brooke-Popham and Percival, together and individually, seemed to have forgotten that the Japanese were working to the plan both sides had drawn up for the conquest of Malaya and the capture of Singapore: Land first in Thailand and then drive south.

Thus, while Singapore was being bombed for the first time on the night of December 7–8, while the Japanese poured ashore into Thailand, while they fought their way ashore at Kota Bharu, the troops who could have swung the pendulum of battle in favour of the defenders, waited for orders that never came.

* * *

Out at sea off Singora, under a moon obscured by clouds, with waves between nine and ten feet high, it seemed impossible that small boats could be lowered and filled with men without being swamped. But lowered they were, and filled they were, tossing like corks on the violent sea, ready to come in under the guiding light of the Singora lighthouse.

The crash of the surf on the shore, the thunder of the waves breaking on the boats, drowned the noise of the engines. There was no need for silence now. So high were the waves that about a third of the Japanese troops were pitched out of their boats onto the shore before they could leap.

It was thus fortunate for them that their landing was un-opposed. Some Thai defence trenches were empty. Lights still burned in the deserted streets. One staff officer ran to the Japanese consulate, but the consul, Katsuno, was asleep. He had been drinking heavily, and when he was awakened, the only words he could say were: "Ah! The Japanese Army!" The next step was the local police station, with an orderly carrying 100,000 ticals of Thai notes in a cloth; the Japanese rightly believed that bribes were better than bullets.

Meanwhile, despite some shelling from Thai forces, Japa-

[4] *The Fall of Singapore* by Frank Owen.

nese planes landed safely on the airstrips. Thai resistance continued until about noon on the following day, but was never much more than token; it ended under the white flag with the announcement: "At the command of Premier Pibul, the resistance of the Thai Army is suspended for the time being."

The chief Japanese agent in Thailand, Major Osone, under his cover as a consulate clerk, had destroyed his secret code book too soon, and thus he could not decipher the telegram which had been sent with details of time and place for the landing. As a result, he had not been able to square the Thai police and army officers; hence the sporadic firing.

He was reprimanded by General Yamashita who next received a visitor, a Thai Army messenger. This go-between was half Japanese, believed to be the illegitimate son of a Japanese nobleman. He smoothed out all further difficulties between the Thais and the Japanese.

Almost immediately, a Japanese reconnaissance plane dropped a message tied to a stone; this reported that a British mechanised column was moving north toward the border. But it did not make contact and the moment was lost.

Down south in Singapore, 600 miles away from Kota Bharu, a message came over the telephone: "Someone's opened fire."

"Who? Us or the Japs?" asked the R.A.F. operations officer.

"Us, I think. No, it wasn't—it was the Japs."

The British planes over the Japanese fleet had been greeted by accurate anti-aircraft fire. Now Kota Bharu air station wanted to know whether it should bomb the troop transports or the cruisers.

"Go for the transports, you bloody fools," shouted the operations officer. But it was too late; the transports had already landed their troops. The sea was behind them, their landing craft as useless as the discarded chrysalis to a butterfly. They had no more need of them; Singapore lay south, and they were on their way.

These first landings occurred just before 4:00 A.M. on December 8, but with characteristic delay, the news did not reach Singapore until 9:45 that morning.

At this point, Brooke-Popham finally realised that it was too late to attempt Matador and decided to adopt the alternative defensive plan, which involved withdrawing south to the village of Jitra, covering the Alor Star airfield. But here more disastrous delays occurred. Brooke-Popham could not find Percival, who had chosen this moment to visit a routine meeting of the Legislative Assembly to let them know what was happening, although he was not clear himself. It was therefore not until 11:30 that Percival gave the order for the withdrawal to Jitra, but due to further unexplained hold-ups the telephone message did not reach the front till 1:00 P.M.[5]

It was another thirty minutes before the withdrawal began, and ten precious hours were lost to the enemy.

Tartly, the official history observes: "The need for a quick decision was not apparently realised at Headquarters, Malaya Command."

This bungling led directly to the disaster at Jitra on December 11 and 12 when tanks, supported by two battalions of Japanese infantry, defeated the 11th Indian Division of III Corps in a matter of hours, with heavy losses in equipment, guns and transport.

The defending troops were inexperienced and undertrained (due to the dubious policy at this juncture of sending trained men back to India to raise more units). But still worse, the indecision over Matador had disastrously eroded their morale. First, the troops had been ordered to dig defensive positions at Jitra. Then they had been ordered to prepare for offence. For two days they stood by in the monsoon rains keyed up for an attack. Finally came the order to return to Jitra. When they did so, in the worst of spirits, they found that their defences had become waterlogged and useless.

There was no local labour to help them—the War Office, as we have shown, had never been willing to pay competitive

[5] The whole telephone link between front line and Singapore, even though this distance shrank daily, was casual to the point of disbelief. Once Brooke-Popham was talking to Percival on a trunk call about a vital military matter. The operator interrupted to say, "Your three minutes have expired, Sir" and cut the connection.

rates—and the troops had to do their own digging. There was never time to get the field telephones working properly across the waterlogged ground, and communications suffered accordingly. By the time the battle started, many of the troops had had no rest for a week, and confidence in their command had gone.

Just as the 11th Division suffered from indecision, so did the small delaying force known as "Krohcol"—Kroh Column—whose task was to go into Thailand at a town called Kroh and seize The Ledge. Krohcol did not get under way until 3:00 P.M. on December 8—hours later than necessary. The padlocked gate at the frontier, on the Kroh-Patani road, was smashed open, and the force advanced.

Thai rifle fire killed the leading scout, and the column was attacked by Thai police, probably Japanese troops in disguise,[6] continuously so that by nightfall, they had penetrated only three miles of Thai territory. The advance continued next morning, still harassed by Thai "police." Six miles further on, at the village of Betong, in the early afternoon, Thai authorities apologised for this "mistake."

For some reason, Lieutenant-Colonel H. D. Muirhead, in command of Krohcol, did not push on. The delay was crucial; next day, the force was attacked in earnest, and vicious hand-to-hand fighting followed before Muirhead decided to withdraw, and the enemy won the race for the vital Ledge.

Operation Matador was an early milestone in a long journey to catastrophe. Now the march back began, the withdrawal to more favourable ground, to previously prepared positions behind the lines; the talk of regrouping and counter-attack, the long haul in retreat.

When Matador was abandoned, the British aircraft at Alor Star, near the frontier, were withdrawn south to Butterfield in Province Wellesley, near Penang. From there six British Blen-

[6] Colonel Tsuji, in a dream, had seen himself advancing south through Thailand in Thai uniform to the confusion of the British. He awoke, thought the idea a good one, obtained specimen Thai uniforms from Bangkok, and dressed one thousand Japanese soldiers as Thai troops and police on the invasion.

heims attacked the enemy landings at Singora. No fighter escort could be spared and the Blenheims, although they inflicted some damage to aircraft on the ground, lost half their number.

In the desperate attempt to check the Japanese advance, a second raid was planned with more planes, but the Japanese struck first. Every aircraft at Butterfield was bombed on the runway except one, piloted by squadron leader Arthur Stewart King Scarf.

In one of the more moving, though lesser-known exploits of the war, for which he was posthumously awarded the Victoria Cross in 1946, Scarf took off alone.

Once in the air he circled the bomb-scarred runway to see if anyone would follow him; but nobody could. There were no planes.

He made his attack on Singora, then brought back his riddled Blenheim, dodging enemy fighters and making a forced landing at Alor Star.

His crew was unharmed, but Scarf was crucially wounded. He was nursed in the Alor Star hospital by his wife, Elizabeth, who had joined the Malayan Government Nursing Service to be near her husband. He needed a transfusion and she gave him two pints of her own blood, but four hours later he died.

The dead cannot speak for themselves, but sometimes their acts speak for them and are their advocate. This was one of those times. The pattern of individual and collective heroism was repeated elsewhere, many, many times, but it could not alter the eventual outcome. British aircraft were bombed regularly as they refuelled and reloaded on the ground. Nothing could be done to prevent this, because the airfields had no anti-aircraft guns and no effective air-raid warning system.

Casualties were so heavy that on December 9, the day after the landings, Pulford decided to withdraw what aircraft he had left in the north.

Kuantan, two hundred miles to the south of the advancing Japanese, was also bombed. Immediately after the raid, the squadron personnel flew off for Singapore in their remaining machines. Seeing themselves thus deserted, the ground staff commandeered the airfield transport and drove for the railway station at Jerantut, some miles away. Large stocks of fuel were left behind for the Japanese. Indeed, so much fuel and so many trucks were abandoned during the retreat south that the Japanese relied on them to transport their troops.

Pilot officer Roy Bulcock wrote later: "I saw a bloody flight-lieutenant soon after the raid started. He ran down to the side road with two friends, blew the door lock off a private car with his pistol, and drove the car on to the main road so fast that he skidded into a deep drain and couldn't get out. Then he held up the Post Office bus with his gun, made all the passengers and the driver get out, and drove off at full speed. For the first and last time in my life I felt ashamed of being an Australian."

On the night of December 7–8, Singapore was bombed. Two air-raid practice alerts had already been held in September, but the rehearsals were not quite like reality. When the Japanese bombers appeared in the night sky, the city lay open to them brilliantly lit up.

It remained that way, for the only man with the key to the building housing the master switches could not be found. The Air-Raid Precaution headquarters was unmanned. Civil defence arrangements were the responsibility of the civil administration and it had no effective liaison with the military for several days after the outbreak of war. Indeed, the sirens only sounded after a personal appeal had been made to the Governor himself.

This episode has called forth much criticism, but according to the private papers of Sir Shenton Thomas, it is largely criticism by hindsight.

"No mention was ever made to me by any service commander on any of the following days about the lights or the alleged failure of the A.R.P. organisation, nor at the meeting of the Legislative Assembly which took place on December 8," he wrote later.

"Surely, if the civil administration had been to blame, I should have been at least questioned: and rightly. Not until five years later was the question raised in the Service despatches.

There was the same silence on the part of the service ministries at home, and of the C.O. [Colonial Office]."

According to Sir Shenton's diary, the Commander-in-Chief, Far East, ordered the first degree of readiness at 3:30 P.M. on December 6, 1941.

"There is no evidence to show that the first degree of readiness provided for a brownout or blackout throughout Malaya, and the application of A.R.P. measures generally, on the outbreak of war with Japan. Such a provision might no doubt have been expected, but, in the absence of proof, its insertion in the Defence Scheme is merely an assumption which ought to be examined in the light of known facts.

"The raid took place at 4:15 A.M. I had therefore only fifteen minutes' warning. . . .

"Whether Percival was at his house or at G.H.Q., he must have seen the lights. So must the other service commanders. I put it to Maltby [General Maltby, in Hong Kong] when commenting on his despatch that it was not 'conceivable that on the night in question the Commander-in-Chief, Far East, the Commander-in-Chief, China, the General Officer Commanding, the Air Officer Commanding and myself should all have gone happily to bed with every light on the island blazing if anyone of us had thought that a raid was even remotely possible. Of course it isn't: it just didn't make sense.' He did not answer.

"Any one of these officers had therefore two and a half hours between the news of the landing and the warning of the raid to request me to have the lights put out. It is obvious that they did not expect the raid, and this is not surprising seeing that we knew that no Japanese aircraft was nearer than French Indo-China, some six hundred miles away. I have heard that to make the raid the Japanese aircraft were fitted with supplementary petrol tanks."

Had a blackout or even a brownout been ordered over Singapore Island, when the first degree of readiness was declared on December 6, then surely one or other of the services would have drawn the attention of the Government to this, because by the night of December 8, when the air raid took place, the street lights would have been burning for two nights against orders.

The officer in charge of civil defence wrote later: "The point is that 'brownout' as a precautionary measure was *not* ordered for the night of December 7–8, and my recollection is that the order was not given on service advice (whether Army or R.A.F. I cannot say). Therefore the A.R.P. was not manned nor were the municipal services alerted in any way. They were in their beds as on any other night in peacetime."

General Percival, in a letter dated May 10, 1947, wrote to Sir Shenton Thomas: "The position, as I recollect, was that the war had not started before midnight, and therefore all lights would normally have been on. Even after the war started there would have been no blackout until the warning was given."

"In other words," wrote Sir Shenton later, "proclaiming of the first degree of readiness did not entail a blackout."

On the evening of Friday December 6, after Brooke-Popham declared first degree of readiness, Thomas told the Colonial Secretary about the movements of the Japanese ships toward Malaya. His colleague asked whether the service chiefs had given any warning or made any suggestion "that we should be on the alert." Sir Shenton replied that they had not.

In any case, many of the street lamps in Singapore were lit by gas. They could only be turned off by a tap high up on each individual lamppost, controlled by men with poles. Thus no "crash blackout" would have been possible.

The British capital ships lay at the naval base where the Japanese airmen saw them, but they were not hit. Indeed, the *Prince of Wales*'s high-angle gun crews were provided with some gunnery practice.

Three R. A. F. Buffaloes were ready to do battle. They had moonlight and searchlights to help them, but their pilots were forbidden to take off because the men firing the anti-aircraft guns were too inexperienced, and it was feared that they might shoot down the British planes instead of the Japanese. In fact, they shot down nothing, but the bombers caused heavy casualties in the crowded city.

In 1937, a committee of service and civilian chiefs was appointed to examine the whole question of building air-raid shelters in Singapore. It was not possible to site these underground because more than half the population were living only a few feet above sea level, and any underground shelters would quickly fill with water. The few areas on higher ground that could have accommodated underground shelters were Chinese burial grounds, and so could not be used.

The Government therefore decided against building any public shelters in Singapore at all. Instead, it planned a policy of dispersal, also followed by the Dutch in the Dutch East Indies. Two camps, at a cost of over a million dollars, were built to accommodate 335,000 people some miles out of Singapore City. They had their own water supply, electric light, communal kitchens and stores of food, with trained camp commandants and wardens, and were built of wood with thatched roofs. When the bombing began, many thousands of people flocked to them for food and shelter.

Public buildings and offices in Singapore were protected with sandbags, and piles of sand were put in the streets for use against incendiaries. Slit trenches were only dug in the last two weeks of the campaign because they filled with water and were a breeding ground for mosquitoes.

Despite this, the casualties caused by lack of shelters were unduly high. The Japanese bombed at will. They hit Tengah and Seletar airfields, and some densely populated parts of Chinatown. Sixty-three people died and 133 were injured. Hours later, Sir Robert Brooke-Popham issued his order for the day: "We are ready: we have had plenty of warning and our preparations are made and tested."

In fact, a considerable amount of work to mitigate the effects of air raids had been done, largely by European women, but later with Eurasian and English-speaking Asiatic women, in the Malayan Ambulance Service, which was constituted in 1940 as an integral part of the Malayan Medical Department. The training was roughly the same as for members of the St. John's Ambulance Brigade in Britain, and all work was entirely voluntary.

Singapore had nearly three thousand members; Kuala Lumpur, nine hundred; and Penang, three hundred. They met each week in posts and depots for practice, and to make bandages and dressings. By the time the Japanese attacked, the Governor could report that there was a branch in each town which contained "a sufficient number of European women to form a nucleus and to give the initiative." European women were also enrolled as transport drivers, and the Army requisitioned all suitable cars in Singapore in late December 1941.

In addition, more than three thousand men and women, nearly all European and Chinese and Eurasians, had come forward as early as July 1941 as blood donors. Even a fortnight before the capitulation they were still queueing up at the rate of 120 a day to give pints of their blood.

European women worked as teleprinter operators, as confidential secretaries and cypher clerks. There were eight in Government House, where, in peacetime, one private secretary had been enough. Besides undertaking this work, often with staggered hours and miles away from their homes, without public transport and forbidden the use of their own cars, many had to look after their own households and young children. In spite of this, the women of Singapore came in for harsh criticism from an unexpected source—from Lady Brooke-Popham when she arrived with her husband in London shortly after the surrender of Singapore.

An interview with her was published in a newspaper in which she was reported as saying: "I went to Singapore as a newcomer after experiencing the London blitz. I was struck immediately by the deadly inertia of the white population. They were utterly dormant. For instance, I asked a certain lady to give me two hours' help with A.R.P. work.

"She told me: 'I am awfully sorry, Lady Popham, but I've

already entered for the tennis tournament. A.R.P. will interfere with my tennis.' They refused to believe that war would come to Singapore. It was parties, bridge and dancing."[7] Soon, it was retreat and then defeat.

❊   ❊   ❊

All this stemmed largely from the inability to risk Matador, first devised in August.

The second crucial setback, the loss of the main fleet, also stemmed from an August decision.

❊   ❊   ❊

In London, on August 8, that year, the Chiefs of Staff, at Churchill's instigation, asked the Joint Planning Staff to con-

[7] After Brooke-Popham's replacement, he was attacked bitterly and quite unfairly in the House of Lords. Although the Labour party before the war had consistently refused to support the services' Estimates, and although their greatest election stunt had been disarmament, Lord Addison, the leader of the Labour peers in the House of Lords, in opening a debate on the war, said:

"I hope the Government will inquire how it came about that this officer in a responsible position could make statements so grievously out of accordance with the actual facts. The only comfort I have—and I do not apologise for my language—is that I am glad that a nincompoop of that kind was promptly removed from his command and succeeded by General Wavell."

At that time Brooke-Popham was on his way home by ship, and was in no position to answer this wounding remark. In fact, of course, he could never answer it because of the rule that forbids a serving officer to take part in public controversy.

Lord Trenchard replied most strongly, deprecating Addison's comments. Addison was throwing stones from a very vulnerable glass house. Not only was he a turncoat politician; he was an unsuccessful turncoat politician. As a doctor, he had joined Lloyd George's Liberal Government, but was sacked because of a disastrous plan he put into operation about subsidising houses.

He became a Socialist in the year of the general strike and had been equally undistinguished as the Minister of Agriculture and Fisheries.

Also, both the parties with which Lord Addison identified himself had together and separately supported the policy of disarmament, which resulted in the nakedness of Singapore to Japanese attack.

sider the whole question of reinforcements for the Far East, especially in terms of capital ships.[8]

In 1921, Singapore had been promised the main fleet within seventy days; now, twenty years on, she would get the main fleet of one battleship, one battle cruiser, before the attack started.

The greatest danger to any capital ships came not from other ships of their size, but from torpedoes fired by submarines or mines. In fact, at the Washington Conference in 1921, which had decided the fatal ratio for East-West naval power, it had been proposed to ban submarines and torpedoes outright.[9]

Nothing came of these proposals, but, as we have seen, the naval powers did agree to stop building capital ships. Japan was ably represented at Washington by Fleet Admiral Tomosaburo Kato, and after the conference the Admiral became Prime Minister of his country.

He stuck rigidly to the naval treaty, and although he died in 1923 his followers were strong enough to uphold his policy successfully against tougher elements in the Army and Navy, even at the London Conference in 1930. Japan therefore put her faith in air attack to compensate for the disparity in capital ship tonnage to which she had agreed in Washington.

Before the First World War she had been buying aircraft from Europe and carrying out her own trials but with such a

[8] Oddly enough, although Alexander Graham Bell had written in 1909 that "the airship will revolutionise warfare," the Wright brothers themselves believed that it would be impracticable to hit a target by dropping bombs on it from an aeroplane.

[9] In 1911, an Italian, Captain Guidoni, actually became airborne in a Farman biplane carrying a 350-pound torpedo; and early in 1914, squadron leader A. M. Longmore took off in his experimental Sopwith seaplane to drop the British Navy's first torpedo. The whole project was pioneered by a brilliant British naval officer, Murray Sueter, later a rear admiral and Conservative M.P. who had devoted his life to studying and developing new weapons, including the tank and armoured car. As early as 1915 three British seaplanes had sunk three Turkish ships in the Dardanelles, but despite this success almost no further effective use was made of the airborne torpedo for the rest of the First World War. Sueter's enthusiasm and foresight were simply not shared by the Admiralty.

high casualty rate that by 1914 nearly all her pioneer aviators had been killed.

In 1918 a rich American gave the Japanese Government a donation of several thousand dollars "with the request that it be devoted to the purchase of flying machines and the training of pilots." The Japanese, in this gentleman's opinion, possessed "qualities which ought to make them the finest aviators in the world."[10] In 1923, at the request of the Japanese, a British mission, headed by the pioneer airman Lord Sempill, went to Japan to organize and train the Imperial Japanese Naval Air Service. (Ironically, forty years later and twenty years after Pearl Harbor, Lord Sempill was given a Japanese decoration for his work.)

The Blackburn Company also sold a number of Napier-engined Dart torpedo planes to Japan. The torpedoes could be powered either by compressed air or by oxygen fuel. The latter was more powerful, but also more dangerous. After experiments, the British Navy decided to concentrate on compressed air.

In 1927, a Japanese naval officer visiting Portsmouth noticed some apparatus on the deck of H.M.S. *Rodney* which he quite wrongly assumed must be an oxygen generator. He reported home to his Government that the British Navy had built an oxygen-powered torpedo, which it had not. His report convinced the Japanese Navy Department to continue trying, and their problems were eventually solved; by 1933, Japan had produced an oxygen-powered torpedo with a speed of 49 knots and a range of 5760 yards, which made all existing models obsolete. This discovery was kept a secret. By 1941, Japanese submarines and destroyers were equipped with a torpedo known as "Long Lance," with a range of 22,000 yards.

At the London Naval Conference in 1930 the powers agreed not to build capital ships for a further five years. According to *The Times* of February 8, "The Government considers battleships a very doubtful proposition in view of their size and cost, and of the development of the efficiency of air and submarine attack."[11] The real reason for the temporary lack of faith in the battleship's future was, however, the world slump, which pre-

[10] Quoted in *Sea Power in the Pacific* by Hector C. Bywater.
[11] *Death of the Battleship* by Richard Hough.

disposed Japan and the United States to agree to build no more battleships, and when, five or six years later, the powers began to rearm, they all began building battleships.

Even so, in 1935, when the Italians attacked Abyssinia, the British Mediterranean fleet withdrew from Malta for fear of Italian air attack.

The third Naval Conference, held in London in that year, was a failure; by this time, the militarist elements in Japan were high in the citadels of power, and preparations had been made—blueprints prepared, building space reserved, materials stockpiled—for the construction of three super-battleships, to weigh 70,000 tons each. As elsewhere, the battleship still had its supporters in Japan.

These ships, it was argued, would put Japan suddenly into a bargaining position. She might not be able to match America in quantity, but for a short time she could match her in quality.[12]

In 1939, Mr. Geoffrey Shakespeare, Parliamentary Secretary to the Admiralty, assured the House that "Modern ships can produce a volume of defensive fire that will drive aircraft to such a height that the efficiency and accuracy of their attacking weapons will be seriously impaired."

This information did not take into account Japan's new attacking weapons for the reason that they were still secret. But, by 1941, the battleship seemed to the British almost to have won its case, for the R.A.F. had attacked the German fleet off Wilhelmshaven at the entrance to the Kiel Canal, with conspicuous lack of success. The pocket battleships *Scharnhorst* and *Gneisenau* escaped untouched; *Admiral Scheer* was hit, but the bombs which hit her failed to explode and the only damage was to the cruiser *Emden*, which was dented by an aircraft crashing into her.

The Luftwaffe attacked the home fleet in the Firth of Forth with similar lack of success, only one bomb scoring a hit, and

[12] In the event, work was well advanced on the third of these super-battleships, *Shinano*, when the Pearl Harbor attack and the battle of Midway showed that aircraft-carriers were more valuable than battleships, and *Shinano* was converted. The three vessels saw no action until 1944, when all three were torpedoed and sunk within six months, *Shinano* on her maiden voyage, and within seventeen hours of leaving port.

that failing to explode. In December 1939, the Battle of the River Plate, which ended with the scuttling of the German pocket battleship *Graf Spee*, appeared as a decisive victory for pure sea power. Hitler seemed wrong in saying, "The day of Britain's sea power is past; aircraft and U-boats have turned surface fleets into the obsolete playthings of wealthy democracies."

Between March and July, 1941, the R.A.F. dropped two thousand tons of bombs on *Scharnhorst* and *Gneisenau* at Brest, but again these caused only superficial damage. In April, Churchill wrote to the Chief of Air Staff that "It must be recognized that the inability of Bomber Command to hit the enemy [battle] cruisers in Brest constitutes a very definite failure of this arm."

The Japanese, however, watching these proceedings in the West with great interest, arrived at quite different conclusions. Before Japan entered the war, of nine capital ships sunk, three had been sunk by gunfire. Of these, the French battleship *Bretagne* had also been trapped in harbour at Oran, and the *Bismarck* had first been crippled by air torpedoes. Only the *Hood*, in fact, was sunk purely by gunfire. The Japanese were impressed with the success of the British air-torpedo attack on Italian vessels in the Mare Grande at Taranto in November 1940. Swordfish aircraft of the fleet air arm from H.M.S. *Illustrious* sank three Italian battleships; later, the battleship *Vittorio Veneto* and the heavy cruiser *Pola* were attacked by five torpedo planes from H.M.S. *Formidable*. Both Italian ships were hit and forced to slow down and the *Pola* was later sunk by surface vessels.

The Japanese were not alone in being impressed by Taranto. United States Navy Secretary Frank Knox sent the following memo to Secretary of War Henry L. Stimson: "The success of the British aerial torpedo attack against ships at anchor suggests that precautionary measures be taken immediately to protect Pearl Harbor against surprise attack in the event of war between the United States and Japan. The greatest danger will come from aerial torpedoing. Highest priority must be given to getting more interceptor planes and anti-aircraft guns, and to the installation of additional anti-aircraft radar equipment."[13]

[13] *The End of the Imperial Japanese Navy* by Masanori Ito with Roger Pineau.

Indeed, as is now known, the Japanese learned a remarkable lesson from Taranto, where the depth of the water was only forty-two feet. Until then, an aerial torpedo had always required deep water to be successfully launched, but the Taranto torpedoes were "rigged" with special wooden fins, which enabled them to run straight in shallow water. The Japanese Admiral Yamamoto applied this lesson to Pearl Harbor, where the depth of the water was forty-five feet.[14]

After the sinking of the *Bismarck*, Churchill cabled to President Roosevelt: "The effect upon the Japanese will be highly beneficial. I expect they are doing all their sums again."

The answer was, unfortunately, that they did not need to; they had all been calculated long before. While in 1941 British Swordfish torpedo planes flew at one hundred miles an hour and dropped their eighteen-inch torpedoes from a height of eighteen feet above the waves, calling for the highest skill and bravery on the part of their pilots, the Japanese had already possessed aircraft capable of dropping twenty-four-inch torpedoes from a thousand feet at a maximum speed of three hundred miles per hour.

When, in August 1941, The British Joint Planning Staff was asked to consider the possibility of sending capital ships to the Far East, it replied that no capital ships could be spared. Such modern battleships as Britain possessed were still needed in home waters to contain the *Tirpitz, Bismarck's* sister ship, *Scharnhorst* and *Gneisenau;* the first in a Norwegian fjord, the last two still safely in harbour at Brest and all a constant anxiety.

On the other hand, it was thought that by February 1942, four old battleships dating back to Fisher's time, of the same class as the *Repulse*, but unmodernized, could be sent, together with an aircraft carrier and ten cruisers. This was the suggestion of the First Sea Lord, Admiral Sir Dudley Pound.

It was appreciated that this force could not, on its own, hold the Imperial Japanese Navy, but, in conjunction with the American Pacific fleet at Pearl Harbor, it could constitute a deterrent.

Churchill strongly disagreed with this plan. Five years earlier, at a private dinner given by Alfred Duff Cooper, the War Minis-

[14] *Admiral of the Pacific* by John Deane Potter.

ter, on February 14, 1936, Churchill had maintained that for the defence of Singapore he would put his faith in fixed artillery and aircraft, rather than a battle fleet. But he still remained obsessed by the sheer physical might of the battleship and he quoted the failure of aircraft to destroy battleships in the Spanish Civil War.

"The extravagant claims of a certain school of air experts have not been fulfilled," he wrote later.[15] Besides, ever since the Dardanelles fiasco in 1915, Churchill had distrusted admirals, and he was determined to assert himself and to prove that his views were right. Thus, instead of accepting the Admiralty's plan for four old battleships and ten cruisers, Churchill pressed for a "formidable, fast, high-class squadron," consisting of one battleship, one battle cruiser and one aircraft carrier. This "would exert a paralysing effect on Japanese naval action," he said, and at the same time reassure Australia and New Zealand.

In this reasoning, it seems possible that Churchill was unduly influenced, if only subconsciously, by the effect that the presence of the three German light battleships already mentioned were having on the British. He found Sir Dudley Pound's proposals "unsound"; the four old battleships would be "floating coffins." For his plan to send a couple of battleships Churchill received the support of the Foreign Office; Anthony Eden, the Foreign Minister (now Lord Avon), stressed the morale-boosting effect of the presence of the battleships.

Pound finally compromised. After all, the battle cruiser *Repulse* would already be in the Indian Ocean, having escorted a convoy for the Middle East around the Cape of Good Hope; and the new battleship, *Prince of Wales,* could be sent to Cape Town. From there she could be recalled home suddenly if necessary, or ordered to continue eastward if possible. The new carrier, *Indomitable,* would join the *Prince of Wales* en route. The Admiralty agreed "reluctantly, as a political measure."[16]

Pound was an ill man and his resolve had weakened. He sometimes appeared to sleep in conference—one of the symptoms of the

[15] In an article in *The Daily Telegraph* on September 1, 1938.
[16] Official Naval History—World War II.

brain tumour that was to cause his death. Churchill used to push through proposals unlikely to please the First Sea Lord while he was asleep, or in a low voice so that he could not hear. Although Pound was always alert to the interests of the Navy, Churchill's most insistent demands could be hard to withstand.

On the following day the Admiralty informed all naval authorities that the battleship was going to Singapore. It may be that Churchill talked Pound over to his way of thinking personally after the Chiefs of Staff meeting.

Admiral Sir Tom Phillips would command the fleet, to be known as Force Z. He was physically small, and someone coined the description of him "all brains and no body." He was fifty-three years old, had joined the Navy in 1903, and was a man of strong will and considerable obstinacy, and fiercely proud of his Service. He was convinced that warships at sea, if properly equipped and well trained, could repel any attack from the air, even by shore-based aircraft. Taranto did not shake Admiral Phillips' confidence; he believed that such an attack on a British base would not have succeeded.

The *Prince of Wales* was a new ship. She was still fitting out when the *Bismarck* made her dash for the freedom of the wide Atlantic; the *Prince of Wales* raced after her with a hundred civil contractors' staff still on board. She was fitted with fourteen-inch guns, the smallest calibre of any battleship afloat. At the London Naval Conference of 1935 proposals were made to limit the calibre of naval guns to fourteen inches. Japan refused to sign the treaty; America agreed not to commit herself until December 1935, in case the Japanese had a change of heart, which they did not. In the meantime, the British Admiralty stuck to the treaty in good faith; this was one of the results.

On August 4, 1941, the *Prince of Wales* had taken Churchill from Scapa Flow to Placentia Bay, Newfoundland, for the Atlantic Charter meeting with Roosevelt. Churchill himself had chosen her for this purpose for he wished to arrive in a new 35,000-ton battleship, defying U-boats and German bombs. The *Prince of Wales* covered most of the distance without destroyer escort; Roosevelt appeared in a ten-year-old 9000-ton cruiser.

The *Repulse* had been laid down in January 1915 and completed within a year. She had visited Singapore once before, in 1923, while on a world cruise, and between 1934 and 1936 she underwent such extensive modifications at Portsmouth that she was nicknamed "H.M.S. *Repair*." In the Second World War her first shots fired in anger were at German aircraft near the Forth Bridge, where she was in drydock. She only fired a few rounds, for there was a strong risk of shooting down the bridge itself. It had been intended to fit to her fourteen of the latest Mark 16 four-inch high-angle anti-aircraft guns in an American yard, but this was never done.

There was mischance when, on November 3, 1941, the carrier *Indomitable*, straight out of the builders' yard and on her ocean trials, ran aground at the entrance to Kingston harbour, Jamaica, and damaged herself sufficiently to necessitate a spell in dock. By this time, the *Prince of Wales* had already sailed, and the expedition could not be called off for political reasons. Australia would have despaired; and the reputation of the new battleship would scarcely have been enhanced if it was decided not to risk her without air protection.

"We are sending our latest battleship, the *Prince of Wales*," Churchill wrote to Stalin, "which can catch and kill any Japanese ship in the Indian Ocean."[17]

Churchill had arranged for Phillips to meet Field Marshal Smuts in South Africa, and when the *Prince of Wales* reached Cape Town on November 16, Phillips flew up to Pretoria.

Smuts believed that the British ships would most certainly be sunk if their arrival at Singapore failed to deter the Japanese from declaring war. "If the Japanese are really nippy," Smuts cabled Churchill, "there is here an opening for a first-class disaster."

The *Prince of Wales* reached Colombo on November 28 and dropped anchor within sight of the *Repulse*. The old, unmodernised battleship *Revenge* was also at Colombo as part of Admiral Pound's proposed force. Phillips decided to leave her there because the Japanese might interpret a force consisting of one new battleship, one old battleship and a battle cruiser, as a

[17] *The Hinge of Fate* by Winston S. Churchill.

last desperate attempt to form a line of battle, whereas two fast ships could only be interpreted as a raiding force.

Two more destroyers, *Encounter* and *Jupiter*, were to arrive from the Mediterranean to make up the escorting flotilla. Having been asked to detach two ships, the Commander-in-Chief, Mediterranean fleet, not unnaturally detached the two oldest vessels under his command. They were in such poor shape that as soon as they arrived in Singapore they were both sent at once to the dockyard for repairs, and replaced by the Australian destroyers *Vampire* and *Tenedos*, the latter an antique vessel built for the First World War and with such a low range that, in the hour of attack, she was unable to accompany the rest of the fleet to the point where it was planned to detach the flotilla, before attacking the Japanese transports.

Such was the British force intended to act as a deterrent to the Japanese Navy, which, at that time, could muster ten battleships, ten carriers, six seaplane carriers, eighteen heavy cruisers, twenty-two light cruisers, one hundred and thirteen destroyers and sixty-nine submarines.

Admiral Phillips took a flying boat from Colombo to Singapore, leaving Captain William Tennant of *Repulse* in command of Force Z. Phillips was anxious to discover what depth of air protection he could expect in Singapore. Phillips believed that "the Japanese air forces, both naval and military, were of much the same quality as the Italian and markedly inferior to the Luftwaffe."

Air Vice-Marshal Pulford, however, told Phillips that he would be able to supply air cover if it was needed.

Pulford told Tennant the same thing when Tennant came to ask later why no fighter planes had escorted the main fleet into Singapore when it arrived on December 2, described in the official communiqué as "H.M.S. *Prince of Wales* and other heavy units." Percival also expressed surprise. Without a carrier to provide air support, this was not a well-balanced fleet.

On December 4, Admiral Phillips flew to the Philippines, in one of the three Catalinas the command possessed capable of making this distance. In Manila, Phillips met the American admiral Hart, General MacArthur, and the Dutch naval representative. Hart's main concern was to keep open his supply lines to Hawaii and the United States. MacArthur did his best to persuade Phillips to bring his fleet to Manila. He also promised that if the Japanese landed in the Philippines he would throw them out again. He did, too, but it all took rather longer than anyone had anticipated in December 1941.

In order to reassure the Australian Government, *Repulse* was ordered off to Darwin for a short stay. As she left Singapore, two Brewster Buffaloes wheeled briefly overhead. They were the first aircraft that Tennant had seen in the Far East.

A few hours after *Repulse* had sailed, Singapore received news of a Japanese invasion fleet in the South China Sea, and Phillips' Chief of Staff, Rear Admiral Palliser, at once cabled his chief in Manila, and Tennant on *Repulse,* urging their immediate return to Singapore.

Pulford sent off a squadron of Australian Hudsons on reconnaissance from Kota Bharu. At 2:00 on the afternoon of December 6, at the limit of their range, the Hudsons radioed confirmation of the report and details of the Japanese fleet—two large convoys steaming west.

❋   ❋   ❋

On the night of the Japanese landings and the air raid on Singapore, the two British capital ships still lay at anchor. Their failure to intervene during the landings puzzled the Japanese, and late on December 8, Rear Admiral Sadaich Matsunaga, in command of the 22nd Air Flotilla, called his squadron leaders together to discuss the best means of attacking the two battleships, which a reconnaissance machine had reported still at the base and undamaged by the night's bombing.

It was arranged for the Japanese bombers to take off at once and destroy the ships at Singapore. But the planes never did go on this mission because that evening Japanese Intelligence learned that the ships had already left. Among the crowds who watched them steam out, the Japanese doubtless had their agents;

at least one radio transmitter was suspected to be operating for them from Singapore. It was sought but never found.

When Admiral Phillips returned from Manila on December 7, the Admiralty signal was waiting for him: "On assumption that Japanese expedition in South China Sea on course indicating invasion, report what action would be possible to take with naval or air forces."

On the following day Phillips held a conference to decide his plans. The situation was serious. Enemy landings had been made, R.A.F. losses were heavy, the Army was hard-pressed and falling back; the whole picture was one of gloom and confusion.

In this situation it seemed he had three alternatives. He could stay where he was at anchor and risk being bombed; he could sail out, away from the action to preserve his vessels against what now appeared to be Japanese air superiority; or he could sail out and attack Japanese ships off the east coast.

The first two alternatives were unthinkable; the third proved impossible. However, at the time it did not seem quite so grim. Given air support and surprise, he believed he could forestall further landing attempts, and this was worth the risk.

He asked Pulford what planes he could give him. Pulford replied that he should be able to give him the reconnaissance he asked for, but could not be certain about fighter protection over Singora. Pulford knew that the airfields in the north were under attack; losses were already heavy; he could not know for sure how many planes he would have left by dawn on the tenth, nor even whether he would have an airfield from which they could fly. The effective range of his Buffaloes was not much more than two hundred miles.

At 4:30, Pulford received a telegram from his station commander at Kota Bharu requesting permission to withdraw his ground forces and remaining aircraft because the airfield was no longer tenable. This meant that he had no airfield left to provide cover for Force Z. One hour and five minutes later, *Prince of Wales* and *Repulse*, accompanied by the four destroyers, *Electra*, *Express*, *Vampire* and *Tenedos*, sailed off into the misty sunset.

Admiral Layton, whom Phillips had relieved as Commander-in-Chief, Far East, only that morning, and who was due to leave for home in the Shaw Savill liner *Dominion Monarch* forty-eight hours later, described the evening departure of the two big ships as a pathetic sight. He added that he did not expect to see them again. Captain Tennant told the ship's company of *Repulse*, "We are off to look for trouble. I expect we shall find it."

At 10:53 P.M. Phillips received this signal from his Chief of Staff, Admiral Palliser, on shore: "Fighter protection on Wednesday tenth will not, repeat not, be possible." He could not guarantee more than one Catalina flying boat for reconnaissance. This was because of the loss of the airfields in northern Malaya, but due to the confused situation Pulford had not been able to tell Phillips this before he sailed. Force Z was thus deprived of one of the basic conditions upon which its full success depended. However, Phillips decided to proceed; in all the circumstances, he could not do otherwise. He could still succeed if the ships remained unobserved throughout December 9. At nightfall on the ninth, they would change course for Singora, leaving the destroyers behind, and make a dash for the coast, arriving at dawn to shoot up the Japanese transports. There might still be a chance to crush the Malayan invasion.

At dawn on the ninth the destroyer *Vampire* reported sighting an unidentified aircraft briefly in the heavy clouds. There was no confirmation of this report, and Phillips decided to disregard it. All day, squalls of rain beat down; low clouds darkened the sky; the hours marched round the clock.

Unknown to Admiral Phillips, however, at 1:40 P.M. on that day, the ships were spotted by the Japanese submarine I 65 south of Pulo Condore Island. The submarine, the most northeasterly ship in a patrol line of twelve between Singapore and Kota Bharu, reported the position, course and speed of Force Z. The Japanese transports still engaged in the landing operations at once withdrew.

Shortly after 5:00 P.M. the clouds began to thin, the mist lifted and the men of Force Z saw three aircraft apparently watching them, far out of range from their guns.

All hope of surprise had now vanished with the sheltering

mists. Admiral Phillips decided that to carry on would be to run an unjustifiable risk, and so he would turn back. He ordered back to Singapore the destroyer *Tenedos* (which had to return in any case because of her limited fuel), and instructed her captain to urge Palliser to send him destroyer reinforcements. In order to confuse the enemy, the other ships would not alter course until nightfall. So Force Z continued north until seven, then changed course for the northwest, as though to begin the dash to the coast. After dark, the Force turned south and reduced speed to save the diminishing fuel of the three destroyers remaining. Phillips was right in not risking his ships, but ironically, in trying to save them, he lost them.

The aircraft they had seen were not from Admiral Matsunaga's 22nd Air Flotilla, but were seaplanes from the two Japanese cruisers *Kinu* and *Kumano* in the squadron commanded by Admiral Kurita. If they saw the British ships, no word of it reached Matsunaga, who had already received the report from submarine I 65 at 3:40.

The news actually came as a surprise to him because the more recent photographic reconnaissance plane had reported that the two big ships were still lying at Singapore. When the photographs were printed and examined, it was found that the pilot had mistaken two large merchant vessels for the two battleships.

Had Force Z continued north for literally a few more minutes, they would have come within lethal range of Admiral Kurita's force of four heavy cruisers, which could certainly have been sunk by the superior British ships, with incalculable results, not only for the campaign, but for the whole of Western influence and authority in the East. But the history of every empire, even every man, is littered with such imponderables; and, as Churchill wrote about the Dardanelles campaign, "the terrible 'ifs' accumulate."

Matsunaga now decided that the British capital ships must be destroyed immediately, at whatever cost, because their presence off the coast of Malaya jeopardised the entire Japanese operation. Aircraft of the 22nd Air Flotilla took off at night to look for Force Z. They had little chance of finding Phillips in the dark because of the complete blackout, and in fact they very nearly attacked

Admiral Kurita's flagship by mistake. The planes returned to their bases, their mission unsuccessful, and then another signal from a submarine altered the whole course of events.

At 2:20 on the morning of December 10, the commander of submarine I 58 saw the British fleet approaching in his periscope.

By this time Phillips, too, had received a signal from Palliser: "Enemy reported landing Kuantan, latitude 03 degrees 50 north."

Admiral Phillips realised at once that for the Japanese to make another landing, two hundred miles further down the coast and behind the British defending forces, would be a most dangerous tactical move, especially as the only main road to the peninsula from east to west started in Kuantan. Therefore, if the enemy should hold this road, all Percival's forces to the north could be isolated.

If Force Z could reach Kuantan in time, he could prevent the Japanese landing because the Buffaloes from Singapore, even with their restricted range, could give him some kind of cover.

Force Z, then, at once changed course for Kuantan. Phillips, believing in the necessity of radio silence, did not tell Palliser what he was doing, apparently assuming that Palliser would realise that his signal would send Force Z to Kuantan, and he would provide fighter cover on his own initiative without being asked. Unfortunately, Palliser did not do this.

Pulford's immediate and anguished reaction, on hearing later that the *Prince of Wales* and *Repulse* had been sunk, was to exclaim, "My God, I hope you don't blame me for this. We didn't even know where you were."[18]

Between dawn and 9:30 the following morning, ninety Japanese aircraft set off from Saigon to seek out Force Z.

The Japanese submarine that had reported the position of the British ships in the middle of the night had, in the confusion, incorrectly estimated their course as southerly, and not southwest. The Japanese bombers, accordingly, flew south to the limit of their range, almost within sight of Singapore without seeing any ships, and then turned back.

The British ships arrived off Kuantan at 8:00 in the morning.

[18] *Someone Had Blundered* by Bernard Ash.

A Walrus seaplane was catapulted off *Prince of Wales* on reconnaissance and the destroyer *Express* sent into the harbour to investigate. There was no sign of a Japanese landing, no sign of anything. *Express* signalled by Aldis lamp to *Prince of Wales*, "All's as quiet as a wet Sunday afternoon."

The midnight signal from Palliser had been a false alarm. It was another of the bizarre ironies that marked the campaign. Some water buffaloes had strayed into a minefield at Kuantan. This set off the charges, causing Indian troops to think the Japanese were landing, which they duly reported to Singapore as a fact.

Admiral Phillips was now five hundred miles from Saigon, and felt himself quite safe from air attack; besides, he was within range of British planes from Singapore. He therefore ordered the fleet back on a northeasterly course in order to investigate the sighting at dawn of what appeared to be a junk or barge towing a number of smaller craft.

Half an hour later, the destroyer *Tenedos*, now far to the south of the main force, radioed that she was being bombed; she had been discovered by the 22nd Air Flotilla. First-degree readiness was at once assumed, and the main fleet changed course to return to base as quickly as possible.

Tenedos, in fact, managed to avoid the considerable number of bombs rained on her, and returned safely to Singapore. Twenty minutes after Phillips had received her signal that she was being attacked, however, Ensign Hoashi, in one of the Japanese reconnaissance aircraft, on the last leg of his search, caught sight of Force Z, and sent out a general call: "Sighted two enemy battleships seventy nautical miles southeast Kuantan course southeast."

Repulse's radar picked up the reconnaissance plane and at once her crew took up action stations. At 11:30 A.M. nine twin-engine bombers appeared on the starboard bow, flying high and in strict formation. As they approached, the high-angled guns of the British ships began to fire.

The planes came on and released their bombs. Tennant in *Repulse* said later he had never seen such accurate bombing.

Eight exploded on both sides of *Repulse*, the ninth hit her amidships and caused damage, but not enough to reduce her speed.

Twelve minutes later, the first torpedo-bombers appeared, with a final and terrible answer to the arguments over the relative values of bomber versus battleship, the irresistible force against the immovable target, that had taken up so much of the Chiefs of Staff's time during their meetings in the 1930s.

Twelve minutes later, "Bomber" Harris' dream of Tom Phillips' future became reality.

Prince of Wales turned to port to comb the tracks—to thread her way through the paths of the torpedoes launched at her—but not in time. A great spout of water billowed from her stern; a direct and mortal hit. Half the ship's machinery was destroyed. The intricate apparatus that controls a mighty warship was paralysed. She signalled *Repulse* she was "not under control."

As the planes wheeled away and the guns fell silent, Tennant asked his Chief Yeoman of Signals what messages about the attack had been sent to Singapore. He was astounded when he learned that no message whatever had been sent. Almost an hour had passed since they had first sighted the enemy aircraft, and even the sluggish Buffaloes could have flown from Singapore in that time.

Tennant thus sent a frantic signal to Singapore—"Enemy aircraft bombing"—and gave the position of the ship.

A few minutes before noon, Japanese bombers again swept in high from the south, concentrating on *Repulse*. Again the bombing was highly accurate, but Tennant's evasive action was again brilliant; all the bombs went wide. Now the torpedo planes came in from the north; *Repulse* swung around just in time to meet the torpedo tracks head on. Another aircraft disintegrated, but *Repulse* emerged unscathed.

Prince of Wales had not been able to do more than watch as *Repulse* had defended herself against the onslaught. At 12:20 another attack developed from the south, with nine planes flying low and heading for her. Three miles away, however, the squadron divided unexpectedly, and one formation of three turned to the left toward *Repulse,* while the other six headed for *Prince of Wales.* Again Tennant brought *Repulse* round to face his attackers, but at the last moment three planes veered suddenly away from an apparent raid on *Prince of Wales* and attacked *Repulse.* Tennant could not avoid both attacks at the same time. *Repulse* was hit amidships. More torpedoes came in, and Tennant ordered "abandon ship." The men slid down the sloping flanks of the battle cruiser as she turned slowly over; few of them escaped the spreading fuel oil. Tennant was still aboard; he was washed away and survived. Phillips went down with his ship.

The Japanese aircraft did not interfere with the rescue work of the escorting destroyers, but signalled to them: "We have completed our task. You may carry on."

All told, 90 out of 110 officers, and 1195 out of 1502 men were saved from *Prince of Wales;* and 42 out of 60 officers and 754 out of 1240 men from *Repulse.*

The total cost of this action that gave Japan immediate naval superiority was the loss of four or possibly five Japanese planes.

At 12:19 P.M. Tennant's emergency signal had been received in Singapore, and seven minutes later eleven Buffaloes of 453 Squadron, which had been ordered to stand by at Sembawang to give air protection to the fleet, took off. They arrived as *Prince of Wales* went down. In the distance, the Japanese planes jettisoned their bombs and disappeared over the horizon. The performance of the Buffalo fighters was so minimal that they could not even catch up with the retreating enemy bombers.

The pilot of the first R.A.F. aircraft on the scene, Flight Lieutenant T. A. Vigors, reported later: "I witnessed a show of that indomitable spirit for which the Royal Navy is so famous. I passed over thousands who had been through an ordeal the greatness of which they alone can understand. . . . Yet, as I flew around, every man waved and put his thumb up. During that hour I had seen many men in dire danger waving, cheering and joking as if they were on holiday at Brighton waving at a low-flying aircraft. It shook me, for here was something above human nature. I take off my hat to them, for in them I saw the spirit which wins wars."[19]

Maybe so, but this was one action lost years before it even took place. The planes were two hours too late because Admiral Phillips relied on his Chief of Staff, Rear Admiral Palliser, to provide air cover at Kuantan *without having been told to do so.* Assumption had taken the place of instruction; this was a prime error.

It is equally unfortunate that no attempt was made by the R.A.F. to confirm the false report of enemy landings at Kuantan, a rumour that led Force Z to destruction. If Pulford had reconnoitred Kuantan, as he should have done, he would have found the ships, and he would not have had to exclaim that evening: "My God, I hope you don't blame me for this. We didn't even know where you were."

If Phillips failed to alert Singapore even when he was actually attacked, it may be that in the excitement he forgot, or assumed that his Chief Yeoman of Signals would do so on his own initiative. When Pulford eventually told him there was no chance of air support at Singora, he should have sailed back to the Indian Ocean, where the ships could have done far more good. Such a retreat might not have pleased Churchill, but it could have saved the ships. *If* . . . Once more those terrible "ifs" accumulate. . . .

On December 9, when the battleships were still steaming through the mist and rain of the South China Sea toward Singora, Churchill was holding a meeting in London to decide what was to be done with the main fleet now that it had not acted as a deterrent, now that the Japanese had actually landed in Malaya.

"I thought myself," Churchill wrote later, "they should cross the Pacific to join what was left of the American fleet. It would be a proud gesture at this moment, that would knit the English-speaking world together. In a few months there might be a

[19] *The Singapore Story* by Ken Attiwill.

fleet in being on the west coast of America capable of fighting a decisive battle if need be."

In the end, Churchill decided to sleep on it. He was awakened by a telephone call telling him the news that the problem had solved itself; there were no ships to send.

Each survivor from *Prince of Wales* and *Repulse* received a gift of about 47 shillings ($6.80) from the Sultan of Johore. The Royal Marines from *Repulse* were reformed as A Company, and the Marines from *Prince of Wales* as B Company, of the 2nd Battalion, Argyll and Sutherland Highlanders, ever after known as the Plymouth Argylls.

On the day following the sinking of the battleships a Japanese aircraft dropped a large bouquet of flowers over the sea in honour of the dead.

This was also the first wreath for the death of the British Empire.

.

Chapter Seven

Now that the main fleet was no more, the defence of Malaya was the Army's concern. Such a situation had never been envisaged, and so was unprovided for; the Army's role was to have been secondary to that of the Navy.

Also, at the start of the campaign, the Army was thinly spread over the peninsula, largely in order to defend airfields that possessed no aircraft.

After twenty-four hours' fighting, only fifty British aircraft were left operational in northern Malaya out of an original total of one hundred and ten. The rest had been destroyed, mostly on the ground, for airfield warning systems and anti-aircraft defences were quite inadequate. As a result, as a means of defence and support for land forces in forward areas, the R.A.F. had now virtually ceased to count.

After thirty-six hours' fighting, Pulford decided to give priority to the defence of the naval base and to protecting convoys. Only ten serviceable British aircraft were left in northern Malaya by that time. The adoption of this policy of withdrawal was premature. No new convoys could be expected to reach Singapore before mid-January. The Army was thus left with no air support, but had to defend useless airfields in an attempt to deny them to the Japanese; in this they were unsuccessful. After sixty hours' fighting, all remaining aircraft were pulled back to defend the naval base.

Now the civilian population of the country saw the superiority of the Japanese in the air. They were soon to see it on land as town after town was abandoned, as the fever of retreat grew stronger and it became less a matter of fighting for the lives of those they had come to defend, but fighting for their own.

The real gravity of the situation was not appreciated in Singapore. Nor were the enormous implications, with Asiatics outnumbered by white men, British and Australian, but still beating them. In fact, when Matador had failed and the two capital ships were sunk, the war in Malaya was already lost, and so were all the Western empires in the East.

But as Ian Morrison so aptly described the atmosphere in the weeks before Japan attacked, "Singapore, alone of cities in the Far East, gave its inhabitants the illusion of security. Aeroplanes droned overhead during the day. The little Buffalo fighters looked beautifully speedy and manoeuvrable. There was hardly an hour of the day when one looked up into the sky and failed to see an aeroplane of some description—a Blenheim bomber, a Wirraway, a Catalina flying boat, a torpedo-carrying Vildebeeste. There was frequent fire practice, when the big naval guns that protected the island would hurl their shells many miles out to sea. After nightfall powerful searchlights played over the water or shone upward into the sky. There were occasional blackout practices. Every Saturday morning the sirens would be tested and would wail piercingly over the city.

"The fighting men of many different peoples were to be seen walking in the streets of Singapore city. . . .

"With all these superficial indications of power it is easy to see how people could feel safe and happy in Singapore. They saw many different uniforms in the streets. Therefore they thought we had enough soldiers. They saw aeroplanes in the sky. Therefore we were strong enough in the air. We had a marvellous naval base. Therefore we had nothing to fear at sea. . . . British statesmen had talked confidently about its strength. It had become the fashion to refer to it as 'the fortress of Singapore.' The legend had already achieved a world-wide currency."[1]

The truth, as Morrison realised, was different. There were no tanks, far too few anti-aircraft guns, even fewer planes.

There was also confusion of purpose among the high command. It was one thing for Churchill to say that "The idea of trying to defend the whole of the Malay peninsula cannot be entertained," but because the naval base was situated on the

[1] *Malayan Postscript* by Ian Morrison.

north shore of Singapore Island, it was vital to hold the whole peninsula in order to prevent the Japanese capturing airfields from which the base could easily be attacked. British policy was therefore to withdraw slowly down the whole length of the peninsula in the forlorn hope that an air force could somehow be built up at Singapore or, failing that, in Sumatra. Thus they provided a spectacle of retirement that showed their strategic and tactical inferiority to a race they had always previously regarded as being inferior to them.

Also, since the official policy was one of slow retreat, the Army was never fighting to the last man, because as many men as possible had to be preserved for the next stand. Consequently, at any danger of encirclement, whether real or imagined, troops were withdrawn—or sometimes withdrew themselves —often from strong defensive positions. These continual retirements seriously affected their morale, and showed to the indigenous population that their protectors were being beaten, with consequent and irretrievable loss of "face."

General Gordon Bennett also discovered, "on questioning several men, that fatigue and the resultant depression is more evident among senior officers than among the men, whose spirits are exceptionally high. They admit tiredness, but feel they are beating the enemy whenever they meet him, and object to the regular withdrawals."[2]

Gordon Bennett, of course, chose the right men to question: his own Australian troops, who were not brought actively into the fighting until comparatively late in the campaign.

Again, according to Gordon Bennett, General Heath "had a stronger personality than Percival and generally managed to impose his will on that of Percival. After the first defeat of 11th Indian Division—at Jitra—he considered withdrawal to a line in southern Johore essential, and that there a stand should be made. Throughout the conferences which I attended, he urged retirements. In fact, one of his brigadiers had been detailed to reconnoitre successive lines of retreat down the peninsula. . . .

"[On one occasion] he urged a withdrawal. I suggested that

[2] *Why Singapore Fell* by Lieutenant-General H. Gordon Bennett.

the only way to deal with the situation was to attack. He ridiculed the idea. I then offered to launch an attack with the Australians. He objected. General Percival supported my idea strongly, but he was unable to convince Heath and the attack did not eventuate."

A British staff officer, during the retreat to the Perak River in the same area, wrote: "It can't go on like this. The troops are absolutely dead-beat. The only rest they are getting is that of an uneasy coma as they squat in crowded lorries which jerk their way through the night. When they arrive they tumble out and have to get straight down to work. They are stupid with sleep, and have to be smacked before they can connect with the simplest order. Then they move like automatons, or cower down as a Jap aeroplane flies two hundred feet above them."[3]

This was bad enough; what could never be eradicated from the minds of the Asiatics who watched them in this position was that this would happen, could happen, was happening.

Before the Japanese landings, the British felt as little dread of the Japanese Army as of the Japanese Air Force. After all, if they had not been able to subdue the militarily weak Chinese in four years, surely they could not offer a very serious challenge?

This was a complete misreading of the facts, for while the Japanese Army held the cities in China they did not control the open country; guerillas lurked in every paddy field.

The British opinion of the Japanese Army was reciprocated. "If we compare the present enemy with the Chinese Army," the Japanese soldiers read in their pamphlet, *Read This Alone and the War Can Be Won*, "we see that whilst the officers are Europeans, the N.C.O.s and other ranks are almost overwhelmingly native, and that consequently the sense of solidarity in each unit between officers and men is practically nil. Much of their equipment is outdated and the fact that the soldiers who operate it are ill trained and without enthusiasm renders it worse than useless. Our opponents are much more feeble than

[3] *Eastern Epic* by Sir Compton Mackenzie.

the Chinese Army, and their tanks and aircraft are a collection of rattling relics."

These comments on the solidarity of the Indian Army were, at the time, and with regard to some units, justified; Indian Army formations had sent their best officers and N.C.O.s back to their regimental bases in India to train the new battalions rapidly being recruited there. Under normal conditions there was more solidarity in the Indian Army than there ever was in India; men of conflicting religious persuasions died together under British and Indian officers. The fact remains that in Malaya the British Army was indifferently trained for its particular task and "without enthusiasm" for it. Russian soldiers would die at Stalingrad; they were dying for Mother Russia. No British wished to die for Singapore, although many brave men did.

The Chinese, in Malaya and Singapore, who had relations with first-hand experience of Japanese conquest, were ready to fight to the death for they were fighting for their homes. A large number of them, under a British officer, Colonel John Dalley, fought fanatically when the Japanese landed on Singapore Island, as we shall see.

The Malays were largely apathetic; the war was "fought over their heads."[4] As Gordon Bennett wrote, "The Chinese showed greater fortitude and courage than either Malays or Indians. Many of the wealthier families contributed large sums to Britain's war loans. Throughout they were loyal to our side. The Malays were weaker in every respect. Though they did not actively help the Japanese, except perhaps in a few cases, they were of little assistance to our side. They seemed uninterested in the war."

This may be true, but the British in retreat gave the native population little to be enthusiastic about. The British had promised to defend Malaya; their rapid withdrawal did nothing to boost the confidence of the Malays. How could they defend any country by running away and leaving it to the invaders? So the Asian population stood on the sidelines and watched two other powers, one the occupying power, the other would-be occupiers, fight down the length of their homeland.

[4] *Britain and South East Asia* by Saul Rose.

They could not influence events, but they wanted to be on the winning side.

After four days' bombardment, Penang's European population was evacuated. Duff Cooper broadcast that the whole population had been evacuated, but this was not so. There was nowhere for the non-Europeans to go; Malaya was their only home.

On February 1, 1942, the Governor, Sir Shenton Thomas, broadcast from Singapore at midnight a message calculated to reassure the Asiatic population.

"Let not the Asiatic population of this island imagine that one day they will find themselves abandoned. That will never be," he said.

"Europeans, Indians, Chinese, Malays—we all stand together side by side, shoulder to shoulder. We will continue to try and send away as many women and children as may wish to leave, whatever their race, and I am glad to say that the Government of Australia has opened the doors of that great country to Chinese and Europeans, subject to a guarantee of good repute, which it will be my government's business to decide. . . .

"I can tell you now that within the last few days substantial reinforcements have been received. They are proof, if proof were needed, that Singapore is intended to be held. All we have to do is to hang on grimly and inexorably, and for not very long; and the reward will be freedom, happiness and peace for every one of us."

"We stand by the ship, gentlemen," he later told the Legislative Assembly. "In any withdrawal or movement of population there will be no distinction of race. We stand by the people of this country, with whom we live and work, in this ordeal." These were fine words, of which Raffles himself would have approved, but when the European women and children sailed back to Ceylon or India from Singapore, to what destination could Asiatic women and children sail? The answer given was: to Australia.

The Australian Government agreed that it was willing to accept 1500 Chinese. But what about the thousands of others? For these, answer came there none. So, when Percival announced on February 1—the same day that the Governor was broadcasting words of reassurance to the Asiatic population—that "The enemy within our gates must be ruthlessly weeded out," every Asiatic man, woman and child became immediately suspect.

When Yamashita, who commanded the Japanese Twenty-fifth Army in Malaya, visited Germany in the summer of 1941, Goering told him that Singapore would hold out for a year and a half, and that five divisions would be needed to attack it successfully. The Japanese, with a more realistic opinion of Britain's military strength in the Far East, reckoned that it would take them three months and four divisions. In the event, it took them seventy days, and three.

The defenders made their first stand at Jitra, a village twenty miles south of the Siamese border; the 6th and 15th Brigades of the 11th Indian Division were to hold what was called "the Jitra line" to protect the airfield at Alor Star, a few miles to the south. But this was, in fact, evacuated by the R.A.F. without word of their intention to the divisional headquarters of the 11th Indian Division.

Percival ordered that the Jitra line must be held to the last man, perhaps impressed by his own Special Order of the Day of December 10: "In this hour of trial the General Officer Commanding calls upon all ranks of Malaya Command for a determined and sustained effort to safeguard Malaya and the adjoining British territories. The eyes of the Empire are upon us. Our whole position in the Far East is at stake. The struggle may be long and grim, but let us resolve to stand fast, come what may, and prove ourselves worthy of the great trust which has been placed in us."

But between the high command, working in relative comfort and safety, and the men actually sweating and fighting in the swamps, under the weeping rubber trees, there stretched not only a distance of nearly six hundred miles, but an immeasurably wider gulf of outlook.

According to the Japanese, Percival's eloquent order produced little result.

The Japanese advanced with ten tanks along a wide asphalt road in streaming rain. It had been raining for days, and the defenders, soaked and wretched, were sheltering beneath the rubber trees. Their guns were not all manned. In the urbane words of Colonel Tsuji, "Through this slight negligence they suffered a crushing defeat."

About fifty Japanese troops, "flashing their swords, charged like shepherd dogs into the darkness among the rubber trees. Voices cried out and groans could be heard sporadically amidst the reports of firearms. Meanwhile, the sounds of engines appeared to move away and they gradually became fainter. . . . The enemy was escaping without even making a sortie, although he had many cannon and machine guns and was menaced only by one small section with a handful of guns.

"We now understood the fighting capacity of the enemy. The only things we had to fear were the quantity of munitions he had and the thoroughness of his demolitions."

The Japanese did not possess large-scale, accurate maps of the area in which they were fighting. The British did—although many of them dated from 1915 and they were out-of-date in the disposition of paths and tracks through rubber plantations—but they were better than the Japanese maps which had been copied from school atlases.

Again, events moved to the Japanese advantage. In an abandoned armoured car, they discovered a map soaked with blood. On it a British staff officer had marked in coloured pencil all the defensive positions around Jitra. The British had thus, unknown to themselves, lost even the basic element of surprise before the battle began. The Japanese knew exactly where to attack. They made full use of this gratuitous and invaluable information.

The defenders "retreated, leaving behind as souvenirs about fifty field guns, fifty heavy machine guns, about three hundred trucks and armoured cars, and provisions and ammunition for a division of three months." The Japanese, prepared for a thousand casualties, actually lost twenty-seven men.

Having overrun the Jitra line so easily, the Japanese found that the bridges over the river defending Alor Star had not been properly blown, and they were able to cross them in less than an hour. They then arrived to find the Alor Star airfield scarcely damaged. Bombs were piled high on the perimeter, and in one of the station buildings bowls of hot soup still stood on the dining-room table. Among the trees fringing the airfield lay a thousand drums full of high-octane petrol. Two Japanese squadrons immediately took over and attacked the retreating defenders. Flying with British fuel in their tanks, they dropped British bombs on British troops.

Indeed, the four main airfields in north Malaya—Kota Bharu, Alor Star, Taiping and Sungei Patani—were all working within a matter of hours of being captured. The Japanese gratefully nicknamed them "Churchill aerodromes."

The new British positions had been reconnoitred, but when the retreating troops arrived, they found that no defence works had been constructed, although a week earlier orders had been issued for a civilian labour force to do this work.

"Whether they had ever assembled and dispersed," wrote Percival later, "or never assembled at all, I cannot say as reports on this point are conflicting." But there was no conflict whatever about reports of the nakedness of the defence position.

The Japanese attacked before any new defences could be prepared. At midnight, the commander of the Punjabis, in the mistaken belief that all the units to his right had been wiped out, decided to retreat.

On December 10, Japanese bombers attacked Penang, the island off the west coast, about five miles south of the Muda River. Penang had neither anti-aircraft guns nor air-raid shelters, and two days later it was decided to evacuate the wounded with all European women and children. Five days later, with cholera and typhoid reported through bomb damage, and with only two battalions available to defend the island against Japanese attack, Heath ordered a complete withdrawal. No demolitions were made. As a result, the Japanese forces which occupied Penang almost immediately found a large fleet of small boats which they later used for landing forces behind British positions. The radio station was not destroyed and so provided a most valuable propaganda weapon for them. If the British meant what they said about standing by the people of Malaya, why were they the only ones to be leaving? This unanswered question made a deep and abiding impression on Asiatic listeners throughout Malaya; many of them had friends or family on Penang Island.

The debacle at Penang was largely a military fiasco. Lieutenant-General Heath, in command of the area, was, in fact, senior to Percival, who held only acting rank. Major-General Barstow had proposed to Heath that the forces withdraw, but such a serious retreat had naturally to be approved by General Percival in Singapore. Percival, understandably, refused to consider this suggestion.

Heath, in the Governor's own words, "considered the matter so important that he felt obliged to travel down by train to Singapore, nearly four hundred miles, to put his view in person, notwithstanding the confusion that prevailed on the Kedah front."

Despite the military withdrawal from Penang, 850 men and women of the local A. R. P. Corps (out of a total strength of 1340) remained on duty helping with such diverse activities as traffic control, police work, the distribution of food and the Auxiliary Fire Service. Telephone operators—Eurasian and Chinese men and women—stayed at their switchboards until the military demolished the power station. The medical auxiliaries and nursing sisters were compulsorily evacuated, mostly against their will, by the Army.

Sir Shenton Thomas wrote later, "The Civil Government in Singapore knew nothing about it, and would not have approved. . . . We should have been able to point out the disastrous effect on morale of such a move."

Sir Shenton Thomas' final telegram to the Resident Councillor, on December 16, contained these words: "In any evacuation, preference should be given to those who are essential to the war effort *without racial discrimination*. . . ."

"Duff Cooper," he wrote later, "was not in favour of the words underlined, but gave way."

On December 23, Sir Shenton received instructions from the

Colonial Office supporting this policy. ("No other was, of course, possible if we were to retain any sort of respect.")

Sir Shenton Thomas always assumed that the order for the wholesale evacuation of the Europeans was given by Brigadier Lyon, who was in command of Penang Island. It was carried out by night "presumably to safeguard the troops, and the Asiatic population awoke on the following day to find themselves alone.

"As a finishing touch, Duff Cooper, in a broadcast on December 22, said that the majority of the population had been evacuated, whereas it was in fact only a small minority. He was, of course, thinking only of the Europeans, and the Asiatics realised this. So did he when I spoke to him about it on the following day.

"Penang was a very discreditable affair, and had a shocking effect on morale throughout Malaya."

What made the abandonment of Penang even more ironic was the fact that Brooke-Popham's order of December 8—"We are ready; our preparations have been made and tested; our defences are strong and our weapons efficient"—had been printed on large posters pasted on walls around the town.

Now that Penang had been abandoned, there seemed no further point holding the Muda River, especially as a Japanese advance threatened to outflank, if not cut off, the 11th Indian Division, so Heath ordered a withdrawal to the Krian River, another thirty miles to the south. It was necessary to go this far because the country between the two rivers was flat and open, favouring the use of tanks, and the defenders had no tanks. The British forces had now retreated one hundred miles—roughly a quarter of the entire peninsula—in little more than a week.

Thus, the pattern for retreat was established. It was not to stop until the surrender of Singapore. Each time the defenders established themselves in positions farther along the road south, Japanese planes would swoop in and bomb them. Then Japanese patrols would surround them, and they would be forced to withdraw yet again. Sometimes the Japanese infiltrated their position from the sides or rear. If this failed, they would by-pass them completely and leave the British troops isolated and forced to withdraw in order to engage the enemy. Whatever the tactics, the end result never varied; the battle burned on down through the peninsula, nearer and nearer to Singapore.

Under the threat, rather than the performance, of Japanese bombing, coolies left the docks and fled away. Troops, unaccustomed to the task, had to unload ships themselves. Railway workers and maintenance men went back to their villages; shops closed, petrol stations ran dry, villages emptied. Gangs of looters pillaged the deserted houses.

General Percival called at a railway station near Kuala Lumpur toward the end of December, and found only the Indian station-master still in his office. He had no signalmen, no shunters, no labourers of any kind. Fear of appearing to collaborate with the British had driven them away; the signs and portents of victory were already all with the Japanese.

Japanese soldiers dressed as coolies and labourers infiltrated defensive positions. Villagers, anxious to be on the winning side, resentful of the way their "protectors" were behaving, laid out arrows of washing or crops or bananas, to point to the British local headquarters, which could then be easily attacked from the air. Troops grew to distrust all Asiatics, for in native dress, it was almost impossible to separate friend from foe; the rift between the races widened.

Some Japanese spoke both English and Urdu, and at night they could call out orders or slang remarks in the hope that a nervous soldier might reply and give away his position.

As the retreat quickened, roads were jammed, exhausted drivers asleep at the wheels of their vehicles after hours without rest or food. Orders came to burn towns and villages to deny them to the Japanese, to scorch the earth, as in Russia. How could these instructions be reconciled with saving the country? It was one thing for the retreating Russians to lay waste their own homeland to deny it to the advancing Germans. It was quite another for Europeans systematically to burn the little huts and bamboo bashas of Malayan and Indian coolies. Often, they could not even speak their language to explain why this was necessary. The feelings of these humble, bewildered locals, seeing their life achievements burn away, needs no elaboration. This was a time that would never be lived down, a memory of a ruling race in terrible retreat that old men would remember and children would be taught.

The Japanese superiority in tactics, in command, in knowing what they were fighting for, bred its own legend of invincibility.

Aboard their troopships from Hainan, the Japanese had lived frugally on soup, rice and barley, pickled radish and dried eel. As they advanced, they lived off the land in a way British and Australians could not possibly do, because they had never been trained to do so, had never been taught which plants and leaves and roots could be eaten and which could not.

For generations, the British had been ordered to interfere as little as possible with local customs, and never to take advantage of local people. The Japanese, completely uninhibited in this direction, speaking as peasants from one Asiatic country to peasants whom they had come to liberate in another, took what they wanted, marching on a handful of rice, chewing leaves, drinking from secret wells. Also, they travelled light in rubber-soled shoes and thin tropical uniforms, while as Spencer Chapman wrote later: "Our own front-line soldiers were at this time equipped like Christmas trees with heavy boots, web equipment, packs, haversacks, water bottles, blankets, ground sheets and even greatcoats and respirators so that they could hardly walk, much less fight."

Bewildered, often without leaders, because the Japanese had been taught to shoot as primary targets European officers leading Indian troops, and so disorganise the soldiers, they fell back, fear and alarm rising like a tide among them with each new disaster. At night, the humid, dripping, breathing jungle was a lonely and terrible place to men brought up in crowded, brightly lit cities.

Here and there they would see tiny flickering flames, the oil lamps of villagers crouched in their bamboo huts, perhaps the glow of fireflies under an immensity of rain and darkness, the night alive with all the strange noises of the tropics; lizards croaking, the cough of frogs in marshes, the creak of branches as wild beasts went stealthily on their way.

There was the fear of being cut off and subjected to nameless tortures by a ruthless and inscrutable enemy. In the popular English-language adventure stories of the day, the Japanese had frequently figured as masterminds of evil. They were unknown, unfamiliar, and to troops who probably had never been abroad before, to be thus transported halfway across the world to face these unimagined hazards, they lived up to their fictional reputations. They were so difficult to see and to recognise; they could melt away into the undergrowth in a way the British Army had not then learned.

Telephone lines would suddenly be cut. Field wireless sets were no smaller than large suitcases—and were constantly and cripplingly affected by moisture, by heat and "blanketing" by trees. The jungle even had an enervating effect on the army compasses; the needles would not always point to magnetic north. Night was thus a time of taut and tightening nerves, and by day, when the troops had to fight again, they were already weary and overstrained in the heat and the sweat and dirt, mentally clouded by the psychological miasma of retreat. The feeling was that this was a nightmare that must somehow end—but how? And when? And where? They could only retreat until Singapore. Beyond that lay the sea. How could they stop before then? The terrible questions chased elusive answers as the retreat went on.

Just after Christmas, at Duff Cooper's insistence, Brooke-Popham was relieved by Sir Henry Pownall as Commander-in-Chief, Far East. Pownall visited the battle area and concluded that "several changes in high places may have provided the solution." Pownall, however, was Commander-in-Chief for only a very few days, and then General Wavell took over as Supreme Commander of all Allied forces in the southwest Pacific. Roosevelt, wanting a unified command, had suggested the appointment. Churchill agreed, flattered at such confidence being placed in a British officer. But he realised the likelihood of early defeat and so, too, did Wavell, who accepted his unenviable command with the classic comment: "I have heard of men having to hold the baby, but this is twins." His appointment was announced on January 4, and Pownall became his Chief of Staff.

Rommel regarded Wavell as the only British general who "showed a touch of genius." As Commander of the huge Middle Eastern theatre which stretched from Kenya to the Balkans, and from Libya to Iraq, Wavell had a power and independence which the Prime Minister often found tiresome. From the outbreak of war in 1939, his responsibilities had included the political, administrative and diplomatic, as well as the military. Although he won the first victories in the Western Desert, he later paid the price for inadequate equipment.

Churchill grew progressively more critical and, in June 1941, replaced him by Auchinleck, claiming that Wavell was "a tired man."

Wavell then succeeded Auchinleck as Commander-in-Chief in India. Churchill sent him directly to New Delhi, refusing all his requests for leave in London, because, in the words of Wavell's biographer John Connell, "he could not have him hanging around London living in a room in his club, and that in India he could enjoy sitting under 'the pagoda tree.'"

As Churchill wrote later, President Roosevelt's suggestion that Wavell become Supreme Allied Commander for American, British, British Empire and Dutch troops in Southeast Asia, was "one which only the highest sense of duty could induce him to accept."

Churchill feared disaster and his fear was well founded.

But this was only shuffling the pack; the game was already lost.

As 1941 closed, the Japanese landed north of Kuantan (on December 29) but were kept from the Kuantan airfleld for five days to allow the first convoy of British reinforcements to unload safely at Singapore. These reinforcements consisted of the 45th Indian Infantry Brigade Group under Major-General J. G. Smyth, V.C.—troops who were, in Percival's opinion, "very young, unseasoned and undertrained, and straight off the ship after their first experience of the sea."

The Slim River was the last natural barrier before Kuala Lumpur, and it was vital to stop the Japanese crossing it to delay the fall of Kuala Lumpur and deny the enemy the use of its airfield until this convoy had been landed at Singapore.

The 12th Indian Brigade held the road and railway to Kuala Kubu. On either side of both road and railway there was dense jungle; and though there had been time to dig weapon pits, wire the defences and erect roadblocks to stop the Japanese tanks, the men were understandably in poor heart. One officer, complaining of the lethargy of his troops, mentioned the depressing, claustrophobic effect of jungle fighting.

"The deadly ground silence emphasised by the blanketing effect of the jungle was getting on the men's nerves . . . the jungle gave the men a blind feeling." And the fact that the silence was periodically broken by the roar of enemy aircraft was no relief at all.

On January 5 the Japanese attacked down the railway line, and were driven back with heavy losses. Next night, tanks and trucks, followed by infantry, attacked along the main road. They were held up at the roadblocks, and several tanks destroyed, before a way round was discovered in the darkness, a number of disused loop roads left when the line of the original main road had been straightened out. The tanks were thus able to work their way round behind the British lines, and so achieved a complete breakthrough, to be swiftly followed by infantry.

The Japanese, as we have said, lived off the land, taking what they needed. British, Australian and Indian defending troops, by contrast, had long supply lines. A broken-down truck could cause chaos for miles. Ironically, with each fall back, they abandoned dumps of food which the Japanese did not have time to eat; they were travelling too fast and left what they could not carry for the men coming behind them.

The Japanese called these other supply dumps "Churchill's Allowance." They captured so much[5] that they did not need to

---

[5] After Slim River, according to Colonel Tsuji, the British abandoned thirteen heavy guns, fifteen anti-tank guns, twenty tractor-drawn guns, six anti-aircraft guns, fifty armoured cars, and 550 motor cars, together with ammunition, rations and medical stores sufficient to service two brigades for a month.

wait for their own supplies of fuel and ammunition, but raced ahead under the order: "Depend upon the enemy for rations."

As Colonel Tsuji wrote later: "We had to be grateful to General Percival not only for provisions for the men, but also for cars and gasolene abandoned in abundance. If such tactics as these could be kept up, then our fighting officers and men would not go hungry." They were and they did not.

Lieutenant-Colonel Spencer Chapman, preparing to organise guerilla warfare behind the Japanese lines, lay in a thicket at the side of the road and watched the Japanese infantry go past him, mounted on bicycles.

"The majority were on bicycles in parties of forty or fifty," he wrote later, "riding three or four abreast and talking and laughing just as if they were going to a football match. Indeed, some of them were actually wearing football jerseys; they seemed to have no standard uniform or equipment and were travelling as light as they possibly could."

This ingenious idea of equipping the advancing infantry with bicycles helped the Japanese advance more than the captured airfields, the stores and all the cars and trucks.

Before the war, cycles had been one of Japan's chief exports. In addition to the thousands the Army brought with them (with expert cycle repairers for each company), they now seized other cycles from villagers, knowing that all the parts—chains, wheels and so forth—would fit. On these cycles they pedalled along the hard, flat, wide, empty roads for up to twenty hours a day. Frequently, in the burning, gruelling heat of noon, their tyres burst. They had no time to repair them; they pedalled south on the rims. By night the noise of hundreds of steel rims grinding through the darkness sounded to already nervous defenders ominously like the rumble of advancing tanks. Back and back they fell, believing columns of tanks were advancing against them. But in the morning the roads were empty again; the cyclists were already twenty or thirty miles farther south.

When the Japanese infantry dismounted to fight, locals were impressed to ride or carry their bicycles for them. Each soldier had a light machine gun and a rifle hung over his shoulder, plus all his equipment, usually weighing between sixty and eighty pounds. Local guides—often from the Japanese plantations of pre-war days—would guide them across difficult country in one of the strangest and most successful advances in military history.

Whereas a truck or armoured car could be halted at a river when the bridge was down, the Japanese simply hoisted their bicycles on their backs and forded the river and pedalled south from the other side.

Too often bridges that should have been blown were not, either because the orders had failed to come through, or the demolition charges were ruined by the rain, or maybe the party detailed to stay behind to deny the bridges to the enemy was itself attacked.

In some cases the Japanese found detonating charges already laid with wires connected to hidden switches. They cut these with their sabres. When a motorised column came to a railway bridge, left unblown because the British thought that since the Japanese had no trains they could not use it, they placed logs of wood their agents had hidden alongside it on the rails, and drove their trucks across.

For the Japanese, the victory at Slim River was "the greatest victory of the Malaya campaign, up to that date"; for Percival, the defeat at Slim River was due to "the utter weariness of the troops, both officers and men. They had been fighting by day and moving by night for a month, and few of them had had any proper rest or relief. To their sheer physical fatigue was added a mental fatigue brought about by the enemy's complete supremacy in the air and on the sea, and by a general sense of futility."

It was unlikely that the Japanese could be held for more than a couple of days north of Kuala Lumpur, and the next hundred miles of country, right down to the Johore frontier, was unsuitable for a defensive action; the roads were too good.

Wavell ordered the 8th Australian Division, which so far had seen no action, to make an all-out stand along the line of the Muar River, some twenty miles into Johore province; the III

Indian Corps could then be pulled back behind this line. Always the emphasis grew on retreat.

On January 13 the second convoy of reinforcements arrived in Singapore, bringing the British 18th Division and fifty-one Hurricane fighters in crates.

The Hurricanes were accompanied by twenty-four half-trained pilots, many of whom had had no combat experience. However, they had to be thrown straight into battle and when twenty-seven unescorted Japanese bombers flew over Singapore a week later, eight were shot down. But such success was short-lived, for against the Zero even the Hurricane was outclassed, as well as outnumbered. This particular batch of machines had originally been destined for the Middle East, and they were further handicapped by special desert air filters, hanging down like a pendulous growth beneath their engines, which reduced the plane's speed by 30 m.p.h. Only at heights over twenty thousand feet did the Hurricane have superiority, and the Japanese were under no compulsion to fly high.

When the Japanese bombers came over next day (at low level) they were escorted by Zeros, which shot down five Hurricanes without loss to themselves. Spitfires would have been the really effective answer, but none were spared from the war in the West.

The Japanese were landing now from the sea on the east coast, and to the weary, retreating British and Australian forces they seemed invincible. The sad tale was illumined by individual acts of heroism; touched with the unselfish lustre of brave deeds, but these were only flashes of glory in a growing tapestry of defeat.

A third convoy of reinforcements reached Singapore on January 22, and a fourth two days later, with nearly two thousand Australians, including recruits with only two weeks' training.

Some had defective rifles, some had never even fired any rifle. These men arrived in time to become prisoners, although in the Middle East 16,600 fully trained Australian reinforcements waited in the depots, and Australia itself possessed 87,000 trained militiamen who might have volunteered for service.

On January 25, Percival ordered the retreat on to Singapore

Island. The last battle was about to begin. Gordon Bennett wrote privately in his diary: "There is no tonic to be gained from any stabilisation of the position. . . . The 'retreat complex' is now here with a vengeance."

Strangely enough, the Japanese Air Force failed to interfere with the actual withdrawal across the causeway. At 7:00 on the morning of January 31 the two remaining pipers of the Argyll and Sutherland Highlanders piped the last of the Australians and Gordon Highlanders across to the island, to the tunes of "Jennie's Black E'en" and "Bonnets over the Border." An hour later the Argylls, who had covered the retreat, followed to the turn of "Hielan' Laddie."

The battle for Johore had been lost, the battle for Singapore was about to begin, with a captive audience of more than one million refugees gathered on the doomed island. "This defeat should not have been," wrote Gordon Bennett in his diary. "The whole thing is fantastic. There seems no justification for it. I always thought we would hold Johore. Its loss was never contemplated." But then none of the horrors in the campaign had been contemplated either.

Percival realised that attack was the best form of defence, indeed, in the circumstances, the only one; but it was too late now. "We must play the enemy at his own game," he announced, "and attack on every possible occasion." But the Indian divisions had no chance to attack. After the cancellation of Operation Matador the spread-eagled defences never had time to recover; the Japanese advanced too quickly.

Churchill could not understand how the Japanese, with no warships whatsoever in the area, constantly forced the British Army to withdraw by threatening its rear with sea-borne landings.

"We have been absolutely outmanoeuvred and outfought on the west coast of Malaya," he wrote on January 22 to the First Sea Lord, Sir Dudley Pound, "and by an enemy who has no warship in the neighbourhood." He asked Pound to explain.

Pound replied: "Where the enemy have air superiority the problem is both a naval and an air one. The rot started at

Penang, where arrangements to put the 'scorched earth' policy into force appear to have completely broken down. The enemy thus had a considerable number of small craft. The enemy have [also] transported motor landing craft overland from Singora." Save on one or two occasions, the Navy was unable to interfere with the Japanese sea-borne outflanking movements; not only would any British warships have been bombed out of the sea, as was the Perak Flotilla, but the decision had also been taken to use what ships the Navy possessed to keep open the sea approaches to Singapore, which was difficult enough. As the Japanese advanced, convoys of reinforcements had to sail the long way round Sumatra.

When Churchill took the blame for the disasters in the Far East on his own shoulders in the House of Commons on January 27, he asked, "Why then should I be called upon to pick out scapegoats, to throw the blame on generals or airmen or sailors, to appease the clamour of certain sections of the British and Australian press?" Basically, Malaya was lost because the Far East came last on the list of official priorities. It ran a poor third to the desert war and aid for Russia—and quite rightly so, in General Percival's opinion: "The choice was made and Singapore had to suffer. In my opinion this decision, however painful and regrettable, was inevitable and right."

In a discussion with the writer, he elaborated this principle: "Supposing we had lost the war in the West and finished up with Germany supreme—and they might have been if they had knocked Russia out—we would have been occupied by Germany. Then what would then have been the use of an empire in the East? . . .

"On the civil side, far too little attention had been paid to the people who did not regard themselves as British, but as Malays and Chinese. The civil side did not seem to realise the complications of fighting in their own country.

"The civilian population were naturally saying to themselves, Who's coming out top dog here?, and they were waiting to see who *was* going to be top dog, so there wasn't very much help from them.

"To start with, it took a very long time to get any overall decisions from the rulers out there, because in the end you had to go to about a dozen different people to get a decision. This occurred time and time again.

"It caused great delays because a lot of these people were pretty dilatory in replying. It took weeks or months to get a decision on general policy regarding the building of fortifications and so on. . . ."

Wavell estimated that had five thousand civilian labourers been organised under British officers able to speak their language, the speed of the Great Retreat would have been greatly reduced. He considered the race was lost by one month.

General Percival thought it was lost "by three weeks, or even two."[6] Yamashita later gave his opinion that the race was even more close-run. He knew reinforcements were on the way; his men were down to one hundred rounds of ammunition each and two bowls of rice a day. A matter of days could have decided it.

Mr. Corbet, of Borneo Motors, expressed the civilian attitude to the fall of Malaya.

"In your heart you had no confidence in your own troops. There had been this all the way down and nobody had stood up to the Japs. You knew it was pretty well all over. You couldn't see any chance of getting away from the Island."

The news that the naval base, the *raison d'être* for defending Singapore, had been abandoned and that demolitions had been begun before the first troops crossed the causeway did little to boost the morale of the British Army.

"This demolition of the docks even before we withdrew from the mainland," said Gordon Bennett, "reflects lack of confidence in our cause," a lack of confidence which the events of the next few weeks was to justify.

On January 19, Wavell told Churchill, "I must warn you that I doubt whether the island can be held for long once Johore is lost." But he expected Singapore to hold out for three months,

[6] In an interview with the author.

believing that the Japanese would not be able to disembark sufficient forces to force a quick surrender.

The island of Singapore is linked to the mainland by an 1100-foot causeway, a stout affair, seventy feet wide at the water-line, with a steel road-and-railway bridge. A seventy-foot gap was blown in this, but the first thing the Japanese discovered when they examined the damage was that at low tide the water over the collapsed part of the causeway was only four feet deep; even a small man could wade across.

The battered army, trailing across the causeway to Singapore, thought it was entering an impregnable fortress, where there would be time to rest and to recuperate from the nightmare of the last few weeks. It soon discovered that Singapore was not a fortress, a fact the Japanese had known for years, but which even Churchill did not know until January 16, when Wavell told him.

"Please let me know," Churchill had cabled on the fifteenth, "what would happen in the event of your being forced to withdraw to the island."

Wavell replied: "Until quite recently all plans were based on repulsing sea-borne attacks on the island and holding a land attack in Johore or further north, and little or nothing was done to construct defences on the north side of the island to prevent an enemy crossing the Johore Strait, though arrangements have been made to blow the causeway. The fortress cannon of heaviest nature have all-round traverse, but their flat trajectory makes them unsuitable for counter-battery work. Much will depend on the air situation."

Churchill was astonished that "no measures worth speaking of had been taken by any of the commanders since the war began, and more especially since the Japanese had established themselves in Indo-China, to construct field defences. They had not even mentioned the fact that they did not exist.

"All I have seen or read of war had led me to the conviction that a few weeks would suffice to create strong field defences, and also to limit and canalise the enemy's front of attack by minefields and other obstructions. . . . I do not write this in any way to excuse myself. I ought to have known. My advisers ought to have known and I ought to have asked. The reason I had not asked was that the possibility of Singapore having no landward defences no more entered my mind than that of a battleship being launched without a bottom."

Yet Singapore had indeed been launched without a bottom. "The fact that no defences had been constructed on the north and west coasts of the island in pre-war days, and only limited defences even after the war started," wrote Percival, "had been the subject of much critical comment even in the highest quarters. It has been imputed to a lack of foresight on the part of successive General Officers Commanding. Such criticism is most unjust. In the first place, General Officers Commanding had no authority to construct defences when or where they liked. Then there was the question of the object of the defences. It was quite definitely the protection of the naval base, not the defence of Singapore Island."

But, in the event, without reinforcements, the two were indivisible; it was not possible to save one and lose the other; it was all or nothing. In the end it was nothing.

In support of Percival's contention that the military had no authority to construct defences when or where it liked, the experience of Major Angus Rose of the Argyll and Sutherland Highlanders may serve as an example.

Major Rose, impatient to cut down a row of banana trees to improve his field of fire, was told that he would have to get written permission from "the competent authority." Major Rose also reported that when the Secretary of the Singapore Golf Club was told that the Club was to be turned into a strongpoint he replied that he would have to convene a special committee meeting.

Despite two meatless days (when, for Europeans, pheasant made an agreeable substitute) it was easy to eat out in style on the island, to eat infinitely better, obviously, than people in wartime Britain. Cinemas and dance halls remained open. There was golf on the links, bridge and tennis in the clubs. The foolhardly optimism scarcely waned as the tide of Japanese murder, rape and devastation moved unchecked down the Malay peninsula. On New Year's Day the *Straits Times*, while regretting that "terrible changes have taken place with a rapidity that still leaves us a little bewildered," proclaimed in its editorial, "We are not overwhelmed; we shall not be overwhelmed. . . . We shall be rejoicing before 1943 comes round."

In January, when the air raids returned, sewers were wrecked and the bodies of air-raid victims had to be hastily buried before they putrefied. But a few streets away, waiters at the Raffles Hotel were laying up clean tables for the dinner and dance. Another hotel boasted "the usual tiffin dance on Sundays." All this at a time when every spare hand could have been used to construct defences.

Sir Shenton Thomas, the Governor, was partly to blame with a "business as usual" broadcast to the country. Late in January, however, he sent a circular to the Malayan Civil Service: "The day of minutes has gone. There must be no more passing of files from one department to another. . . . The essential thing is speed in action. Nothing matters which is not directly concerned with defence. . . ."

The *Straits Times* commented: "The announcement is about two and a quarter years too late."

Where stood the military through all this?

Not till December 23 did General Percival arrange for reconnaissance of the north shore of the island to select defence positions against possible landings, and nothing more was done that month. Not until Wavell arrived on January 7 was work actually put in hand. On January 19, Churchill decreed: "The entire male population should be employed upon construction defence works. The most rigorous compulsion must be used, up to the limit where picks and shovels are available."

But it was not until January 28—three weeks later—that a detailed *plan* for the island's defences was brought out, not until January 29 that compulsory labour regulations came into force, not until January 31—with the surrender only two weeks away—that Whitehall finally gave Singapore a free hand to fix wages and conditions.

By then most of the civilian labour had fled away. There were no coolies around to be paid the newly agreed wages for work that never was done.

Unaware of these particular difficulties, also unaware that Sir Shenton Thomas was against having defences on the island because he believed their construction would be bad for civilian morale, Churchill sent a long memo to General Ismay, for the benefit of the Chiefs of Staff, on January 19. This memo ran: "I must confess to being staggered by Wavell's telegram of the sixteenth. Merely to have seaward defences and no forts or fixed defences to protect their rear is not to be excused on any ground. I warn you this will be one of the greatest scandals that could possibly be exposed. . . .

"Let a plan be made at once to do the best possible while the battle in Johore is going forward. This plan should comprise: (a) an attempt to use the fortress guns on the northern front by firing reduced charges and by running in a certain quantity of high explosives if none exists; (b) by mining or obstructing the landing places where any considerable force could gather; (c) by wiring and laying booby traps in mangrove swamps and other places; (d) by constructing field works and strongpoints, with field artillery and machine-gun cross-fire; (e) by collecting and taking under our control every conceivable small boat that is found in the Johore Strait or anywhere else within reach; (f) by planting field batteries at each end of the Straits; (g) by forming the nuclei of three or four mobile counter-attack reserve columns upon which the troops when driven out of Johore can be formed; (h) the entire male population should be employed on constructing defence works. The most rigorous compulsion is to be used; up to the limit where picks and shovels are available; (i) not only must the defence of Singapore Island be maintained by every means, but the whole island must be fought for until every single unit and every single strongpoint has been separately destroyed; (j) finally, the city of Singapore must be converted into a citadel and defended to the death. No surrender can be contemplated."

The next day Churchill sent a cable to Wavell: "I want to

make it absolutely clear that I expect every inch of ground to be defended, every scrap of material or defences to be blown to pieces to prevent capture by the enemy, and no question of surrender to be entertained until after protracted fighting in the ruins of Singapore City."

Wavell replied, on January 21: "Points in Chiefs of Staff telegram have all been considered, and are in hand as far as possible."[7] But, of course, Churchill's vision of protracted fighting in the ruins of Singapore City was essentially unrealistic. There could be little question of making a heroic last stand in the ruins of a swarming city with a million refugees, where two thousand civilian casualties were being counted each day. As Percival said in his appeal to Wavell on February 13, the eve of surrender: "There must come a stage when in the interests of the troops and civilian population further bloodshed will serve no purpose."

That stage came within hours.

At the same time, as Churchill called on the defenders of Singapore to fight to the last, however, he also realised that too much could not be expected. On January 20 he had cabled Ismay: "Should Singapore fall, quick transference of forces to Burma might be possible. As a strategic object, I regard keeping the Burma Road open as more important than the retention of Singapore."

The next day he added: "What is the value of Singapore (to the enemy) above the many harbours in the southwest Pacific, if all naval and military demolitions are thoroughly carried out? On the other hand, the loss of Burma would be very grievous. It would cut us off from the Chinese, whose troops have been the most successful of those yet engaged against the Japanese."

Churchill did not share President Roosevelt's high opinion of Chiang Kai-shek's army, but for the sake of India it was important to keep the Japanese out of Burma, and to keep China in the war, for twenty-three Japanese divisions were effectively

---

[7] The Japanese knew that Singapore was clogged with civilians, both inhabitants and refugees, and so considered it unlikely that the island would be defended to the last man and the last round.

tied down in China. This was obvious to Wavell, who considered the loss of Singapore of relatively minor strategic importance compared to the loss of Burma. But any ideas that Churchill may have entertained of diverting reinforcements from Singapore to Burma were scotched by the Australian Government.

On January 23 the Australian Prime Minister, John Curtin, cabled Churchill in alarm: "After all the assurances we have been given, the evacuation of Singapore would be regarded here and elsewhere as an inexcusable betrayal. Singapore is a central fortress in the system of the Empire and local defence. Even in an emergency, reinforcements should be to the Netherlands East Indies and not Burma. Anything else would be deeply resented, and might force the Netherlands East Indies to make a separate peace."

"The Australian War Committee," complained Churchill, "could not measure the whole situation." But what it could measure was the distance from Singapore from its north coast, and, in fact, Yamashita had planned to drive on down across the Pacific to Australia, where, copying his campaign in Malaya, he would land troops on either side of the coastal cities, with deliberate diversionary landings elsewhere to draw away the scanty defending forces.

"With even Sydney and Brisbane in my hands, it would have been comparatively simple to subdue Australia," he told his biographer after the war. "I would never visualize occupying it entirely. It is too large. With its coastline, anyone can always land there exactly as he wants. . . .

"I could have poured in enough troops to resist effectively any Anglo-American invasions. Although the Japanese General Staff felt my supply lines would have been too long, so would the American or British lines. They might never have been able to reach the place at all. We could have been safe there forever."

Tojo would not accept this, arguing, as Yamashita said, that his supply lines would be too long, and too vulnerable; and, in any case, Tojo was more interested in going West to meet up with advancing German forces, possibly in the centre of India. Australia could wait; its turn could come.

Meanwhile, the decision was taken to hold on to Singapore for as long as possible; reasons of face played a considerable role in this. "The effect that would be produced all over the world," said Churchill, "especially in the United States, of a British 'scuttle' while the Americans fought on so stubbornly at Corregidor was terrible to imagine." Again, the comparison was unfair: Corregidor was a natural fortress and Singapore a teeming city on a marshy island.

Singapore had one week's unexpected grace while the Japanese forces on the other side of the Strait planned their attack. General Yamashita made his advance headquarters in a room at the top of a tower in the Sultan of Johore's palace. From this he could look down through wide glass windows over the narrow strip of water at the naked north coast of Singapore Island. It was a supremely good position to see the entire battlefront, and after the surrender a British prisoner was asked why the palace tower had never been shelled. The reply was that "no one imagined any army commander would be so rash as to choose such an obvious target as his headquarters."

From this vantage point, high above the treetops, the Japanese watched as the weary men of the Malaya campaign began to build defences. Lieutenant-Colonel Steedman, C.R.E., 11th Indian Division, whose engineers had been blowing up bridges all down the peninsula, found that not only had no trenches been dug, but there was no barbed wire available on the north side of the island. He went at once to the Base Ordnance Depot in Singapore City to collect some barbed wire and start putting it up, but his mission was unsuccessful; he had arrived at the depot on a half holiday.

Now the Japanese prepared for their assault. They wheeled up every gun they possessed, 440 in number, and all through each night, just before they attacked, each heavy gun fired one hundred rounds, and each lighter field gun twice this number.

The defenders, even without knowledge of the fearful weight of shells that would soon rain in on them, dug trenches in the mud of Singapore Island north shore without much confidence in the outcome. They had come to Malaya to defend the naval

base; their comrades had died in the jungle to defend the naval
base, but now the Navy was about to blow it up. The air was
thick with rumors and a sick feeling of fantasy and disbelief; this
could not possibly be happening, but it was, it was.

Churchill sent a memo to Ismay on February 2 stressing that
"What is indispensable is: first, the naval base should be completely wrecked; and secondly, the fortress guns should all be
destroyed. The preparations for the above demolition ought not
to cause alarm, because they are all in military areas, from which
the public is rigorously excluded." The public was excluded,
agreed, but it could hear the thunder of explosions over the walls,
and see the enormous towers of smoke, the funeral pyres of all
the empires of the east, which darkened the noon skies and turned
the rain black with soot. These sounds and sights of imperial suicide filled even the bravest hearts with dread.

For Churchill, the naval base was of secondary importance
now that the main fleet had been sunk. He was thinking of
Singapore as the bastion of Empire, the Gibraltar of the East, the
fortress that never was. On December 10, only two days after
the initial Japanese landings, Churchill had sent the following
signal: "Beware lest troops required for ultimate defence of Singapore Island and fortress are not used up or cut off in Malay
peninsula. Nothing compares in importance with the fortress."

He wrote to Ismay: "Over the last two years I have repeatedly
shown that I relied upon this defence of Singapore against a
formal siege, and have never relied on the Kra Isthmus plan
[Operation Matador]." "The idea of trying to defend the whole
of the Malay peninsula cannot be entertained." In essence,
Churchill's view was that while huge forces would have been
necessary to defend the whole peninsula, with the forces at his
disposal, Percival might have been able to defend Singapore
Island for quite a long time. This was why General Heath wanted
to withdraw all the way to Johore after Jitra.

But Percival was fighting to defend the naval base, and to defend the naval base he felt that he had to defend Malaya. Dobbie
had said as much in 1937, when Percival was his Chief of Staff.

In his Despatch to Parliament after the war[8] Percival repeatedly insisted: "Our object remained as before; i.e., the defence of the naval base," but by the end of January, with the base under constant artillery and aircraft attack, this objective had to be abandoned. All there remained to defend now, for as long as possible, was Singapore itself, the island and the city on the island.

Churchill and Percival were, in fact, fighting two different wars; twenty years of muddled thinking, of procrastination and indecision in the East, of assumption usurping proof at home, had confused the issue beyond easy understanding. In London, it was imagined that Singapore was as rigid as a rock; bombs could burst against it but it would emerge in the end, a symbol. And that was really all it could claim to be; a name synonymous with power, standing for a greatness that had already ebbed away. The only thing rigid about Singapore lay in the minds of the men who had devised the unworkable plan for its defence long before it was ever attacked.

If Churchill thought that "preparations for the above demolitions ought not to cause alarm, because they are all in military areas," he was wrong. The Army knew all about the naval demolitions; so did the civilians. Their knowledge did nothing to improve the situation.

"The worst part," said a signalman, "was that we heard the Navy had gone and they had started blowing up the naval base. The floating dock had been sunk in Johore Strait. My mate said, 'What the hell? Time we were getting weaving. We're supposed to protect the naval base; now they've blown it up and ratted, so what are we waiting for?' Then our skipper came up and said for us to take the truck to the base and get any spare stores we could find. The Navy's evacuated, he said, so it's a fair scrounge. . . .

"We got to the naval base and there were a few sailors knocking about. It was open shop for anybody who liked to go there."

Ian Morrison, the *Times* correspondent, also visited the base

[8] Published as a Supplement to the London *Gazette,* February 20, 1948.

and described it as "my most tragic memory of the whole Malayan campaign."

The looting that went on apparently unchecked was indicative of a complete breakdown of leadership on the part of officers. Morale was so adversely affected that on February 5, Percival called a press conference and tried to explain why the base had been evacuated. There was only one convincing reason that everyone already knew: the battle to save it had been lost. The conference was not a success.

Churchill believed that Percival had 100,000 men on Singapore Island; in fact, he had about 85,000, of whom 15,000 were noncombatants. But Wavell agreed with Churchill's view that there were enough troops on the island to throw the Japanese off it when they landed. In any case, the Japanese would not be able to land very large forces if the Strait was properly defended; Wavell based his plans on this factor. The causeway had been blown up—although not effectively—and it could be raked with fire.

Percival did not control enough fighting troops to defend the whole seventy miles of perimeter coastline. His defence of the island would have been better based on preventing large numbers of Japanese troops landing by being ready with strong counter-attacks. Instead, however, he decided to spread his men along the coast in an attempt to prevent the Japanese landing at all. He did not have sufficient troops to do this, and the strategy failed. Montgomery, after Dunkirk, had faced a similar problem; he had made no attempt to cover the whole coast of Kent and Sussex, but held a strong counter-attacking force at a strategic position inland, ready to fall on invading troops wherever they should land—a policy which had greatly impressed Churchill when he toured that area.

Percival's decision was based on the fact that the morale of his troops was already low, and if the Japanese actually landed on the island it would sink further. He did not feel they were determined enough to launch a strong counter-attack. His lack of confidence in them was to some extent justifiable. But the

men, on the other hand, could only be as good as the officers who
led them; the arguments tended to cancel each other out.

"Gordon Bennett," wrote Percival later, "was not quite so
confident as he had been up-country. He had always been very
certain that his Australians would never let the Japanese through,
and the penetration of his defences had upset him."

Next, having adopted what was in the circumstances a bad
plan of defence, Percival made the further mistake of concentrating more troops on the northeast coast of Singapore Island than
on the northwest, where, because of the lie of the land and the
absence of heavy guns, an invasion was most likely.

Wavell had visited Singapore on January 20, and had warned
Percival that the northwest coast of the island was the weakest
link and, therefore, the place where an attack was most likely.
He suggested that the British 18th Division, which, if lacking
experience of local conditions, was the freshest and strongest
formation available, should be placed on the northwest coast; the
8th Australian Division, the next strongest, on the northeast
coast, and what was left of the two Indian divisions would be
held in reserve.

Percival replied that he believed the main Japanese attack
would be on the northeast coast and he proposed to have the 18th
Division there, with the Australians on the northwest. Wavell
allowed Percival to dispose his troops as he thought fit, believing
that Percival, the man on the spot, and the man who had studied
the problem the longest, knew best. Wavell's appreciation and
control of the situation was handicapped throughout the campaign by having his A.B.D.A. headquarters in Java, where radio
and telegraphic communications were primitive.

Gordon Bennett, who was given command of the vital northwest area with the 8th Australian Division and the 44th Indian
Brigade, the one weakened by 1900 untrained reinforcements,
the last arrivals on Singapore Island, and the other only partly
trained, was not happy.

"To hold the Australian front," he wrote, "I have only four
reliable infantry battalions and two companies of the well-trained
machine-gun battalion. This area is the most uninhabited part of

the island. I held a conference of brigade commanders . . . all
agreed that we were undermanned. I realised the unfairness of
asking them and their men to fight with such meagre resources.
. . . The northwest part of the island is thickly covered with
timber, mostly rubber, with thick mangrove growing right down
to the water's edge. The posts, which are many hundreds of yards
apart, have a field of fire of only 200 yards."

The big gaps were patrolled by Dallforce, Chinese guerillas
trained by Colonel John Dalley, director of the Intelligence
Bureau, Malayan Security Police. These were men who had
buried political differences and secret society feuds to join common cause against the Japanese.

Colonel Dalley had suggested the formation of guerilla units
in 1940, but his proposal was ignored until December 1941, when
somebody found his report and sent it to General Heath. Dalley
was told to form his force, but by then it was rather late. Even
so, he managed to group his guerillas, known—after him—as
Dallforce, just before Christmas.

Spencer Chapman, who had been in Singapore for months
trying to persuade Shenton Thomas to allow him to organise
guerilla units which would operate throughout Malaya, in Siam,
Indo-China and even Hong Kong, had also been refused permission to do so. The Governor said that the plan was neither
practical nor desirable. He added that he had conferred with
Percival, and Percival agreed with him. In any case, the Chinese
Communists must not be armed, for the Malayan Communist
party was illegal at the time, and even to admit the possibility of
a Japanese attack would be disastrous for Asian morale. Now, too
late, hastily and with improvisation, these men were to do what
they could.

Dalley became a hero for the Chinese; they called him "Dalley
Sin Sang." Many of the men he recruited he had previously
caught and jailed. Now they prepared to fight or die in the
mangrove-covered shores of Singapore Island. They were fighting
for their country and they had no thought of surrender.

Dallforce was not properly armed; the British Army had left
behind so much equipment on the mainland that there was little

to spare. It was hoped, however, that the arrival of the *Empress of Asia*, with a full cargo of rifles and automatic weapons, would remedy the situation. But even in this particular, the defenders were disappointed; the *Empress of Asia* did not arrive.

She was an old ship, coal-fired, with some malcontents among the crew. In Cape Town the captain tried to discharge these men, but no replacements could be found. Complaints about poor conditions and inadequate fire-fighting equipment came to a head when the stokers learned that they were bound for Singapore. As the old ship approached Singapore, one of a convoy of four, on February 5, she fell astern, and as she did so, Japanese bombers singled her out for attack. She was set on fire from bow to stern. The captain ran her aground on a sandbank, and sent distress signals to Singapore harbour.

The Malays, who normally manned the local tugs, had already fled, but a number of European civilian volunteers took their place. Thanks to them and the work of the Navy, who took off most of the *Empress'* crew, there was very little loss of life.

But the heat from the blazing ship was so intense that it was impossible to tow her off, and neither she nor her precious cargo could be salvaged.

The last days, the last hours, before Singapore fell were touched with apocalyptic scenes. There were no deep air-raid shelters or concrete surface shelters, unless those built privately, because the marshy island was waterlogged, and, in any case, in the words of the official historian, "sufficient open spaces in which to construct above ground the large number of shelters needed, did not exist."

Because of this, civilian casualties from bombing were severe. As in Penang, the streets were crowded with people who ran out from their ramshackle houses, either to see the planes, not realising their danger, or in an attempt to escape from the threat of being buried beneath their houses. Between raids, the bodies of victims would be piled on trucks and buried—as they had been buried during the Plague of London three centuries before—in mass graves. Many were interred in the old Bukit Timah Cemetery, often without any burial service.

One day, a stray bullet hit the driver of an army truck carrying ten British soldiers. The truck skidded and overturned into the swollen canal by the junction of Bukit Timah Road and Kampong Java Road. The soldiers, trapped inside, were all drowned. No men could be spared to removed the bodies until after the surrender.

Other canals and ditches were clotted with oil from the streaming storage tanks, blocked with the bloated bodies of air-raid victims and animals. Looters roamed the streets; sometimes they were groups of soldiers with sub-machine guns or rifles. Other deserters, often drunk with whisky stolen from deserted liquor shops, besieged the docks, and in some cases forced women and children off the outgoing ships at the point of a gun, to take their places themselves.

One British deserter, bearded and without his rifle, arrived in the last days at the Chartered Bank of Raffles Place. From inside his filthy uniform he produced bundles of notes of various currencies which he said he wished to deposit.

"Everybody was taken aback at this grim incident," wrote one who was there, "for we knew its implications."

These implications of defeat and despair were not lost upon the million other refugees who crouched wretchedly in hollow drain pipes, in ditches, in locked houses, anywhere for shelter against the rain of bombs and shells.

Many streets were impassable. Cars, abandoned after their owners had escaped in them from up-country, blocked the roads for miles, bumper to bumper. Frequently, a bullet or shell would hit one and then petrol in their tanks would catch fire, making them blaze like torches, one igniting another.

Anti-aircraft guns were mounted on the pavements. House-holders beseeched the soldiers to remove them in case they attracted Japanese fire. (Similar incidents were reported before the fall of France. Then, peasants dragged farm carts across airfields to stop British planes taking off, in case of reprisals.)

All around the island, and in Singapore City, fires raged, and although the fire brigade worked day and night, it could not hope to control them. From the second week in February, when the naval base oil tanks were set alight, a pall of smoke darkened the entire scene and enshrouded the city so that at mid-day the sky was as dark as dusk. This pall completely obscured the moon at night, and even dyed the rain, staining uniforms, surrealistically turning white faces black, symbolic tears for the end of an empire.

"Singapore was burning and mutilated. . . . It had the air of an abandoned city for the reason that thousands of soldiers, with no fight in them at all, were congregating on the Esplanade, Raffles Reclamation and other open spaces. They were being massacred by machine-gun fire from Japanese bombers. Some of these gunners were to be seen throwing hand grenades from low-flying planes."[9]

Queues of Europeans waited day and night outside the bungalow of the shipping manager at the top of Cluny Hill, for tickets aboard any available ship anywhere—Ceylon, Java, Australia. The queue was rarely less than three quarters of a mile long and six deep, but only a handful of the ships carrying out these women and children would ever reach safety. They were dive-bombed, shelled, machine-gunned.

So the stage was set for the final act of the tragedy. On February 8, at 10:30 P.M. the Japanese invasion began, under the enormous thunder of their guns. As the first of the landing craft were sighted, this should have been the signal for a blaze of British searchlights to light up the Strait, the signal for an equally savage barrage of artillery to rip apart the wooden boats as they came on slowly, weighed down in the water, their outboard engines put-putting in the flickering glare of exploding Japanese shells.

Unfortunately, 22nd Australian Brigade headquarters had ordered that the shore searchlights were not to be turned on without direct permission from unit commanders. It was feared that they would immediately be shot at and destroyed.

Permission was never given, due, it is said, to telephone failure; so the searchlights were saved but not used. Nor did anyone telephone the artillery batteries inland to ask for the obvious

[9] From the eye-witness account of Dr. J. B. van Cuylenburg.

barrage. Indeed, not until a few infantry SOS flares went up in the dark did some of the guns open fire; and by then the enemy had already established a firm footing on the island. The rest of the artillery never even saw the flares.

Granted that many of the telephone failures were due to the extensive Japanese bombardment, why was radio not used to alert the artillery? The sets were there, the distance involved was only a few miles; the message could have been made but it never was. General Percival has called this "a strange and unfortunate reluctance to use the wireless." To this day, it remains unexplained. There is a curious parallel to this in the fatal radio silence of Admiral Sir Tom Phillips when the *Prince of Wales* was attacked.

So the Australians on shore fought in the darkness, but were powerless to stop the enemy landings.

During the night of February 8–9 the Japanese landed 13,000 troops on the island and a further 10,000 after daybreak. This was a remarkable achievement—a characteristic blend of determination and ingenuity. The landing craft had nearly all been carried overland down the west coast of Johore to avoid detection at sea. In addition to special armoured craft, each of which could take forty men, the Japanese used portable collapsible boats made of plywood with rubber joints, which one man could assemble in two minutes. Each of these was powered by an outboard motor and could transport over a dozen troops. If roped together in threes these boats could also carry artillery. It was the night of the little ships, a sort of Dunkirk in reverse.

Japanese who had no boats swam across the Strait, holding rifles and ammunition above their heads. As General Percival was later to comment ruefully: "There can be no doubt that preparations for this attempt on Singapore Island had been made a long time before the war started." They had; they even included roads built through the Japanese-owned rubber plantations in Johore, all leading south to the sea.

By one o'clock in the morning, the 22nd Brigade was ordered to withdraw. In so doing, many men were lost in the mangrove swamps and jungle. What should have been an orderly withdrawal degenerated into a disorganised and desperate escape. The Chinese volunteers patrolling the gaps between the thinly spaced defensive positions did not withdraw.

A gunner in one of the artillery units guarding Tengah Airfield saw Australians come running down the road toward him.

"It is the most vivid memory I have of the Singapore campaign," he wrote later. "They came moving at a half-trot, panic-stricken. It was pouring with rain and most of them were only in shorts. Few were wearing boots, and most of the men's feet were cut to ribbons. They'd come across rivers, through mangrove swamps, through the bush and out onto the road. They'd scrapped everything that could hold them back. They'd thrown aside their rifles and ammunition . . .

"Among them was one Aussie soldier fully equipped: rifle, ammunition, cape, shirt, shorts and boots. He came across the road to three of us who were standing watching.

"'What's happened?' we asked him. He looked at his fellow Australians.

"'They're finished,' he said. He was quite calm. He was a boy of about nineteen, a private. He seemed sorry for his mates.

"'Can I join up with you blokes?' he said. He came along with us. The others had lost control. They were panting, incoherent, a rabble."

Another astonishing incident was the abandonment of the Johore causeway by Brigadier D. S. Maxwell of the 27th Australian Brigade. Again, it was a case of fearing the worst and retreating, an act that precipitated an even worse calamity.

As early as 11:00 A.M. on February 9, Maxwell was seeking permission to withdraw from the vital causeway sector. He feared that the Japanese on the far side of the Kranji River might attack his sector in the rear. This was most unlikely, since they had two good roads leading straight to the heart of the island, and unless they struck completely unexpected difficulties they would hardly trouble to cross a mangrove-fringed river instead. Gordon Bennett quite rightly refused the request. But that evening, the Japanese landed on the near or east side of the river and once again Maxwell grew anxious about being cut off.

Yet his troops were fighting magnificently and at midnight,

when they found themselves concentrated in a strong defensive position across the neck of the Kranji peninsula about 500 yards from the shore, they had fought the Japanese to a standstill.

Many of the Japanese, landing in the mangrove swamps by the river, had been fried in a flood of burning oil when the Australians opened the tanks of the Kranji oil depot. The water blazed from bank to bank like some Old Testament vision. If this had been done earlier it would have been infinitely more effective.

Indeed, the Japanese were so worried about their own position, in the face of this heroic resistance, that, had this opposition been maintained, they were going to abandon their attack and attempt to land next day at a different point.

Yamashita ordered his crack troops, the Imperial Guards, to cross and land in the mangrove swamps near the north of the Kranji River. They hesitated, for their commander, Nishimura, had a personal feud with General Yamashita. After the Muar River battle in the previous month, when Australians and Indians fought with fierce fanaticism, when the brigade commander of the 45th Indian Brigade had died personally leading a bayonet charge, when the fighting had been so ferocious that out of a total of 4500 defenders only 450 Australians and 400 Indians had been able to fight through the swarms that threatened to cut them off from their main force, the Guards had lost some stomach for war. This small defending force had been pitted, with only hand weapons, against tanks, aircraft and heavily manned roadblocks, and by sheer defiance had held up the advance of Yamashita's entire army.

The Japanese Imperial Guards thus felt they had lost face, and in the East there is nothing more damning to lose. They showed their feelings by indulging in one of the most sickening atrocities of a campaign already surfeited with unnecessary slaughter: they beheaded 200 wounded soldiers whom the retreating Indians and Australians were unable to reach to carry off through the jungles.[10]

[10] Other wounded men, hiding in the forests, saw this act of mass murder. Although taken prisoners themselves, they survived to give evidence against the Japanese Imperial Guards at a war crimes tribunal after the war.

In the fighting, the commander of the 3rd Regiment of Guards was wounded. Years previously, Yamashita had commanded this regiment and now he chose the officer to replace him. Nishimura was annoyed by this, for it was one of the Guards commander's traditional rights and privileges to nominate his subordinate commanding officers. Although Yamashita sent his own personal staff officer to Nishimura to assure him that his decision had not been intended as a slight, Nishimura would not accept this explanation: he believed he had been insulted, and so, like a sulky child, he would make things as difficult for Yamashita as he could.

Now, when it was essential for the success of Yamashita's attack on Singapore that the Guards advance instantly, he hung back. He was offended that the Guards had not been chosen to lead the attack, instead of being used as second-wave troops. He therefore delayed his advance.

Yamashita, in his own account, says: "I ordered the Imperial Guards . . . to cross the Strait. . . . Then their commander asked for further orders from me. . . . I received a message from him that his troops were hesitating to cross because of oil flames on the surface of the water. It looked to me as if he was still upset about not being able to lead the attack. I ordered him to do his duty. . . ."

Yamashita crossed the Strait himself with his staff. There was only one small barge with an outboard engine for them. They were so crowded that they did not even have room to crouch down against the bullets and the shells that whistled through the air above their heads. They had to stand upright, holding on to each other's shoulders. His deputy Chief of Staff actually fell overboard and had to be hauled back into the boat.

When they landed, Colonel Tsuji, climbing up the swampy bank in the darkness, stood on something that yielded beneath his foot; there was a cry of pain and alarm. He shone a torch. They were walking over rows of British prisoners, captured by the first wave of Japanese. Having no time to corral them they had simply roped them together; they lay, hopeless and defeated, under the feet of the advancing Asian army.

Then, incredibly, at 4:30 A.M., the resistance suddenly subsided; Maxwell had decided to withdraw. Worse, Western Area Headquarters, which officially controlled this part of the operation, knew nothing of this new intention. General Bennett later denied that permission was ever given.

This withdrawal had far-reaching consequences, for the enemy was not only able to consolidate his landings, but was left with a 4000-yard gap to push through.

This tragic blunder opened the way for the abandonment of another vital defensive position, the Jurong Line on the western part of the island, a high ridge of land about three miles long running north–south between the sources of the Kranji and Jurong rivers. Even though anti-tank ditches had scarcely been dug, the Jurong Line could have formed a natural bottleneck—or stronghold—against enemy advance from the west.

Now, because of the withdrawal, its rear was threatened. At this point, Brigadier H. B. Taylor, who held the centre portion of the Jurong Line, received a copy of some "secret and personal" withdrawal plans which had been drawn up by General Percival, and which were intended to be acted upon only under certain circumstances. Unhappily, Taylor construed these as a direct command to withdraw. The upshot was a general evacuation of the Jurong Line and the whole strong defensive position collapsed, although the Japanese had done nothing more than probe it with advance troops. The position was now hopeless and defeat simply a matter of days.

On February 10, Wavell flew in from Java on his last visit to Singapore. He called upon the headquarters of the chaotic Western Area, and there he, Percival and Bennett were forced to scuttle for cover beneath a table ("an unedifying spectacle," recalled Percival) when a Japanese bomber scored a direct hit, but fortunately with a bomb that failed to explode.

A far worse shock awaited Wavell when he saw the state of the Jurong Line.

He ordered an immediate counter-attack, this time against Percival's better judgment. The attack failed because it came too late; there were heavy casualties.

By then the air arm in Singapore had ceased to exist. Shortage of aircraft had, all along, been the crucial weakness in the defence of Malaya. They received less than a third of the planes they had asked for, and those that did arrive were greatly inferior to the Japanese planes.

Even so, with adequate early warning, the Hurricanes and even the Buffaloes (which took more than half an hour to climb to 30,000 feet) might have stood a chance of competing with the enemy. But one by one the Japanese had overrun the relatively primitive early-warning stations on the mainland, and after the shutdown of the Mersing station in mid-January (some time before the site was lost to the enemy) the R.A.F. pilots always found themselves at a profound tactical disadvantage—behind and beneath the enemy.

As Percival wrote later, the R.A.F. men went "unflinchingly to almost certain death in obsolete aircraft which should have been replaced many years before."

"My attack on Singapore was a bluff—a bluff that worked," Yamashita admitted in his diary. "I had 30,000 men and was outnumbered more than three to one.[11] I knew that if I had to fight long for Singapore, I would be beaten. That is why the surrender had to be at once. I was very frightened all the time that the British would discover our numerical weakness and lack of supplies and force me into disastrous street fighting."

But the British never did. When Yamashita's assembled artillery began to fire through the night of the first assault, Percival was certain that reinforcements had arrived, with new supplies of ammunition. He considered that the Japanese barrage was as

[11] General Percival, in his estimate of the numbers opposing him, wrote: "I have seen it stated that 100,000 British surrendered to 30,000 Japanese. That, of course, is sheer nonsense.

"Does anyone seriously think the Japanese would be so foolish as to try to win the prize they wanted so badly with 30,000 men? It is safer to say they employed 150,000 men in Malaya, although some Japanese reports suggest a much higher figure. They also employed two tank regiments probably containing 200 to 300 tanks.

"For their attack on Singapore, the Japanese employed 68,000 combat troops in addition to other units. There can be little doubt that at the end of the campaign there were over 100,000 Japanese troops on Singapore Island and in south Malaya."

heavy as anything encountered on the Western Front during the First World War. He was no bluffer and he did not conceive that Yamashita could be as worried as he was himself. He limited his own big guns to twenty rounds each through the night, anxious to husband ammunition against the prospect of a long siege.

Had he guessed that Yamashita's director of supplies, Colonel Ikatini, had reported he was so short of ammunition and petrol that a long siege of Singapore "would probably fail," that Ikatini had actually suggested that the attack should be postponed, how different the picture of catastrophe would have appeared.

The Japanese *blitzkrieg*, although never approaching the severity of the blitz on London, caused complete chaos in the crowded, huddled slums of Singapore. The city's normal population was 550,000; now, because of refugees, it had swollen to approximately twice this figure. The Japanese used anti-personnel bombs, and one eye-witness recalls seeing "eight decapitated bodies in one street . . . I looked at the drains on each side of the narrow street. They were full of water, bloody water."

The four airfields on Singapore Island were under merciless attack. The three in the north—Tengah, Sembawang and Seletar—could also be shelled from the mainland and rapidly become unserviceable.

This only left Kallang in the south, which, being built on reclaimed land, oozed mud through every bomb crater. All the bombers had been withdrawn to Sumatra on January 27, and the fighters that could still fly soon followed. Only a handful of Buffaloes and Hurricanes remained to provide defence against dive-bombers' attack when the Japanese invaded the island on February 8.

To have left behind any more fighters would have been to invite their certain destruction, as Wavell explained to a somewhat irate Churchill. On February 9, the R.A.F. brought down six bombers with only one loss. Next day, the last fighter flew off. The R.A.F. claimed 183 enemy aircraft destroyed during the campaign. Had Percival been able to prolong the defence of Malaya by two or three weeks more, the story might have been very different. Two aircraft carriers, carrying ninety more Hurricanes, were due before the end of February. And even though the Hurricanes were technically inferior to the Japanese planes, their numbers would have helped enormously—both tactically and psychologically; for by now troops and civilians were cowed and resigned to defeat.

On February 10, Churchill sent Wavell a cable:

"I think you ought to realise the way we view the situation in Singapore. It was reported to the Cabinet by the Chiefs of the Imperial General Staff that Percival has over 100,000 men. It is doubtful whether the Japanese have as many in the whole Malay peninsula. In these circumstances, the defenders must greatly outnumber Japanese forces who have crossed the Straits, and in a well-contested battle they should destroy them.

"There must at this stage be no thought of saving the troops or sparing the civilian population. The battle must be fought to the bitter end at all costs. Commanders and senior officers should die with their troops. The honour of the British Empire and of the British Army is at stake. With the Russians fighting as they are and the Americans so stubborn at Luzon, the whole reputation of our country and our race is involved."

Wavell put Churchill right about the numbers Percival actually had under his command, but agreed that he "should have quite enough to deal with the enemy who have landed if the troops can be made to act with sufficient vigour and determination." No one would dispute the numerical superiority of the defenders, but quantity was not all. Their calibre and the quality of their leaders also counted; so did the quality of their arms. The fact was that, after two months' retreating, to fight back without subconsciously anticipating yet another withdrawal was virtually an impossibility.

However, Wavell, whatever his own views, dutifully passed on Churchill's strictures in a Special Order of the Day.

"It is certain that our troops on Singapore heavily outnumber any Japanese troops who have crossed the Straits. We must destroy them. Our whole fighting reputation is at stake, and the honour of the British Empire. The Americans have held out on the Bataan peninsula against far heavier odds; the Russians are turning back the picked strength of the Germans; the Chinese, with almost a complete lack of modern equipment, have held back the Japanese for four and a half years. It will be disgraceful if we yield our boasted fortress of Singapore to inferior enemy forces."

To make assurance double sure, Percival issued his own version of Wavell's Special Order.

"In some units," he said, "the troops have not shown the fighting spirit which is to be expected of men of the British Empire. It will be a lasting disgrace if we are defeated by an army of clever gangsters, many times inferior in numbers to our own."

This was the first time that discomforting words like "yield" and "defeated" appeared in official orders. The comparisons drawn by Churchill and Wavell were, in fact, unfair. China and Russia are infinitely larger than Singapore, and although the Americans at Bataan were heavily outnumbered, the terrain favoured them, forcing the Japanese to attack from the front and preventing the use of encircling tactics as practised in Malaya and Singapore. Nor did the Americans face crack Japanese units until after the fall of Singapore, for it was imperative that they first capture this hub of Far Eastern defence.

Two days before the fall, on February 13, the last of the small ships, about fifty of them altogether, sailed from Singapore harbour carrying refugees. Scenes at the quayside were chaotic, with much overcrowding and boat-jumping. In some instances, armed deserters, as previously mentioned, forced women off the gangplanks to make way for themselves.

Some priority was given to trained officers and technicians who could carry on the fight in Sumatra or Java. General Percival also insisted on places being given to the women of the Military Nursing Service. He had heard how the Japanese had dragged nurses out of their hospitals after the fall of Hong Kong and raped them.

Most of the fifty little ships ran into the Japanese navy and air force before they reached their destinations. One naval launch carrying Rear Admiral Spooner and Air Vice-Marshal Pulford was chased by a Japanese destroyer. They beached on an islet, where a boatload of Japanese sailors followed them ashore and smashed their engines. Marooned on the barren tropical island, without food or any sort of contact with the outside world, more than half, including Pulford and Spooner, died of starvation and sickness.

In Singapore City, as the enemy noose tightened around the narrowing defensive perimeter, disorder and confusion mounted. Stragglers looked for their units. Deserters skulked in damaged buildings or went out in gangs looting, rifles slung across their shoulders, shirts crammed with tinned food and cigarettes. After more than two months of day and night retreat, too many had lost the will to fight. One observer described the Municipal Building as "solid blocks of Australians sitting on the stairs."

The ultimate catastrophe was now imminent. Civilian casualties were around two thousand a day as the town was raked by artillery and bombing, and machine-gunning by low-flying aircraft. Singapore General Hospital was crowded with dead and wounded; nurses working round the clock were soaked in the blood of the casualties. The sky was black with smoke as oil and rubber supplies were burned.

At noon on February 13, Sir Shenton Thomas' ban on liquor came into force. Altogether, 1,500,000 bottles of spirits and 60,000 gallons of the Chinese Samsu spirits were destroyed, so that the Japanese should not seize them, and then, inflamed with liquor, repeat the atrocities that had marked the fall of Hong Kong. The streets and gutters of Singapore streamed with alcohol and rain.

Rumour and despondency were everywhere.

Now a new danger threatened—shortage of water, for breaks in the conduits as a result of the continuous bombardment proved too numerous to repair.

At 2:00 P.M. on February 13, Percival held a conference at his underground headquarters, Fort Canning. It was hot and stuffy; the place was packed, and the air-conditioning system could not cope. By then, both Heath and Gordon Bennett advocated surrender, but Percival would not agree. He did, however, send a telegram to Wavell at his headquarters in Java, pointing out: "There must come a stage when in the interests of the troops and civilian population further bloodshed will serve no purpose. Would you consider giving me wider discretionary powers?"

Wavell, following Churchill's instructions, replied on the fourteenth, "Continued action essential," but informed Churchill of the position: "Have received telegram from Percival that enemy is close to town and that his troops are incapable of further counter-attack. Fear resistance not likely to be very prolonged."

Early on the fourteenth a complete breakdown of water supplies became imminent; there might be enough left in the reservoir for twenty-four hours or at the most forty-eight hours. Shenton Thomas, fearful of epidemics in the desperately overcrowded city, cabled the Colonial Office about the situation.

Churchill replied to Wavell thus: "You are, of course, sole judge of the moment when no further result can be gained at Singapore, and should instruct Percival accordingly."

As the end neared, Gordon Bennett did not care for the idea of fighting to the last. He was essentially a "civilian" soldier. There were many such senior officers in the A.I.F. because the regular army had been pared to the barest nucleus. They had been out of harness in the years before the war, and lacked proper training in modern warfare, and held, in addition, a most individual attitude to the military chain of command. On the morning of February 14, Gordon Bennett issued orders, unknown to Percival, and the Malayan High Command, that because of ammunition shortage his artillery was to fire only in defence of the Australian perimeter. There was little thought for the 1st Malaya Brigade, fighting gallantly to Bennett's south in the area of the Alexandra Military Hospital.

Their task of defence became impossible, and Bennett's order thus contributed indirectly to a peculiarly revolting horror in the hospital when Japanese troops stormed in, insisting that the building had been used as a firing point. By way of reprisal they bayoneted medical orderlies and patients, one of whom was actually on the operating table.

Bennett's second extraordinary action was to send a cable to his Prime Minister in Australia to advise him that "in the event of other formations falling back, and allowing the enemy to enter the city behind us," it was his intention to surrender "to avoid any further needless loss of life." Again, Gordon Bennett did not tell Percival of his decision to surrender, nor did he tell his Prime Minister of his other intention, which was to escape from Singapore.

It was not until after the war, when Percival, released from a prison camp in Manchuria, learned of this "surrender" telegram. His restrained verdict on Bennett's behaviour was: ". . . a most extraordinary procedure. No doubt he was perfectly entitled to communicate with his own Prime Minister but surely not to inform him of an intention to surrender in certain circumstances, when he had not even communicated that intention to his own superior officer."

The Japanese had for some days been dropping leaflets urging Percival to surrender. Now a Japanese reconnaissance plane dodged the anti-aircraft fire to drop a message in a cardboard tube tied with red and white streamers. It had been written by a staff officer, Lieutenant-Colonel Sugita, who had a knowledge of English. He had studied in America and was Yamashita's senior Intelligence officer.

The Japanese Commander to the British Commander.

In a spirit of chivalry we have the honour of advising your surrender. Your army, founded on the traditional spirit of Great Britain, is defending Singapore, which is completely isolated, and raising the fame of Great Britain by the utmost exertions and heroic fighting. I disclose my respect from my inmost feelings.

Nevertheless the war situation is already determined and in the meantime the surrender of Singapore is imminent. From now on resistance is futile and merely increases the danger to the million civilian inhabitants without good reason, exposing them to infliction of pain by fire and sword. Furthermore we do not feel you will increase the fame of the British Army by further resistance.

From first to last our counsel is that Your Excellency will cease to think of meaningless resistance, and from now on, yielding to our advice, promptly and immediately will suspend the action extending over the whole British battlefront. It is expected that you will take measures to dispatch an army messenger as stated below.

If on the contrary you continue resistance as previously, it will be difficult to bear with patience from a humanitarian point of view, and inevitably we must continue an intense attack against Singapore. Ending this advice we show respect toward your Excellency.

1. The army messenger's route of advance shall be by the Bukit Timah road.

2. The army messenger, hoisting a white flag as well as the British flag, will be escorted by a number of soldiers as a protection.

(Signed) Japan's Army Commander,
Lieutenant-General Tomoyuki Yamashita

*   *   *

Almost unseen beyond the early morning darkness, Japanese aeroplanes wheeled insolently, black-winged against the gloom, the roar of their engines rising and dying as they turned. Some flew so low over the anti-aircraft guns on the pavement of Beach Road that the crews threw out hand grenades at the gunners.

From the north came the cough and bark of mortars, and then the loose rattle of machine guns. Streets were empty of people, who crowded in home-made air-raid shelters, fashioned largely out of huge drain pipes. Abandoned cars and broken-down army trucks stood where their drivers had left them, many ablaze. Shop windows had splintered from the bombing; the pavements glittered with the sharp spikes of glass that no one had cleared away. The goods in the windows had long since disappeared: in the outskirts of the city the looters were at work.

Many roads were impassable, blocked by fallen lampposts, pocked with shell craters and bomb holes, latticed with the overhead tramway lines, telegraph wires and cables. Houses blazed along North Bridge Road; Capitol Flats was a concrete torch. Officials in the upper floors of the Cathay Building, Singapore's only skyscraper, were burning papers; the smoke billowed out of the open windows, to add to the smell of oil, the stench of decay from blocked drains, burst sewers and the unburied dead. The air was heavy with imminent defeat.

In the underground conference room at Fort Canning, the British military headquarters, at 9:30 on that morning, half a dozen men, officers and civilians, sat with pale, tired faces around the oval table. The air felt dead, used up. A fan from the middle of the ceiling beat its slow, heavy blades above their faces.

Percival sat at the head of the table. He had begun the day with Holy Communion; it was his daughter's twelfth birthday. Now he had to face the most crucial decision of any military commander in modern British history; whether to fight on—hoping reinforcements could arrive by sea to save the hemmed-in garrison of this indefensible island, ludicrously publicised for nearly a generation as the Gibraltar of the East—or to surrender.

First, *could* he hold on? Were his men able to do so—and if so, for how long and with what hope of relief? No one could say with certainty. The Japanese controlled the air and the sea approaches. Many soldiers, no one even knew just how many, had flung away their arms. Others had formed armed gangs, determined to fight their own way out, with a looted fortune if possible. The majority, outgunned, outgeneralled, outmanoeuvred, outfought, had lost faith in any possible victory.

The Director-General of Civil Defence, the Inspector-General of Police, the Water Engineer, all gave their reports to Percival. None had anything of comfort to say. The only petrol at their disposal was in the tanks of what few military trucks remained in running order. They had some small arms ammunition, but very little ammunition for the 25-pounder field guns, and virtually none in reserve for the anti-aircraft defences.

Stores of food for the forces—nearly 100,000—would not last more than a few days, possibly a week. Civilians who had retreated from the fighting up-country were now packed thirty to a room. The water situation was very grave. The two reservoirs on the island would not last for more than twenty-four hours. Five gallons out of every six being pumped into them were pouring away through smashed conduits and pipes. Once the water failed, no date could be given for its resumption. On top of all this there was the frightening prospect of epidemic through lack of sanitation and the unburied dead, whose corpses were being ripped to pieces by starving dogs, abandoned by their masters.

Such was the physical situation; the moral one was even worse.

This was not Mons or Dunkirk. There was no room left for anyone to retreat: Percival could either attack at this late hour of the battle, or he could surrender. He had no other alternatives. If the troops he commanded could mount an immediate counter-attack with all available men, regain control of the reservoirs and the supply dumps of food in the centre of the island, near the village of Bukit Timah, five miles northwest of Singapore City, and from there force the Japanese from the heights they commanded, they might yet, in the British idiom, win the last battle.

But the question, inspiring as it might be to ask, was really only rhetorical. The troops were exhausted and dispirited. Cohesion and command had gone; the retreat had lasted too long; there had been too many mistakes; too many excuses. Confidence in their leadership, in their weapons, in themselves, had evaporated. They were a long way from home in a hostile, alien land, where the indigenous people they had come so far to defend seemed indifferent as to who won or lost. This battle had been lost long ago, before the first guns began to fire. Only one course remained: surrender.

As the officers debated, a messenger brought in a telegram from Wavell in Java:

"So long as you are in a position to inflict losses and damage to enemy and your troops are physically capable of doing so, you must fight on. Time gained and damage to enemy are of vital importance at this juncture.

"When you are fully satisfied that this is no longer possible I give you discretion to cease resistance. Before doing so all arms, equipment and transport of value to the enemy must, of course, be rendered useless.

"Also, just before final cessation of fighting, opportunity should be given to any determined bodies of men or individuals to try and effect escape by any means possible. They must be armed. Inform me of intentions. Whatever happens, I thank you and all troops for your gallant efforts of last few days."

Percival decided to seek terms of surrender.

Three officers were detailed to take a car and drive toward Japanese headquarters outside Bukit Timah. They were Major-General Newbiggin, Captain Wylde and the secretary to Sir Shenton Thomas. To one side of their car they lashed a pole with the Union Jack; to the other, a strip of sheet as a white flag of truce. They drove in silence through the ruined empty streets toward the centre of the island. Civilians had locked themselves in their homes; curtains were drawn as though if they could not actually see the horrors of imminent defeat, they did not exist.

As the officers approached the village, Japanese sentries of the 5th Japanese Division halted them; the Japanese officer, Colonel Sugita, appeared. The officers explained their mission to him, while the Japanese soldiers watched them with impassive faces.

Sugita sent back the message to Tomoyuki Yamashita's headquarters. Yamashita replied briefly: "We accept their surrender. The Japanese commander will meet them at 1800 hours."

The officers hoped that Japanese envoys would visit Singapore City to discuss or accept the cease-fire. Yamashita would not hear of this. General Percival, as commander of the defeated army, must come out himself to seek surrender. He was determined to extract the maximum publicity from his victory and inflict the maximum of humiliation on the vanquished. As an Asiatic he knew the effect that this would have on the Indians and Chinese and Malays. The British, who had created Singapore from a buried mangrove swamp, thick with mosquitoes, and made from it one of the world's richest commercial cities, and the greatest naval base in the East, must be made to bow down before people smaller physically than themselves, weaker economically and fewer in number. This chance to humiliate them might not easily return.

Also, Yamashita did not quite believe that General Percival could really be seeking surrender. He knew Percival commanded an army of Australians, British, Gurkhas and Indians, with locally raised forces, roughly three times as powerful as his own three divisions, which totalled about 30,000 men.

In this situation, he feared that this offer of surrender was simply a ruse to give the British time to move men and ammunition to more strategic positions. And indeed, other commanders less scrupulous and gentlemanly than General Percival could so have used it, and could conceivably have turned the balance to victory.

A more ruthless adversary, when the three emissaries returned with the exact position of the Japanese commander, could have wheeled round what guns he possessed and issued all the ammunition available. Then, taking advantage of the psychological relief that swept through the Japanese Army at the prospect of an end to the fighting, plus the gain of hours of rest by talk of terms, he could have opened up on their target.

It would not have been honourable, not British, but it would have been war; more important, it might also have been successful. But a commander who would have contemplated this would not have been in this last extremity.

Yamashita did not know that Percival's Intelligence about the Japanese was so poor that it could virtually be discounted. A small Intelligence group had existed at Army Headquarters in pre-war days, but in the previous year it was decided that the Army should share the responsibility of Intelligence services with the Royal Navy; their headquarters were close together and theoretically work would not be duplicated. The Army thus ceased to have its own Intelligence arrangements and was dependent on what crumbs of information the combined service allowed them. As a direct result of this almost unbelievable situation, Percival was under the impression that Yamashita had "five and probably six divisions available for their attack on Singapore."[12] Taking the Japanese division as comprising 20,-000, he calculated that Yamashita must have about 100,000 troops against him. In fact, he had a third of this number.

Yamashita wrote in his diary later that day: "When the message came of the enemy surrender offer, I was very cautious about it. I was afraid it might be a trick. I ordered the British commander with his chief of staff and interpreter to meet me at 1800 hours. I also ordered a guard of one thousand armed soldiers to protect us at the meeting place."

In addition, Yamashita ordered Japanese planes to patrol the skies over Singapore in case British reinforcements were on their way by sea. If sighted, they were to be sunk.

The British officers returned to Fort Canning and reported the Japanese conditions to General Percival. His ciphers and other secret papers were burned; orders were given to smash open liquor stores and destroy any remaining stocks of spirits. Paper money from the banks had already been removed and destroyed. Not all the money was burned—in case the situation improved and the British needed it, after all.

With two brigadiers, all wearing tropical uniforms of khaki shirts and knee-length shorts of that time, and steel helmets, one officer carrying a Union Jack and another a white flag of truce, they set out by car for Bukit Timah.

The place for surrender was the assembly building of the Ford Motor Company's factory outside the village. This had been damaged by shells and part of the roof had caved in; many windows were without glass.

The evening was hot and sultry; the factory smelled of charred wood, burned rubber and gasolene. Yamashita had purposely selected it because it was the biggest covered building in the area—indeed it was one of the largest on Singapore Island—so that as many spectators as possible could witness the almost unbelievable victory he and his army had achieved, and the abject and humiliating surrender of what had been almost universally

[12] General Percival's Despatches.

believed to be an impregnable fortress, built by superior European skills and defended by the white man's superior strategy, to an Asiatic army one-third the size of the defending force.

This was the most decisive blow so far in the battle between white and coloured people, between rulers and the ruled, East and West, the old order and the new. Yamashita was anxious that its importance should not be underestimated.

A long table covered with a white cloth was set up in the middle of the hall. The two generals were to sit with their staff officers, and a Japanese interpreter. On the concrete floor orderlies had chalked squares and written inside them the names of the Japanese officers who would witness this historic scene, according to rank and precedence.

Japanese war correspondents, newsreel cameramen and official army photographers crowded around the outer perimeter to record in print and picture the details of the surrender.

General Percival arrived. He was kept waiting for nearly thirty minutes before the Japanese contingent appeared. Thus it was approaching seven o'clock before the victor and the vanquished formally shook hands on being introduced by the Japanese interpreter. They then sat down.

As Yamashita dictated his terms of surrender, he casually kicked off his long leather boots to ease his feet, a sign of the apparent indifference in which he held the British delegation.

In fact, Yamashita's bland and expressionless face concealed considerable anxiety. Because of his extremely bad supply situation, he had only one hundred rounds of small arms ammunition for each of his soldiers. Rations were also extremely meagre. His troops were existing on two bowls of rice a day, often seized at bayonet point from villages and local storehouses. When these supplies were exhausted, they held nothing in reserve.

Their plan, as we have seen, had been to travel light, living off the land; to seize arms, tanks, guns, petrol from the retreating forces. But while this had proved admirable for a swift and ruthless attack, its success depended on speed and movement. It was no way to win a long siege. Unless Yamashita had a

quick victory, he felt he could still be defeated. British reinforcements were expected; a matter of days could tip the balance.

Yamashita had eighteen tanks, including tracked Bren gun
carriers captured from the British, and a small army to hold the
whole of the Malay peninsula against any—admittedly unlikely—
local uprising or the arrival of reinforcements. He could not
risk any delay or stalling.

For both generals, for diametrically different reasons, every
hour, every minute, was vital.

Accordingly, Yamashita talked fast and bluntly. The Japanese
version of their talks, which was reprinted in the *Manchester
Guardian* on April 17, 1942, gave this account of their conversation.

General Yamashita: I want your replies to be brief and to the point.
I will only accept an unconditional surrender.

General Percival: Yes.

General Yamashita: Have any Japanese soldiers been captured?

General Percival: No, not a single one.

General Yamashita: What about the Japanese residents?

General Percival: All the Japanese residents interned by the British
authorities have been sent to India. Their lives are fully protected by the Indian Government.

General Yamashita: I want to hear whether you want to surrender
or not. If you want to surrender I insist on its being unconditional.
What is your answer? Yes or no?

General Percival: Will you give me until tomorrow morning?

General Yamashita: Tomorrow? I cannot wait and the Japanese forces
will have to attack tonight.

General Percival: How about waiting until 11:30 p.m. Tokyo time.

General Yamashita: If that is to be the case, the Japanese forces will
have to resume attacks until then. Will you say yes or no?

General Percival: (made no reply)

General Yamashita: I want to hear a decisive answer and I insist on
an unconditional surrender. What do you say?

General Percival: Yes.

General Yamashita: All right, then. The order to cease fire must be
issued at exactly 10:00 p.m. I will immediately send one thousand

Japanese troops into the city area to maintain peace and order. You agree to that?

General Percival: Yes.

General Yamashita: If you violate these terms, the Japanese troops will lose no time in launching a general and final offensive against Singapore City.

Percival asked for a guarantee of the safety of the lives of the English and Australians who remained in the city. Yamashita replied: "You may be assured of that. I will positively guarantee it."

Afterwards, he wrote his own private account of this meeting in his diary, which he kept every day of the campaign.

"On this occasion I was supposed to have spoken to Percival rather abruptly. If I did, it was because I now realised that the British Army had about 100,000 men against my three divisions of 30,000 men. They also had many more bullets and other munitions than I had.

"There have been many versions and rumours about my behaviour at this meeting, including the story that I said to him, 'All or nothing.' This is not true. But I knew that if the battle was to be fought in the streets of Singapore, there would be many casualties among the civilian population, and I did not know how long we could carry on, as our munitions were very low. I was preparing an all-out attack on that night and their surrender offer came as a surprise.

"After making a promise to meet me, the enemy commander was half an hour late; when the time came to talk, he accepted the unconditional surrender but asked me to postpone the cease-fire until the next day.

"It looked to me as if the British Army wanted to delay everything, but they still estimated the Japanese forces as more than they really were. They seemed to assess our force at about five divisions.

"I was afraid in my heart that they would discover that our forces were much less than theirs. That was why I decided that I must use all means to make them surrender without terms.

My interpreter was very poor. Obviously, he did not know about my worries and he also had difficulty with technical army terms. I became irritated, as I wanted to bring the matter straight to a conclusion, and I told my interpreter, 'I want to hear nothing from him except yes or no.'

"I am afraid that in my anxiety I emphasised the 'yes' or 'no' in English too much. The interpreter also emphasised the words very loudly when he repeated them to the British commander. This, however, did end the matter quickly and Percival agreed to my demand for unconditional surrender.

"The reporters who heard my words 'yes' or 'no' thought I was being haughty. . . . I have no excuse for that, but I have been annoyed ever since by the newspapers reporting with such glee how I spoke so harshly and with such fierceness. I have never tried to make any excuse for it publicly, but I would like people to know my real state of mind on that occasion."

Yamashita's adjutant also wrote his account of that surrender.

"The meeting between the two army commanders ended at 1900 when the enemy accepted unconditional surrender. Yamashita stood up and again shook hands with the enemy commander. He was surrounded by cameramen and war reporters. He told me afterwards that he wanted to say a few kind words to Percival while he was shaking hands with him, as he looked so pale and thin and ill. But he could not say anything because he does not speak English and he realised how difficult it is to convey heartfelt sympathy when the words are being interpreted by a third person."

The Japanese guarantees were not observed. Their treatment of the Chinese, whom they seemed to regard as mostly Communists, was, if anything, worse than their treatment of the Europeans and Australians. When Singapore fell, most of the Chinese were segregated into barbed-wire compounds. Some escaped with confiscation of their property. Others were less fortunate, for the Kempetai, the secret police, soon began their work.

Hundreds of Chinese were driven in trucks to the east coast of the island. There they were ordered to go down on the beach and dig their own graves with bamboo sticks or with their hands. Afterwards, they were lined up in ranks, standing with their backs to the graves, and shot. Any who still remained alive were bayoneted.

News of these atrocities came from one Chinese boy who was among those driven out there to be shot without trial and for no given reason. He stood behind a grown man, and the bullet from the Japanese rifle, passing through the heart of the man in front of him, went harmlessly over his shoulder. The weight of the corpse falling back pushed him into the grave.

The Japanese soldiers shuffling through the mud thought he was already killed, and by some error did not completely fill the grave. As a result, the boy could breathe, could still see a small patch of sky. All day he lay under the weight of the dead man. When darkness came, he crawled out of the grave, along a monsoon drain built to carry away the rush of water during the rainy season, and eventually he reached the safety of a Chinese village, where he explained what had happened to him and was given food and shelter.

The British had organised volunteers among the civilians in Malaya. One company was made up of Englishmen, another of Scots, a third of Eurasians, a fourth of Chinese, and so on. When the Japanese entered Singapore, the Chinese officer commanding the Chinese company of volunteers advised them to abandon their uniforms and to change into civilian clothes. He considered that it would thus be impossible to identify them as troops.

Unfortunately, they neglected to destroy their nominal register, which fell into Japanese hands. All the men whose names and addresses appeared on it were visited and ordered to report outside St. Joseph's Institution in a children's playground at nine o'clock on a certain day. They did so, and to their surprise only received a mild lecture on the virtues of co-operation with the Japanese.

As the officer finished his talk he declared that special jobs would be found for them in the New Greater Asia Co-Prosperity

Sphere. They should thus return on the following morning at nine o'clock when full details of these jobs would be available.

By nine o'clock on the next day, only a relatively small number had arrived. The others, relieved that the Japanese appeared to be much more lenient than the British had led them to believe, were late, and arrived in time to see the early comers being driven off in Japanese trucks. None of them were ever seen again. Punctuality on this occasion meant death; being late, a new lease on life.

* • #

So the Army and the Navy and the Air Force in Malaya passed into captivity. There was no official inquiry into the catastrophe. It was judged impossible to hold one during the war, although the Americans had held one over Pearl Harbor.

"I certainly thought," wrote Churchill, "that in justice to the officers and men there should be an enquiry into all the circumstances as soon as the fighting stopped." But the war ended and nothing was done. By now, most of the leading participants are dead, and as Churchill said, "It may well be that we shall never have a formal pronouncement by a competent court on the worst disaster and largest capitulation in British history."

Exactly one hundred years earlier, in January and February 1842, the British Army in Afghanistan had suffered an almost equally humiliating defeat. Even then their weapons were outdated against those of the fierce but primitive tribesmen; the British smoothbore flintlock muskets, firing at ten yards range, did "little or no execution," and out of 40,000 soldiers, only one European, an army surgeon, was not captured or killed.

Afterwards, a report on the disaster listed, among its causes, "making war with an ill-prepared force, without a safe base of operations; want of forethought, placing the magazines in indefensible positions; great military neglect and mismanagement after the outbreak of hostilities."

An enquiry into the fall of Singapore would have given the

same reasons. In a hundred years, nothing had been remembered, nothing had been learned.

Lacking a formal pronouncement, however, the reader can at least assess what the disaster meant to the allied cause—and the British Empire, and French and Dutch possessions in the East.

The manpower loss was immense. In the Malayan campaign the British, Indians and Australians lost a total of 138,708 soldiers of whom more than 130,000 were prisoners of war, often subjected to barbarous treatment. The Japanese casualties throughout Malaya were 3507 dead and 6150 wounded. For the capture of Singapore the figures were only 1715 dead and 3378 wounded.

The fall of Malaya and Singapore led directly to the collapse of the Dutch East Indies. Burma was overrun within weeks and the Japanese tide swept on, up to the Indian frontier. Taking this, plus the fall of Hong Kong (almost 12,000 men) and the naval and air force casualties into account, the British Commonwealth lost—killed, wounded or taken prisoners in the East between December 8, 1941 and March 8, 1942—no less than 166,-500 men. The comparable Japanese total was only 15,000 men.

There was, too, the incalculable economic loss to the Allies. The rubber, tin and oil—large proportions of the world output—so badly needed, now went to the enemies of the Allies.

Strategically, the disaster meant that the Royal Navy now had no base in the East nearer than Ceylon or Australia. Both these countries, along with India and New Zealand, were also now directly threatened and the Japanese attack on Burma was greatly facilitated.

Then there were the political consequences. New Zealand and Australia, having been assured so often that Singapore could never fall, would not be allowed to fall, felt that the British had failed them. After the war it was to the United States that they turned for their security. In India, the move to political independence was given powerful impetus among leaders who now saw a chance to play the British off against the Japanese. In China, there was disillusion that the British had crumbled so quickly when the Chinese had been enduring war with the Japanese for four and a half years. Throughout the East the psychological effect on the oriental mind was widespread and deep.

The surrender was marked by a wild outbreak of looting in Singapore.

"The inhabitants," explained Colonel Tsuji, "were giving vent to the feelings of hostility that more than a hundred years of coercion had aroused." This was not so: they were thankful still to be alive, and the more aggressively spirited among them were taking what they could while they could, before the Japanese could stop them.

Two days after Singapore fell, Wavell commented: "The trouble goes a long way back: climate, the atmosphere of the country (the whole of Malaya has been asleep for at least two hundred years), lack of vigour in our peacetime training, the cumbrousness of our tactics and equipment, and the real difficulty of finding an answer to the very skilful and bold tactics of the Japanese in this jungle fighting."

After General Percival and his officers had left the Ford Motor Company, the victorious Japanese staff returned to their headquarters. All the maps on the operations room table had been cleared away. In their place, on a white tablecloth were spread the tidbits of a Japanese cocktail party: chestnuts, dried cuttlefish, bottles of wine.

"You have done a good job," Yamashita told them approvingly. "Thank you very much. From now on you can drink Sake whenever you like."

Outside, in Singapore, the bronze statue of Stamford Raffles was coming down. In its place a war memorial, the Shonan Shinto Shrine, was set up on Bukit Timah heights.

When the plans for the invasion of Malaya and the capture of Singapore had been made, the Japanese had estimated that if they began on Meiji Setsu—November 3, the anniversary of the birth of the Meiji Emperor—they should capture Singapore by Kigensetsu—February 11, which was the anniversary of the crowning of Japan's first emperor, Jimmu, six hundred and sixty years before Christ.

They were only three days behind their unofficial schedule[13]; they had much on which to congratulate themselves. And when the casualty lists were compiled, they found they had even more: for a total of only 1715 killed in the battle for Singapore they had inflicted the greatest Asiatic defeat on a European power since the bearded, fierce horsemen of Genghis Khan had threatened the city of Vienna seven centuries before.

Now they set about changing the citadel of white supremacy which had succumbed so easily.

The name of Singapore was changed to Shonan—The City of Light. One hundred and thirty thousand British, Australian and Indian troops were moved into prison camps, and the Japanese flag flew above Government House and Fort Canning.

The Japanese also asked for the Union Jack that had been carried to the surrender.

"It doesn't exist," came the reply from the British officer believed to have it. "I burned it that night on the ramparts of Fort Canning, looking toward England and home."

In fact, it was hidden in Changi Jail. It was brought out during the next three and half years for the funeral of British and Australian prisoners who died as captives.

In September 1945, when the tide of war turned and Singapore was freed again, that flag was run up over the city once more. But, as Colonel Tsuji wrote, "The halo of victory must shine on the Union Jack, but today there remains little vestige of its glory of former times."

[13] In April 1944 they hoped to capture Imphal on the India-Burma border by the nineteenth of the month—Emperor Hirohito's birthday. They failed. This defeat proved pivotal to their dreams of conquering India.

Postscript

CROMWELL'S Ironsides had been successful largely because they knew what they were fighting for and loved what they knew. Percival's men had no such inspiration. As General Percival admitted, a "sense of futility" haunted the British Army. Few knew why they were fighting; after the first few days, fewer still thought that they could win.

Always inadequately armed, often half-trained, sometimes badly led, Indian, Australian and British units had fought against veteran Japanese soldiers, men with a mission, who were convinced of their superiority, who believed that if they should die fighting they would go at once to a soldier's heaven.

"If the trumpet give an uncertain sound, who shall prepare himself to the battle?" In Malaya, the trumpets of war sounded uncertainly all through the sad campaign, until at last the bugles called "Stand down."

For the Japanese, there was no doubt of the success of their mission, the justice of their cause, the last outcome. They were the new empire builders.

"We embark now upon that great mission which calls upon Japan, as the representative of all the peoples of the Far East, to deal a resolute and final blow to centuries of European aggression in these lands," ran the pamphlet *Read This Alone and the War Can Be Won*.

This was, of course, propaganda; Japan was the last of the non-Communist imperialist powers. She was to be the hub of the Greater East Asian Co-Prosperity Sphere; the nations she liberated from white man's rule were to be cast in strictly subordinate roles under her jurisdiction. Japan went to war simply to further her own military and imperialistic ends. The opposition seemed weak and largely employed elsewhere. Such an opportunity had not occurred before and might never occur again. So she took it, and she used it.

Her propaganda deceived many Asians as, of course, it was intended to, for the task of conquering their countries would be all the easier if the invading forces were hailed as liberators, and the defenders as the oppressors.

Subhas Chandra Bose saw India's salvation in Japan; and so did nationalist leaders in Burma and the Dutch East Indies. The propaganda also deceived many sincere Japanese; the idea of a New Order in Asia, after all, sprang from Kanji Ishihara's Federation of 1931: Asian shall speak peace unto Asian, and in the event of war between America and anyone else, Asia should remain neutral.[1]

"The English, French, Americans, Dutch, Portuguese and others sailed into the Far East as if it were theirs by natural right, terrorised and subjugated the culturally backward natives, and colonised every country in the area. These territories were taken by a handful of white men, and their tens of millions of Asian inhabitants have for centuries, down to our own day, suffered constant exploitation and persecution at their hands.

"The peoples of the Far East trust and honour the Japanese, and deep in their hearts they are hoping that, with the help of the Japanese people, they may achieve national independence and happiness. . . . The reason why so many peoples of the Far East have been so completely crushed by so few white men is, fundamentally, that they have exhausted their strength in private quarrels, and that they are lacking in any awareness of themselves as a group, as peoples of Asia.

"The aim of the present war is the realisation, first in the Far East, of His Majesty's [the Japanese Emperor's] august will and ideal that the peoples of the world should each be granted possession of their rightful homelands. To this end the countries of the Far East must plan a great coalition of East Asia, uniting their military resources, administering economically to each other's wants on the principle of co-existence to the common

---

[1] Colonel Tsuji, who wrote so illuminatingly of Japan's advance through Malaya, is now a prominent figure in the Japanese Toa Renmei Undo movement which has the aim that "Asians must never again fight Asians."

good, and mutually respecting each other's political independence. Through the combined strength of such a coalition we shall liberate East Asia from white invasion and oppression. "The present war is a struggle between races."

So ran the propaganda. But, in practice, the performance was rather less praiseworthy than the promise. Japan had been a medieval state less than a century previously, and its thin veneer of civilisation was soon to be rinsed away in blood.

The peoples of Southeast Asia learned early that they had exchanged old masters for new of a very different calibre. So unpopular did the Japanese conquerors make themselves in Malaya that even ten years after the war it was still not wise for a Japanese to be seen alone in that country. Famine followed upon neglect; and not till the Rising Sun began to set were the conquered nations to win some measure of "political independence."

"We should have assisted the development of independence in the oriental nations controlled by Britain, Holland and America for centuries," Colonel Tsuji admits. "Promotion of the independence of the occupied countries was not considered until too late for effective action. . . . Incomprehensibly [however, as a result of the Japanese victories in 1941 and 1942] India, Pakistan, Ceylon, Burma, Indonesia and the Philippines achieved independence soon after the end of hostilities. These Asian peoples who were emancipated by the fall of Singapore will eternally pronounce benedictions on their benefactors."

There was nothing "incomprehensible" about the way the former colonies achieved independence after the war. The nationalists of Indonesia and Burma had already been given a taste, however illusory, of self-rule. In Indo-China and Malaya, an underground resistance fought for liberty. Before the fall of Singapore, few Asians had dared to fight for such a cause. The Japanese showed Asia that "domination by force must be overthrown by force." Thirty-six years earlier, in 1905, Japan had defeated Russia and so proved that an oriental nation could humiliate a European nation.

The Western powers were strong; and in the Asian colonies there was little nationalist opinion. But two suicidal wars weak-

ened the European powers. The psychological effect of the First
World War should not be overlooked. As the former British
Prime Minister Harold Macmillan once pointed out, when the
Europeans brought hundreds of thousands of their Asian subjects
to France, mainly to work behind the front lines, "They brought
them to see their masters destroying themselves."[2]

Lord Salisbury, once a prominent member of the Conservative
hierarchy, comments[3] that "the unrestricted electorates of today seem mainly interested in politics only insofar as it directly
affects their own daily lives. They are too concerned with this
to bother about events thousands of miles away."

In a letter to Mr. Gladstone one hundred years ago, an eminent
authority on colonial history wrote: "When the Roman eagles
retreated across the Danube, it was not the loss of Dacia but the
satisfaction of the Roman people at the loss that was the omen
of the Empire's fall."

This comment is true of the negligent attitude of the British
at home to their imperial outposts in the years before and after
the Second World War. The Empire was something to deride;
a kind of Victorian Boy Scout dream; a music-hall joke. It became fashionable to desecrate Britain's imperial achievements.
And all these comments sprang from a well of ignorance that
has still not run dry.

There can be no question that, in the fullness of time, the
countries of Southeast Asia would have become "self-governing,"
even if there had never been a Pacific war, or the collapse of
Singapore.

The Japanese victories of 1942 and the Allied victory of 1945
simply precipitated the granting of "independence" and "democracy" to countries either not ready or unable to run their own
affairs. As events since then in Asia and Africa have proved,
democracy that comes too soon is no democracy; if it does not
bring chaos and violence, then there is a rapid move to dictatorship. Sometimes, as in Indonesia, there has been both.

All Eastern colonies crumbled at the Japanese onslaught in

[2] In an interview in the London *Sunday Times,* February 9, 1964.
[3] From the *Sunday Times,* January 26, 1964.

December 1941. In the Philippines, American forces under General Douglas MacArthur were pushed back to the Bataan peninsula and the fortified island of Corregidor. Manila was declared an open city to save it from destruction and was occupied by the Japanese on January 2. MacArthur escaped by submarine, and his army surrendered after a gallant resistance.

General Wavell arrived in Batavia on January 10, and established A. B. D. A. (southwest Pacific) Command headquarters at Bandoeng, the Dutch Army Headquarters. He did his best to face up to the Japanese attack, organising an air striking force at Palembang consisting of sixty bombers and fifty Hurricane fighters, mostly manned by the Australian Air Force, but what could be done was so little and too late.

On February 14, the day before Singapore surrendered, 700 Japanese paratroops dropped on Palembang. Two days later, following the loss of Singapore, Wavell cabled to Churchill: "Burma and Australia are absolutely vital for the war against Japan. The loss of Java, though a severe blow from every point of view, would not be fatal. Efforts should not therefore be made to reinforce Java, which might compromise the defence of Burma or Australia."

Churchill agreed. A week later, the Combined Chiefs of Staff informed Wavell that there would be no reinforcements for the Dutch East Indies; Java was to be defended by the troops already there, and A. B. D. A. Command headquarters should be moved from Bandoeng. Wavell said that he thought A. B. D. A. Command should be dissolved; this, too, was agreed.

"The defence of the A.B.D.A. area," Wavell told Churchill, "has broken down and the defence of Java cannot possibly last long. It always hinged on the air battle." And so General Wavell left Bandoeng, by air, piloted by an American who was provided, for navigational purposes, with a railway map.

On March 8, the Dutch surrendered. Eight thousand British and Australian troops and 5000 British and American airmen accompanied them into captivity.

The break-up of A.B.D.A. following the Japanese invasion of the Dutch East Indies, and Australia's not unnatural refusal to

allow Australian reinforcements to be diverted there, made the
fall of Burma certain. Burma, against Wavell's better judgment,
had been part of A. B. D. A. Command, at the insistence of
Chiang Kai-shek. Wavell, however, did not think the Japanese
would invade Burma until the conquest of Malaya was complete.
As it was, the land invasion of Burma began on January 16; and
Wavell had to deal with it from his A. B. D. A. Command headquarters, 2000 miles away in Java.

Communications between A.B.D.A. headquarters and Burma
were so poor, even by radio, that messages had to be passed by
way of India. As a result, Wavell was always acting upon out-of-
date information. The defence of Burma was bedevilled at this
time by such chaotic organisation of command that it became a
sort of yo-yo for the Chiefs of Staff.

When war started, Burma was the responsibility of Far East
Command in Singapore. Then, on December 11, Burma was
switched to India Command. There it could have remained. But,
with the setting up of the ill-fated A.B.D.A. (which was itself
dissolved on February 25), Burma was again plucked away from
India Command and not handed back until six days after the
fall of Singapore.

Burma, with a population in 1941 of about 17,000,000, lies
sandwiched between China on the east and India on the west.
It was politically separated from India in 1937 and achieved a
measure of self-government. The country is small compared to
these vast nations on either side, and not unlike a tadpole in
shape with a long thin tail; the coastal strip of Tenasserim
stretching to the south and bordering Siam. Nonetheless, Burma
covers an area of some 240,000 square miles, equal to that of
Belgium and France combined.

In the desolate north, lie the mountains which are part of
the great Central Asia mountain mass, sometimes known as the
Roof of the World. In the centre of the country are plains, and
paddy fields dotted with pagodas. Along both east and west
frontiers run more mountain ranges covered to a height of 6000
feet, and sometimes more, by tight-packed green jungle.

Running north–south between the mountain ranges are the val-

leys with the three main rivers. The Irrawaddy flows from the
mountains down the central plain for more than 1000 miles. With
its tributary, the Chindwin, which joins it for the last 400 miles,
it empties into the delta of Rangoon, capital city and main port
with a cosmopolitan population of 500,000. To the east of the
Irrawaddy is the Sittang River and east of that again the third
main river, the Salween, which rises in China and flows into the
sea at Moulmein in Tenasserim.

The defending troops fought in tough climatic conditions, enduring at one moment thirst, heat and dust, and then, in the
monsoon, soaked to the skin, pestered by leeches that sucked
their blood and mosquitoes that poisoned it with malaria. At the
start of the war, drugs such as mepacrine, were not available,
and malaria and other tropical diseases took as heavy a toll as
the Japanese. Also, the British and Indian troops were often inexperienced in jungle fighting. Many had trained for the immensely different conditions of desert warfare. They depended
too much on motorised transport, and except in open country
this could not be used off the roads, of which there were not
many. Again, as in Malaya, they were strangers in a strange
land; they were not fighting for their own homes, and the natives
did not greatly assist them to fight for theirs.

Road communications between Burma and India were primitive, consisting of little more than a few tortuous tracks through
the mountains, liable to blockage by landslide or flood according to the season of the year.

On the Burma-China border, the main road communication
is the Burma Road, which crosses the frontier some 200 miles to
the northeast of Mandalay. On the Burma-Siam border there is
a road to Kengtung in the Southern Shan State—a route so devi-
ous that the Japanese made no attempt to use it.

By conquering Burma the Japanese hoped not only to cut off
China from her war supplies, but also to invade India.

Again, in Burma there were the brave words, the promise without performance. The General Officer in Command, Lieutenant-
General Kenneth McLeod, announced: "In the air, on the sea,
and on the land, Burma is ready to repulse any foe. It is with

every confidence that I call on the soldiers to face the enemy with calmness and courage. We shall throw back the invaders, and free Burma forever from the threat which has dawned to-day."

The Governor, Sir Reginald Dorman-Smith, was somewhat more wary. Burma, like Malaya, was singularly unprepared to defend herself. In August Brooke-Popham had paid a visit, and been assured by McLeod that any Japanese attack would be across the Shan State in central Burma rather than through Tenasserim in the south. Events proved this to be an unfounded and costly misconception.

Wavell had paid his first visit to Burma at the end of October, and in his Despatch on "Operations in Burma" reported, "I was very greatly concerned by the extent of unpreparedness in Burma's defences which I became aware of during my visit."

The extent of unpreparedness in Burma's defences applied to the Air Force as well as the Army. The R.A.F. had only one squadron of Buffaloes for the whole country, and the Royal Indian Air Force a flight of obsolete machines. Fortunately, there was also an American air base. But paradoxically, the American air base was not there to defend Burma; it was there for the benefit of Chiang Kai-shek. On it was stationed part of the American Volunteer Group, a mercenary formation under the command of Major General Claire Chennault, a stocky, pugnacious Texan whose gallant soldiers of fortune were known (from their unit sign) as the Flying Tigers. The rest of the formation was in China. All had had considerable experience of fighting the Japanese for their employer Chiang.

Their aircraft, first-class Tomahawk fighters, were landed at Rangoon and sent over the Burma Road by truck to China in pieces to be assembled there. Later, the aircraft were assembled at Rangoon and flown to China, but their armament still went by road. Eventually, Chennault asked Dorman-Smith if his planes could be armed in Burma. Dorman-Smith, realising that the presence of armed American fighters could only be good for Burma, asked for permission, but Brooke-Popham refused to allow this on the grounds that it would antagonise the Japanese.

The Burmese Prime Minister, U Saw, a colourful character who figures largely in the story of Burmese nationalism, told Dorman-Smith that Chennault could use Magwe, a civil aerodrome by the Irrawaddy some 250 miles north of Rangoon, and not under the Governor's or Brooke-Popham's jurisdiction. And so when the Japanese bombed Rangoon, Chennault's fighters were on hand to attack them. They acquitted themselves well in the defence of Rangoon. In two months, 130 enemy aircraft were destroyed.

Victoria Point, the most southerly airport in Tenasserim, and a staging post from which British planes had been flown to Malaya, fell to the Japanese on December 15—a week after the Malayan and Siamese landings.

The Japanese attacked Burma over the mountain passes used by the old kings of Burma in their wars with Siam, and not, as the British had predicted, across the Shan hills. Tavoy fell on January 19. Mergui, one hundred miles to the south, was thus cut off. The next day, the small force at Mergui was evacuated by boat. The Deputy Commissioner, F. H. Yarnold, told the Governor afterwards: "We will never be able to hold up our heads again in Mergui."[4]

Next month, the Japanese occupied Moulmein after a fight lasting only twenty-four hours. Now Rangoon was threatened; civilians were evacuated; lunatics were freed from the asylums.

The first Rangoon air raid had occurred on the morning of December 23. The city was not entirely unprepared for this, having had forty minutes' warning, but the warning system was probably unique. It consisted of a number of Burmese perched on platforms up trees in Tenasserim. They telegraphed a warning to Rangoon when enemy bombers appeared overhead. According to Dorman-Smith's aide-de-camp, Eric Battersby, one of these lookouts was taken by the local peasants for a hermit. They brought him offerings of food, which they reverently laid at the foot of his tree. The lookout found the profession of holy man more profitable than that of lookout, neglected his military duties and was dismissed.

There was only one anti-aircraft gun at Rangoon, and this

[4] *Last and First in Burma* by Maurice Collis.

an ancient one. When the Japanese bombers appeared, this weapon went into action. It scored one hit, with its first shot. The two fighter squadrons, the Royal Air Force Buffaloes, and Chennault's Tomahawks, engaged the enemy with some success.

The civilian casualty rate was appalling, for the native population, unused to aerial bombardment—and, indeed, the sight of so many planes in the sky at one time was in itself a novelty—did not take shelter but stayed out in the streets to watch the Buffaloes and Tomahawks. In the second raid, no less than twenty-one Japanese aircraft were shot down, and six Buffaloes.

After the bombing, 100,000 Indians left Rangoon to walk to India, a distance of some 500 miles through rough country. Unknown numbers, in spite of strenuous attempts by the Government to supply them with food and medical stores, died on the way. The roads were clogged by these refugees, and as they went they spread panic and terror like an infection among the villages through which they passed.

The 7th Armoured Brigade, which Wavell had been able to divert from its original destination of Singapore just before that city fell, landed in Rangoon docks, to find that all the coolies had disappeared. The men had to unload their tanks and equipment themselves.

In the haste and confusion of withdrawal the 17th Indian Division was bombed and machine-gunned by the R.A.F. in mistake for Japanese.

Crossing the railway bridge over the Sittang River, between Moulmein and Rangoon—on planks laid Japanese fashion across the rails—a truck slipped at four o'clock in the morning, and blocked the track for two and a half hours. The impatient traffic queue stretched back for six miles, and then, with daylight, the Japanese began to attack it. Part of one brigade, the 48th, which had not crossed the river, held the bridgehead successfully; but on the following night rumours spread that the Japanese were actually over the river further north and going to take the bridge from the other side. Accurate communications in all the chaos were impossible and the rumour was accepted as fact.

As a result the bridge was blown at 5:30 in the morning, leaving thousands of British and Indian troops on the wrong side of the river. They had to swim across the 600-yard-wide swollen current, or cross it on logs, or in any way they could devise. Many reached the Rangoon side without boots and rifles, and only in their underwear. More non-swimmers were abandoned, and they went off to seek some easier place to cross.

Churchill decided to send General Alexander (now Field Marshal Lord Alexander) to Burma. Alexander, who took command on March 5, had been the last British commander off the beach at Dunkirk in 1940 and was said to bear a charmed life. He was a man of enormous ability but, as in Malaya, men were not enough, however brave or brilliant. The British were lacking modern equipment; they were fighting a twentieth-century war with the leftovers of Victorian campaigns.

Dorman-Smith had arranged for large-scale demolitions to be undertaken at Rangoon on March 1. The Government had already been evacuated to Mandalay, and Alexander's predecessor, General Hutton, wanted to withdraw what was left of his Army. Wavell would not allow him to do so, underestimating the Japanese, and overestimating the strength and stamina of the retreating defenders.

"There seemed to be no reason why Rangoon should not continue to be held at least long enough to enable the reinforcements on the way, 63rd Indian Infantry Brigade and a field regiment, to be landed," said Wavell, and the demolitions were postponed. When Alexander arrived, Wavell instructed him to disregard Hutton's advice to leave Rangoon. On the day after his arrival, however, Alexander realised that Hutton was right and Wavell wrong: the Japanese were threatening to cut the Pegu Road to the north and this could maroon him in the capital.

This threat was duly carried out on March 6. On the following day, Alexander led his men out of Rangoon, in a long line of motor transport, the Magwe Royal Air Force wing providing air support. The column moved north along the Prome Road—and met a Japanese roadblock. Capture seemed inevitable, but the Japanese did not attack the column's flanks and by next day

they had disappeared. The Japanese force was, in fact, moving
west to attack Rangoon from the northwest, had set up the roadblock as a precaution against being cut off, and when Alexander
and his men appeared, they did not realise that Rangoon was
being evacuated. The withdrawal north continued safely.

Now an American general came on the scene: Joseph "Vinegar
Joe" Stilwell, who had reached Lashio by way of India on March 3.
Stilwell was a tough West Pointer, sixty years old at the time,
canny and caustic, who viewed the world with a highly critical
eye through his steel-rimmed spectacles. About this time he gave
up chain-smoking—he claimed he had to pause for breath climbing a 1 in 2 mountain gradient after smoking—and so he took
to sucking acid drops. The change was appropriate; he was
remarkably caustic in his remarks and outlook.

His task was to command the Chinese armies in Burma—if
Chiang Kai-shek would let him. Roosevelt's principal object in
sending an American general to Burma was to keep Chiang Kai-
shek in the war. Stilwell's first task was to persuade Chiang to
sign an order appointing him Commander-in-Chief of the Chinese armies.

He saw the Generalissimo on the sixth and wrote in his diary
afterwards: "I asked about the general plan for operations in
Burma and he said there was none. Wavell had not made any
agreement with him, so the Chinese troops were just waiting
for direction." This, of course, was not so. Wavell had seen
Chiang before Christmas and they had agreed on a plan of
campaign. Stilwell wanted to move the Fifth Army, commanded
by General Tu Yu-ming, down to Toungoo, for there was still
only one Chinese division, the 200th, at Toungoo, and there
were four divisions to an army.

"What a mess," Stilwell wrote. "How I hate the Limeys. And
what a sucker I am."

He thought it was wildly funny that the Japanese should have
the British Raj on the run.

Stilwell's arrival brought several new conflictions to an already
overcomplicated and collapsing front. If Alexander ordered Stilwell to move one division, Stilwell had to give the necessary

orders through General Lo Cho-ying, Commander-in-Chief of the
Chinese First and Sixth Armies. But General Lo Cho-ying could
not pass on the order until Chiang himself gave his blessing.
Also, Lo was forbidden to approach the Generalissimo directly,
and had to apply to General Lin, a liaison officer, at Lashio. In
turn, Lin had to approach a superior liaison officer, General Hou,
whose headquarters were at Maymyo, the summer hill-station
in the north. General Hou could then approach the Generalissimo
directly and ask for his approval. None of these elaborate arrangements made for speedy decisions.

Alexander was able to rethink his position after the fall of
Rangoon on March 9, for the Japanese called a temporary halt
to consolidate their victories. The 1st Burma Division and 17th
Indian Division were combined to form 1st Burcorps, under
Lieutenant-General "Bill" Slim (now Field Marshal Lord Slim)
a quietly determined west-country man, and the future leader of
the Fourteenth Army which was to reconquer Burma.

Slim arrived to take up his command on March 19. By now,
superior numbers were beginning to tell heavily in the air,
despite the extraordinarily gallant against-the-odds battle fought
by the Flying Tigers and the R.A.F. At one time, at the end of
February, the Japanese had actually had to suspend bombing
at Rangoon, for their casualties were so heavy, but by mid-
March the Japanese had some four hundred aircraft in the air,
compared with an Allied total of around seventy.

The Japanese eventually launched a two-pronged attack northward, against the British at Prome, in the west, and against the
single Chinese 200th Division at Toungoo in the east. Stilwell
ordered this division to fall back, to avoid being surrounded,
and the rest of the Fifth Army was to advance southward to
meet it. When the Chinese abandoned Toungoo, Alexander
had to withdraw from Prome, moving out on April 1. This was
awkward, for Chiang had threatened to recall his troops altogether if the British left Prome. In vain Stilwell tried to rally
the Chinese. "They'll do nothing unless I can somehow kick
them into it," he wrote in his diary. "The pusillanimous bas-

tards. . . . The upshot is that I am the stooge who does the dirty work and takes the rap."

Unfortunately for Stilwell, Roosevelt held a high and over-enthusiastic opinion of the Chinese. Churchill had occasion to write: "At Washington I had found the extraordinary significance of China in United States minds, even at the top, strangely out of proportion. I was conscious of a standard of values which accorded China almost an equal footing with the British Empire, and rated the Chinese armies as a factor to be mentioned in the same breath as the armies of Russia. I told the President how much I felt United States opinion overestimated the contribution China could make to the general war. He differed strongly."

On April 3, Mandalay was bombed. Fires broke out and again there were heavy casualties among terrified locals who could not understand what was happening. Arrangements were made to move the civil Government to Myitkyina, but this was a bad choice, because the only way to leave Myitkyina was by air. On April 1, however, Alexander had told the Governor that he planned to send some of his forces through Myitkyina to China, with the Chinese Fifth Army; the Government would leave Burma with them. This plan had to be revised when the Japanese launched their attack on the Shan State in the east, upon which the Chinese Sixth Army disintegrated.

On April 22 a Japanese motorised column began moving north toward Lashio, thus cutting off Myitkyina. Two days later, Alexander visited the Fifth Army headquarters twenty-five miles south of Mandalay, and learned that the army was breaking up, and so decided on a prompt withdrawal across the Ava bridge, over the Irrawaddy, to prevent a second Sittang fiasco. He offered Stilwell and the Chinese Fifth Army asylum in India, but Chiang Kai-shek had to be referred to before any decision could be taken, and by the time he had made up his mind, it was too late. The remnants of the Fifth Army escaped in disorder across the mountains into India or China.

At a conference held in Shwebo on April 30, Stilwell admitted that Alexander had no option but to get out of Burma, and quickly. First Burcorps crossed the Chindwin at Kalewa, and was extricated without mishap by May 20. Stilwell himself was at a loss what to do, for his command had evaporated. On May 2 he left with his staff for Shwebo in jeeps, making for Myitkyina, but they were unable to reach the town as the railway was cut. The small party destroyed their jeeps and set off for the Chindwin on foot, crossing the wide river in dug-out canoes and escaping to India over the Naga Hills, where the tribesmen, although wild, were friendly. Armed with a stick, Stilwell had led his men on foot through one hundred forty miles of tortuous jungle. He reached Imphal on May 20, and told an Associated Press reporter: "I claim we got a hell of a beating. We got run out of Burma and it was as humiliating as hell. I think we ought to find out what caused it, go back and retake it."

The Japanese had now reached the Indian frontier. The richest jewel in the British Empire's crown seemed there to be taken. But behind them, their lines of communication stretched to the limit, they could not use the enemy's equipment forever. The sky now opened and the monsoon poured down its rain indiscriminately on both sides; the tide of invasion of the Japanese could go no further forward.

In the months and years ahead, the British and Indian forces would gather their strength, and, slowly at first, then with increasing speed and momentum, they would drive the Japanese down through the jungles the way they had come.

But while this was inevitable, with the speedily growing resources of the Allies, the British, as the world's most important imperial power, had treated their peoples of the East to an unprecedented exhibition of their own humiliation and ineptitude.

Malays, Chinese, Burmese, Indians by the hundred thousand, had watched in horror and surprise as their recent rulers were driven down from alleged strongholds in northern Malaya to surrender in the illusory fortress of Singapore, and then on up from the south of Burma, north to the gates of India. Never in all imperial history had such a spectacle been staged before, nor watched by so vast and attentive an audience.

The tens of thousands of Indian refugees who blocked the Burmese roads with handcarts, motor cars or on foot, with all their belongings on their backs, spread these terrible tidings among their relations in India. Doubtless, they often exaggerated the British lack of success in arms against a brother Asiatic race, because in so doing they minimised their own terror and cowardice. But there was no need for exaggeration: the facts were grave enough.

Subject peoples had watched the British destroy their own myth. Now nationalism, which had been either nascent or non-existent, surged to maturity. If one Asiatic power could so humble the greatest imperial power in the world, then other Asiatic countries could at least run their own affairs, conduct their own governments, secure their own future without European control, without having to feel that they were somehow inferior, second-class citizens, that the white man was supreme. He may have been once, but he was not any more. They had seen him break and run; they had seen him steal and loot; they had seen him beaten by his own inventions, and with fear and despair in his eyes. They had seen the proud humbled and those who were high brought low.

They had seen all this and they would remember.

Thus the events in Southeast Asia set the pattern for imperial retreat; the long sojourn of the West in the East, the long rule, was ending, and the East was for the dark.

In Asia, the Japanese encouraged nationalism for their own political ends and ambitions. At the other extreme, the United States, largely guided by Roosevelt's own peculiar views and prejudices, and by a general vague, if unfocussed feeling of affinity for colonial peoples, because America had once been a colony, helped to complete the process of imperial decline, a dwindling of authority that has since cost the West extremely dear in men and money and influence.

Independence came to India; and that country, which had never been cohesive until the British had welded one nation out of many warring states, immediately split in two, amoebia-like, to form India and Pakistan. Two million people are estimated to have died in the riots—religious, political, communal—that marked the birth pangs of these two independent nations.

Burma became a republic. The Dutch moved out of Indonesia, the French finally abandoned Indo-China and the city of Saigon, which they had built as the Paris of the East.

But as the imperial powers packed their bags and sailed West, with varying degrees of sadness or relief, other plunderers were due to arrive, for politics, like nature, abhors a vacuum and the weak will always be pillaged by the strong.

In less than a decade, much that had been achieved in all these countries—through generations of gradual evolution towards self-government in the British case—dissolved and melted away to such an extent that when one returns after five, ten or twenty years, it is to live in the shadows of the past. The post-independent achievements of these countries are the best argument for the old days, which can never come again; the years when a few thousand European administrators superimposed on Asia the structures of the West and made them work.

The Indian subcontinent is reduced to infinitely lower standards of living than it enjoyed thirty years ago. Famine stalks the land; corruption, ever present, has increased enormously, the rich are richer, the poor infinitely more needy.

Burma, which under British rule had enjoyed law and order and such unexpected sophistications as one of the world's first air-conditioned trains in the 1930s, is now a country seemingly bent on retreating from the twentieth century, with China an uneasy predator, watching the warring factions, the disagreements, the overwhelming inefficiency and inertia.

Frequently, rail services out of Rangoon are stopped by roaming marauders; travellers are warned that they drive on the roads outside the city boundaries at their own risk.

Indonesia, naturally prosperous, with immensely valuable natural resources of oil, tin, rubber, rice and much else, has sunk, after twenty years of growing chaos and corruption, under Sukarno's ludicrous and psychotic regime, to the status of a land of delusion. It has still to prove it can govern itself with anything approaching the efficiency of the old colonial powers.

All over Southeast Asia today the Communist threat is strong. South Vietnam is only held against the Communists by a vast American outpouring of money and men. At least one argument advanced for the American commitment there is the "domino theory": South Vietnam falls, then Cambodia falls, Laos falls, Thailand falls, Malaya falls, Burma falls.

So today the United States, in the name of anti-Communism, can find herself supporting regimes far more repressive and inefficient than any of the old empires in the East. If the clock could be set back twenty or more years it is difficult to believe that the same mistakes would be repeated.

Responsible and moderate American opinion has certainly changed its view since the overly sanguine days of 1945 and after. As *Life* magazine commented on February 4, 1966: "By and large . . . the United States now seems to have been wrong in assuming, when it pressed for an early dissolution of the colonial empires after World War II, that democracy would be the natural substitute of White rule.

"Ready-or-not independence suited our anti-colonial attitude and also our fear that Africa would go Communist unless its people got the 'Uhuru' they demanded."

❂   ✱   ❂

Now that Americans, with their commitments in the East, with their grip on the reins of world power, their fusion of authority, commercial profitability and political responsibility, are held to be imperialists, some words of Franklin Delano Roosevelt make strange and ironic reading.

"Don't think for a moment, Elliott," he said to his son during the last war, "that Americans would be dying in the Pacific tonight, if it hadn't been for the short-sighted greed of the French and the British and the Dutch. Shall we allow them to do it all, all over again? . . .

"When we've won the war, I will work with all my might and main to see to it that the United States of America is not wheedled into the position of accepting any plan that will further

France's imperial ambitions, or that will aid or abet the British Empire in its imperial ambitions."[5]

Although Roosevelt did not live to see the winning of the war, his views were shared by most members of his country's government.

Before he met Winston Churchill, his future ally and a man of rather different views on the subject of empire, aboard the battleship *Prince of Wales* in Placentia Bay, Newfoundland, in August 1941, Roosevelt also told his son what he considered he should do.

"The British Empire is at stake here. . . . We've got to make it clear to the British from the very outset that we don't intend to be simply a good-time Charlie who can be used to help the British Empire out of a tight spot, and then to be forgotten forever. . . . I think I speak as America's President when I say that America won't help England in this war simply so that she will be able to continue to ride roughshod over colonial peoples. I can't believe that we can fight a war against fascist slavery and at the same time not work to free people all over the world from a backward colonial policy. . . . The peace cannot include any continued despotism. The structure of peace demands and will get equality of peoples."

At the Mansion House, London, after the North African landings, Churchill was to say: "Let me make this clear, in case there should be any mistake about it in any quarter. We mean to hold our own. I have not become the King's First Minister in order to preside over the liquidation of the British Empire." But, whether he liked it or not, that was in fact what Churchill did.

The outcome of the Atlantic meeting was the Atlantic Charter, Clause Three of which ran, "They [Great Britain and the United States] respect the right of all peoples to choose the form of government under which they will live; and they wish to see sovereign rights and self-government restored to those who have been forcibly deprived of them."

The author of Clause Three was Churchill himself. He en-

[5] *As He Saw It* by Elliott Roosevelt.

larged on what he meant in the House of Commons: "At the
Atlantic meetings we had in mind, primarily, the restoration of
the sovereignty, self-government and national life of the states
and nations of Europe now under the Nazi yoke. So that is
quite a separate problem from the progressive evolution of self-
governing institutions in the regions and peoples which owe
allegiance to the British Crown."[6]

This was not, however, quite what Roosevelt visualised. In
February 1942, the month Singapore fell, he said: "We of the
United Nations are agreed upon certain broad principles in the
kind of peace we seek. The Atlantic Charter applies not only
to the parts of the world that border the Atlantic, but to the
whole world; disarmament of aggressors, self-determination of
nations and peoples, and freedom of speech, freedom of religion,
freedom from want and freedom from fear."

As he told Elliott privately: "I've tried to make it clear to
Winston that while we're their allies and in it to victory by
their side, they must never get the idea that we're in it just to
hang on to the archaic, medieval ideas of Empire. . . . Great
Britain signed the Atlantic Charter. I hope they realise the
United States Government means to make them live up to it."

Cordell Hull, who shared Roosevelt's views, wrote: "We had
definite ideas with respect to the future of the British colonial
Empire, on which we differed from the British. It might be said
that the future of that Empire was no business of ours; but we
felt that unless dependent peoples were assisted toward ultimate
self-government and were given it when, as we say, they were
'worthy for it and ready for it,' they would provide kernels of
conflict."

Life magazine toed the Roosevelt line and in October 1942
warned Britain that the United States would not allow her to
hang on to an empire.

The Americans felt most strongly about India and Hong Kong.

"The United States," wrote Churchill, "had shown an increasingly direct interest in Indian affairs as the Japanese ad-

[6] *The Far East in the Modern World* by Franz H. Michael and George E.
Taylor.

vance into Asia spread westward. The concern of the Americans with the strategy of a world war was bringing them into touch with political issues on which they had strong opinions and little experience."

Roosevelt raised the question of India during Churchill's visit to Washington in December 1941, but Churchill, in his own words, "reacted so strongly and at such length that he never raised it verbally again."

Towards the end of February 1942, the President sent Averell Harriman to see if there was any prospect of an agreement between the British Government and Indian nationalist leaders. Three days before the Japanese attack on Pearl Harbor, the British had suddenly released all their political prisoners, Nehru among them, but even so, after Churchill's remarks in the Commons about the Atlantic Charter, many Indians felt that Britain never intended to let India go. Gandhi, moreover, was still implacably determined to continue the struggle for immediate independence.

The British had made India by uniting many small independent states, and they wanted to leave a united India behind them. This to them seemed a reasonable enough desire, and represented the attitude of the Churchill Government, of Conservative and Labour members alike. Congress (Hindu) and the Moslem League members in India took a different view.

"Let the British withdraw from India," said Gandhi, "and I promise that Congress and the Moslem League will find it in their interest to come together."[7] It was undoubtedly in their interest, but could they ever come together in fact? Gandhi's vision was a pipe dream, as events showed when the British did withdraw, and communal hatred between Hindu and Moslem, unrestrained by the moderating British presence, reached a climax of violence, in which an estimated two million people died. Today, what was once a united India is divided by fear and frustration over the future of Kashmir, occupied by India but with an overwhelming Moslem majority, and in 1965 the cause of an Indo-Pakistan war.

[7] *The Last Years of British India* by Michael Edwardes.

Even the imminent prospect of Japanese occupation in 1942 failed to bring Congress and the League together. The League was more afraid of Congress than of the Japanese; just as Chiang Kai-shek's obsession with the Communists had allowed the Japanese to overrun much of China, so in India the League concentrated on the wrong danger.

Although the British did their best to rally Indians to the defence of their country and although 2,500,000 men and women volunteered for the fighting services and fought with loyalty and courage, others, intent on saving their own skins, felt that if Japan was winning the war they ought to be on the same side.

Of the nationalist leaders, only Rajagopalachari (later to become the first Indian Governor-General) bravely and publicly called for "whole-hearted resistance to the Japanese and the transfer of full responsibility to a council of national leaders." Nehru hoped Britain would win the war but was not prepared to lend her a hand. Gandhi, living in an intellectual cocoon of his own, preached non-violence.

Chiang Kai-shek and his wife came to India in February 1942, to whip up support for the Allied cause, but the Indian Nationalist leaders were more interested in persuading Chiang to take up their case with the British Government. As soon as the British War Cabinet realised this, Churchill wrote to the Generalissimo, asking him not to see Gandhi as he had intended.

Chiang agreed, but Roosevelt and the Generalissimo, although at a far greater physical distance from each other, kept closely in touch, and Chiang's visit probably led to Averell Harriman's mission to Churchill. As a result of Harriman's visit Churchill had to tell Roosevelt that the position in India where there were Moslems and Untouchables as well as Hindus, was more complex than the President imagined. Churchill, in fact, actually sent Roosevelt a bundle of documents giving minority points of view, for Roosevelt, as Elliott admitted, was prone to oversimplification.

"The colonial system means war," Roosevelt declared. "Exploit the resources of an India, a Burma, a Java; take all the wealth out of those countries but never put anything back into them; things like education, decent standards of living, minimum health requirements—all you're doing is storing up the kind of trouble that leads to war. All you're doing is negating the value of any kind of organisational structure for peace before it begins."

The British, who now were trying belatedly to publicise their achievements in India, were reaping the harvest of years of neglect. They had overcome apathy, corruption, hostility and the ageless inertia of the East. Roads, railways, schools, hospitals and cities had been built and maintained at a level of efficiency that today is only a memory. But intellectually the anti-colonialists had held the field for too long, and a whole generation had grown up to believe in their propaganda.

On March 11, 1942, four days after the fall of Rangoon, Churchill announced that he was sending Sir Stafford Cripps to India. Cripps was "to satisfy himself, on the spot, by personal consultation, that the conclusions upon which we are all agreed, and which we believe represent a just and final solution, will achieve their purpose." The "conclusions upon which we are all agreed" referred, of course, to the Government's plan to prepare Indians for eventual independence. As Churchill explained in a letter to the Viceroy, Lord Linlithgow, "It would be impossible, owing to unfortunate rumours and publicity and the general American outlook, to stand on a purely negative attitude, and the Cripps mission is indispensable to prove our honesty of purpose."

Cripps was chosen because he had been interested in India for a long time; he was a lawyer like Nehru, a vegetarian like Gandhi, and a deeply religious man. At a press conference held as soon as he arrived in India, Cripps promised independence for India after the war, within the Commonwealth or not, as India wished.

"Moslems and the native princes," he said, "could choose whether to join India or to form separate states of their own." Cripps could not promise instant independence, as demanded by Congress, partly because nationalist leaders were not wholeheartedly pro-British in the war, but he was ready to set up an "interim government," with the Viceroy in charge of defence. Cripps's suggestions were rejected by Congress, which, like the British, still hoped for a united India; but they were readily accepted by the Moslem League, allowing as they did for a separate Moslem state—Pakistan.

Gandhi dismissed Cripps's offer of independence after the war as "a post-dated cheque on a bank that was obviously failing." Japan was clearly on the point of winning the war; even as the talks went on, Japanese planes were bombing Indian towns. It might be better, thought Gandhi, to talk to the Japanese. According to Cripps, Gandhi persuaded Congress not to accept the offer of an interim government.

Stafford Cripps was accompanied by an American, Colonel Louis Johnson, who was meant to report back to Roosevelt on what happened. Indians, however, did not see how America, with her hands full in the Pacific, could possibly help them.

When Churchill heard that Cripps had failed to talk Indian nationalists round to his view, he wrote to him: "The fact that the break comes on the broadest issues and not on tangled formulas about defence is of great advantage."

Roosevelt did not see it that way.

"I regret I am unable to agree with the point of view that public opinion in the United States believes that the negotiations have broken down on general broad issues. Here the general impression is quite the contrary. The feeling is held almost universally that the deadlock has been due to the British Government's unwillingness to concede the right of self-government to the Indians, notwithstanding the willingness of the Indians to entrust to the competent British authorities technical, military and naval defence control.

It is impossible for U.S. public opinion to understand why if there is willingness on the part of the British Government to permit the component parts of India to secede after the war from the British Empire, it is unwilling to permit them to enjoy during the war what is tantamount to self-government."

Churchill immediately replied: "I did not feel I could take

responsibility for the defence of India if everything had to be thrown into the melting-pot at this critical stage."

He expanded on this in a letter.

"The human race cannot make progress without idealism," he wrote, "but idealism at other people's expense and without regard to the consequences of ruin and slaughter which fall upon millions. This was no time for a constitutional experiment. Nor was the issue one upon which the satisfying of public opinion in the United States could be a determining factor."

When Cripps had gone, Nehru announced: "We are not going to surrender to the invader. In spite of all that has happened, we are not going to embarrass the British war effort in India." But Gandhi wrote on May 10, "The presence of the British in India is an invitation to Japan to invade India. Their withdrawal would remove the bait. Assume, however, that it does not, Free India would be better able to cope with invasion. Unadulterated non-co-operation would then have full sway."

And Congress, tutored by Gandhi, resolved to meet any Japanese invasion with peaceful non-co-operation.

Secretly, however, Gandhi had been plotting an even less terrifying welcome for the Japanese. In fact, if the Japanese had invaded, Gandhi would have been ready to talk. Congress would have assured the Japanese "that India bore no enmity" toward them. Nehru's vague protests were overruled; and the only leading Congressman to resign was Rajagopalachari, who was followed by seven rank-and-file members.

Police raided the All-India Congress Committee's offices and Gandhi's plans for welcoming the Japanese were discovered. As a result his fellow members of the Committee were quietly arrested and Congress was officially outlawed. In Britain, Labour and Liberal M.P.s without full knowledge of the situation, but vocal as ever, vehemently protested against this outrage; in India, there was rioting.

The future of India was thereafter left in British hands, but Americans made a valiant effort to "liberate" Hong Kong, an effort not appreciated by the local population. The United States had something of an ulterior motive in this, for their policy was to make Chiang Kai-shek's China a great power, and to do everything possible to court the Generalissimo's good opinion.

Before the Pacific war began, Henry Morgenthau, Jr., United States Secretary of the Treasury, had even suggested that the British should be persuaded to sell Hong Kong to China; the United States, he explained, could lend China the money. Roosevelt went a step further. According to Harry Hopkins, during Atlantic Charter talks, he "once or twice urged the British to give up Hong King as a gesture of goodwill."[8] Hopkins' story is corroborated by Lord Halifax, British ambassador in Washington during the war.

In March 1943, in Washington, Roosevelt told Anthony Eden that he did not want "a commitment made in advance that all those colonies in the Far East should go back to the countries which owned or controlled them prior to the war." Eden asked whether the United States intended making any similar "gestures."

Roosevelt was also trying to persuade the Dutch to get out of their Southeast Asian colonies, and Queen Wilhelmina had agreed to treat the Dutch East Indies just as America treated the Philippines.

"The point is," the President told his son Elliott, "that we are going to be able to bring pressure on the British to fall in line with our way of thinking, in relation to the whole colonial question." The British, however, did not fall in line with any of Roosevelt's plans for Hong Kong, although they did promise to give up rights and privileges on the mainland of China, which were also enjoyed by the U.S.A. At the first Cairo Conference, Chiang Kai-shek had spoken to Roosevelt on the subject: "We will support his [Chiang's] contention," said Roosevelt to Elliott, "that the British and other nations no longer enjoy special empire rights to Hong Kong, Shanghai and Canton. . . . As far as China is concerned, the only earnest of our good faith that he expects is that when Japan is on her knees we make sure

[8] *The White House Papers of Harry L. Hopkins* edited by Robert E. Sherwood.

that no British ships come into Chinese ports. Only American warships. And I've given him my personal assurance that that's what will happen."

It was, of course, all very well for Britain and the U.S.A. to give up the privileges they had so far enjoyed in China, for China was at the time occupied by the Japanese. Chiang Kai-shek, however, thought he might be able to take over Hong Kong when the Japanese left, for Hong Kong was obviously part of China and that half of Britain's ninety-nine-year lease of the vital New Territories on the mainland had run out.

At Yalta in February 1945, Roosevelt talked to Stalin about the East. Neither Churchill nor Chiang's mouthpiece were present at this meeting. Roosevelt told Stalin that he thought Chiang should be given Hong Kong after the war. The President wanted Stalin's help in the Japanese war, and felt that Stalin would insist on the British giving up this colony as a pre-condition.

An Allied Combined Civil Affairs Committee was set up to administer territory recaptured from the Japanese and the Committee would, in fact, call on the former colonial powers to help in the task of administration. Hong Kong, however, happened to be in Chiang Kai-shek's province, and not therefore—or so the Americans claimed—subject to the A.C.C.A.C.

Just how much one man's personality and individual leadership can achieve in a situation equally as dangerous as the debacle at Singapore is illustrated by the achievement of Franklin Gimson (later, Sir Franklin Gimson, and a post-war Governor of Singapore) when he was in Hong Kong before, during and after the surrender.

Franklin Gimson arrived there in 1941, shortly before the Japanese attack, with the appointment of Colonial Secretary, actually the chief executive officer under the Governor, and as such responsible for advising the Governor on matters of policy.

Franklin Gimson was cast in the mould of earlier empire builders; he was physically strong, with great personal and moral courage, and always remembered that his duty lay as much towards the indigenous people of the country in which he worked as to his own countrymen.

After service in the First World War, Gimson had spent much
of his career in Ceylon. Initially, he had been Secretary to the
Minister of Education. Later, he organised aid for villagers during a serious malaria epidemic, and then had charge of a general election under the Manhood Suffrage, where although the
electorate was largely illiterate, he devised ballot papers they
could mark against a sign for their candidate, because they
were unable to read his name.

He was put in charge of the Labour Department, under a
Ceylonese minister, and there met hostility from European planters because he conceived it to be his duty to foster the trade-
union movement, then starting in Ceylon, while the planters
feared for labour troubles that they believed the unions would
provoke.

"In those years—1937 to 1941—I regarded the growing interest
in trade unions as a sign of the growing nationalism in Asia,"
Sir Franklin told me. "What had impressed me very much indeed was a pamphlet by Sir Harold Butler, Director-General of
the International Labour Office, in which he said: 'When the
history of the twentieth century is written, in spite of the rise of
Nazi Germany and Fascist Italy, the most important factor
will be the rise of nationalism in Asia.'"

In recognising this, Gimson became unpopular with European
superintendents of the tea estates, but he had the sympathy of
the Colonial Office in London, which posted him to Hong Kong.

As a defensive position, Hong Kong had been written off by
the British as long ago as 1921. Even so, and despite overwhelming odds and unexceptional leadership by the army commander, plus logistic catastrophes (as a result of one, although
Canadian reinforcements arrived, their equipment went to Manila) Hong Kong held out against vastly superior Japanese air
and land forces from December 7 to Christmas Day, 1941.

Both the Americans and the British had broken the Japanese
cypher code before the war, and, under no illusions about Japanese intentions, extensive air-raid shelters had been built in
Hong Kong, enormous tunnels dug beneath the rocks and rationing schemes prepared. This was in sharp contrast to the lack of

preparedness obtaining in Singapore with just as much warning of Japanese intentions.

Hong Kong's Governor, Sir Mark Young, was a man of vigour and enthusiasm, and also the colony's Commander-in-Chief. He had been a prisoner of the Germans in the First World War, and while realising the vulnerability of Hong Kong, he knew that every day it could hold out against attack was vital, for each day would pin down Japanese troops who would otherwise be free to attack Malaya. Also, in late 1941 there was still hope that, if attacked, Hong Kong would be relieved by the American fleet. In the event, of course, this proved impossible because the fleet was destroyed at Pearl Harbor.

It must be remembered that, before the Japanese attack, Britain was fighting on her own against Germany and Italy. America was not directly involved, and however benevolent her neutrality, she was still technically neutral. Had the Japanese been wise enough not to attack Pearl Harbor, as well as European possessions in the East, then British influence would have been even more speedily and possibly permanently annihilated. There is little doubt that Japan could then have swept south under Yamashita's plans to invade Australia and New Zealand, and could also have gone west to meet up with Nazi forces, as was visualised, somewhere in India.

By attacking Pearl Harbor, and so forcing the United States into the war, Japan assured her own defeat. But, as the pamphlet *Read This Alone and the War Can Be Won* put it, "At stake in the present war, without a doubt, is the future prosperity or decline of the [Japanese] Empire.

"Slowly, little by little, like a man strangling his victim with a soft cord of silken floss, America has been prohibiting the export to Japan of oil and steel. Why such cautious methods? The reason, perhaps, is a fear that to deny all supplies at one stroke might drive Japan, in desperation, to invade South Asia. And if the rubber and tin of the South were to be seized by Japan, it would create a situation far more intolerable to America than even the present lack of steel and oil is to Japan. America's

policy so far has been one of weakening Japan without rousing
her to violent indignation.

"We have already, perhaps, left things too late. If we remain
patient a moment longer Japan's aircraft, warships and road
transport may be forced to a standstill."

In British consultations with the United States—and at the
time of the Japanese attack, Churchill was actually in Washington—the British Government had given guarantees that they
would defend every inch of their territory. The argument was
that Britain could not expect America to come to her aid if
Britain was not prepared to defend her own overseas possessions. Thus even the indefensible had to be defended; hence the
importance of holding on in Hong Kong for as long as possible.

As Sir Franklin Gimson told me: "To give up our overseas
possessions without every effort at resistance would nullify any
claims to their restoration at the end of the war, and Hong Kong
could scarcely have remained British territory, in view of the
pressure America would, and did, exert on Britain to return it
to China."

Gimson found that the attitude of many Europeans in Hong
Kong in 1941 was that of Europeans in the treaty ports of
Shanghai, Nanking and Tientsin in China, where they had enjoyed special concessions and came to regard British consuls as
being paid simply to protect the interests of British merchants,
and to smooth over any difficulties or altercations they might
have with the indigenous Chinese authorities.

They could see little difference between a treaty port and a
British colony, and so felt that the British Government had a
special duty to safeguard their own interests in preference to
safeguarding the interests of the native population.

Neither the Governor of Hong Kong nor Franklin Gimson
could agree with this narrow view, but it persisted and when
Hong Kong surrendered and the Europeans entered captivity,
many maintained, against all argument, that it was the duty of
Britain to send out a ship from England simply to repatriate
them. They were also highly critical of the Hong Kong Govern-

ment, although before the war they had not all been among the first to help in carrying out emergency measures.

The Japanese deported Sir Mark Young from Hong Kong to another prison camp, and so as the senior Government official left in Stanley jail, Gimson came in for considerable bitterness, recrimination and even personal hostility among the internees.

Initially, a number of Americans were also interned in Stanley, but they were repatriated in June 1942, in exchange for Japanese interned in the United States. Speaking to them before they left, Gimson said: "When you are drinking the victory toast, just remember the hardships you shared with us here in Stanley."

To Gimson this was a perfectly ordinary phrase, but the attitude of expecting eventual victory seemed new to his fellow European internees, who asked him why he had referred to it. After all, the British had not been successful in France or Crete, and victory at Alamein was still five months ahead. Gimson nevertheless retorted: "Isn't it obvious we are going to win?"

"Won't the Japanese be annoyed?" asked the faint-hearted.

"I don't mind whether they are annoyed or not," Gimson replied. "*We are going to win.*"

As he said later, "That revolutionised the whole of their feelings. Before this, they were thinking entirely of repatriation."

Shortly afterwards, a petition was circulated around the camp, which the prisoners signed, asking Gimson to speak for them as their leader. He accepted full charge and had a committee of representatives elected by the other internees, but the final authority in any decision rested with him.

Before this, the European internees were curiously ambivalent in their attitude toward captivity. Although prisoners, they still felt themselves superior to their Japanese captors, and many still believed that the only way to deal with Asiatics was by banging a fist on the table and demanding something.

Gimson believed in the diplomatic approach, which, during his time in Ceylon, he had proved produced better results. After all, as he says, "From the Japanese point of view *they* were victorious; we were defeated. We were in no position to argue, or to expect better treatment as Europeans than they would give to Asiatic people themselves. . . .

"Many internees were living in the past; they never for a moment imagined that Britain hadn't still the authority it had in the 1920s or even before that, and they thought my approach was wrong.

"At one time, three of them went up to one of the Japanese commandants and said, 'You've fed us like pigs and housed us like swine.' The Japanese weren't so much furious as astounded. They didn't understand."

Once, after a long interrogation, a Japanese N.C.O. asked Gimson whether he thought they were being badly treated.

To gain time he replied, "That is a difficult question." The interrogator retorted that it was not; he was to answer immediately.

Gimson said: "We are ignorant of the conditions in Hong Kong. If they are better than in Stanley, then we are badly treated. If they are worse, we are well treated. I do not know."

All the Japanese said was, "Ah."

Later, Gimson learned that, in other camps, any suggestions that the Japanese were guilty of inhuman treatment would have resulted in arrest and possible execution.

On another occasion, Gimson was before the commandant, asking for some minor concession to be given to a man who had been removed from the camp. He was told that it was impossible.

"The matter is finished," said the Japanese.

"No," retorted Gimson, "this is by no means the end."

The officer angrily asked him to explain this remark.

Gimson replied: "This refusal will be raised at the peace conference, and I shall be interested and highly amused to see what the reactions will be."

He then repeated his request. This time the Japanese bowed his head.

"It is granted," he said.

Some time afterwards, a young Eurasian internee was accused of stealing sugar from the camp godown. Under Japanese interrogation, he said that the Japanese guards had helped him. Gimson was called before the commandant, and told to take charge of the youth himself, in order to avoid his being ill-treated by the guards if he remained in the cells.

Over forty-four months of internment, Gimson established himself as a leader, purely by his character and the strength of his personality. During the final few months of the war, he and his committee, together with a few of his senior officers, prepared plans for their action when the Japanese surrendered. They buried these plans in a bottle beneath the floor of the camp building, so that if anything should happen to them they could still be acted on by the others.

In mid-August 1945, news spread through the camp that the war was over. No Japanese newspaper was available to confirm the rumours, but the attitude of the Japanese to their captives changed, and confidence in the ultimate triumph for the Allies left no doubt in the minds of the internees who were the victors.

As their representative, Gimson sought an interview with a Japanese commandant to confirm or deny these rumours.

"I do not know their accuracy," Gimson said, "but the majority of internees have no doubt that peace has been declared. In consequence, incidents might arise if the guards adopted their usual attitude of arrogance and violence. If I could make a definite pronouncement I could counsel restraint and patience and also exercise the greater authority now imposed in me as a leading official of the Hong Kong Government."

The Japanese officer drew himself up and replied: "His Majesty the Emperor has taken into consideration the terms of the Potsdam Conference and has ordered hostilities to cease. In other words"—pointing to Gimson—"you've won; we've lost."

Gimson wrote the news on a sheet of paper and pinned it on the camp notice board.

The Representative of Internees has been informed by Lieutenant Kadowaki that hostilities have ceased. This information was contained in a broadcast from Tokyo received on August 15 which stated that the Government of Japan had accepted the conditions set out in the announcement by the Allied Powers which was issued at Potsdam on July 26.

Until official instructions are received the administration of the camp will continue as at present. During the next few days the situation is likely to be somewhat tense and internees are strongly urged to refrain from anything in the nature of demonstration, cheering and so on. The guards are to remain on duty. They have received instructions to refrain carefully from any action likely to lead to incidents, and the hope is expressed that internees will exercise every restraint in their contact with them. The Representative of Internees has accepted responsibility for the maintenance of discipline within the camp, and trusts that his confidence in the good sense and dignity of our people will be justified.

The danger of any attempt to leave the camp precincts cannot be over emphasised.

As senior official of the Hong Kong Government, Gimson told the Japanese: "I will take charge of the administration."

"The Japanese," he wrote later, "were not prepared at first to agree with my view of this new sphere of responsibility which I claimed to be in the position to assume, and stated that the future of Hong Kong was not decided. There was no certainty it would continue to be British.

"I replied that this view was merely their expression of opinion with which I was not concerned. I intended to carry out those duties to which I had been appointed by H. M. Government. I required accommodation for myself and for my officers, and also use of the wireless station."

Such was Gimson's personality, his air of authority and his standing as the acknowledged leader of the civilian internees that the Japanese agreed.

Gimson had just returned to his quarters, when a Chinese civilian came to see him. He brought with him a telegram from the British Embassy in Chungking. This had originated in London and it instructed Gimson "to assume authority . . . Policy of His Majesty's Government is to restore British sovereignty and administration immediately. . . . It is open to you to assume administration of government. . . ."

As a result of what this civilian told him about international events and trends, Gimson—who had been out of touch for nearly four years—immediately realised that the Japanese opinion that Hong Kong might not continue to be British was based on fact. He called a meeting of the senior members of the administration in the jail, and explained the situation to them. The Chief Justice of Hong Kong, Sir Athol MacGregor, administered the oath of office to Gimson so that he became virtually Governor of Hong Kong.

His first task was to send an urgent message to the British Government in London to say what was happening. The nearest diplomatic radio post was in Macao, the Portuguese colony some miles away on the Chinese coast.

An ex-internee volunteered to take the message to Macao in a Chinese fishing boat. He was successful, but on his way back, the vessel was intercepted by pirates. The crew hid him under a pile of dried fish, and he returned unharmed.

Next, Gimson broadcast over Hong Kong radio a message assuring his listeners that life in the colony would soon return to normal. He then made contact with the commanding officers of the Navy, the Army and the R.A.F. who had been released from P.O.W. camps.

"After a day or two had elapsed," he wrote later, "my officers and I were transported by bus from Stanley to the town centre of Hong Kong to take charge of the administration of the colony, after an interval of nearly four years of Japanese occupation.

"This journey, more than any other incident of this momentous period, filled our hearts with more emotion than we had previously experienced, and made us appreciate to the full the truly providential survival after enduring the privations of the Japanese regime.

"Our route took us through the fishing village of Aberdeen, and my most vivid memory of it is the sight of the faces of the Chinese there, who, at the noise of the approach of the bus, cast their eyes down to avoid possibly meeting the glances of its Japanese occupants. The faces were slowly raised, and beaming smiles appeared in answer to ours as our identity was recognised."[9]

Gimson did not know at the time that his action had prevented Hong Kong being taken over by Chiang Kai-shek's Chinese troops, for, as a result of the Cairo Conference, it had been agreed that since Hong Kong lay in Chiang Kai-shek's sphere of command, any arrangements for the surrender of the Japanese there were to be subject to his approval.

In the House of Commons, Churchill, by then out of office as Prime Minister and now leader of the Opposition, knowing that Hong Kong was in the Chinese sphere of influence, asked Prime Minister Clement Attlee what was happening to Hong Kong. Attlee was able to reply: "I have just heard that we have received a broadcast from Mr. Gimson saying that he has assumed authority."

American Air Force planes were dropping leaflets over Hong Kong advising prisoners to remain where they were until the arrival of relieving forces. The internees ignored these leaflets and left camp to try to reorganise their businesses and their pre-war careers.

One of the results of this came as a surprise to members of the relieving forces when they landed some days later. They were met with copies of the *Chinese Morning Post,* a local daily newspaper produced under British management, and under a British editor!

But in the few days immediately following the Japanese surrender there was no sign of any British forces. The Japanese had recovered from their initial shock of defeat, and were becoming more truculent. It was not impossible that they would defend Hong Kong against the relieving forces.

Gimson's fear was that the Chinese army would enter Hong Kong. "But they made no attempt to do so," he said later. "I don't know why Chiang Kai-shek did not, but he accepted the fact that I had taken control. He must have been completely nonplussed by this, and if he had attempted to assume military control, he may have wondered what my reactions would have

[9] Private papers of Sir Franklin Gimson.

been. Anyway, we had no representations of any kind from anybody."

There was no guarantee that this state of affairs would continue, so another ex-internee went out by sampan to contact the British fleet. He reported that they had no plans of the minefields outside Hong Kong; nor had they orders to enter the harbour. After ten days of mounting anxiety and bewilderment, Gimson visited the Japanese liaison officer between his temporary government and the Japanese commanders to ask him if they had received any news. They showed him a signal reporting that a British plane from an aircraft carrier would be landing at Kai Tak aerodrome in Hong Kong. A Japanese officer should be present to fly back to the aircraft carrier to receive instructions about the entry into Hong King harbour of the British fleet.

The Japanese officer told Gimson: "We have no authority to negotiate. A message is to be sent that the despatch of the plane would serve no useful purpose, and so entry would be refused."

Gimson would not accept this position. The officer then explained that Kai Tak aerodrome was under water and so a plane could not land. Gimson pointed out there had been no rain for three weeks; this excuse could not be accepted.

The Japanese still refused to send a man to meet the plane. Gimson told them that when they replied to the British message they must add that they would not obey Gimson's own request; failure to do so would be treated as a criminal offence.

The Japanese officer consulted his superior, and finally agreed that he would meet the plane himself. He did so, accompanied by a British naval officer just out of the P.O.W. camp.

On the way back, owing to engine trouble, their plane had to make a forced landing in territory occupied by Chinese guerillas. The guerillas surrounded it at once, and seized the Japanese. One man drew a knife to slit his throat. The British pilot protested that the Japanese was his prisoner. At this, the Chinese immediately handed the knife to him.

"Here, take this," he said. "*You* cut his throat."

Fortunately, a quick repair got both the plane and the Japanese officer out of trouble.

On the following day, the British warship H.M.S. *Swiftsure* entered the harbour. Gimson still feared that some Japanese fanatics might open fire, but they did not. Later, a naval officer called on Gimson and took him to the flagship where, in his own words, he "gratefully transferred to its Admiral the responsibility for the government of Hong Kong."

The British Prime Minister sent a personal message to Gimson: "I have learnt with admiration of the energy and spirit with which you, after your long ordeal in Stanley, first of all took the initiative and have since supported Admiral Harcourt in restoring British administration.

"I should like you and your civil officers to know the high value I attach to your indomitable courage and splendid service."

Had Gimson not used his initiative and resource, Hong Kong would have been taken over, first by the Nationalist Chinese, and then by the Communists. Instead, it remains one of the few possessions and thriving enclaves of the West in the East, with thirty-three years of its lease still to run.

Looking back now, nearly a quarter of a century after these events, Sir Franklin Gimson wrote[10]: "I brushed aside the refusal of the Japanese authorities to agree with my suggestion that I was determined to re-establish British administration. I am sure that my decision would not have met so readily with acquiescence unless the Japanese authorities were in no doubt that I had the authority and the influence to do so. This authority and influence had been impressed on the Japanese throughout the whole period of the camp.

"Incidentally, in Singapore, the Governor had told his officials to de-associate themselves from the administration of the camp owing to the disrepute into which the government there had fallen. No official assumed control and no one came forward to establish a British administration prior to the arrival of the relief force. . . .

"The amazing thing to my mind is that the whole story makes for coherency. One action appeared to follow in a natural sequence from the other, possibly because my attitude was based

[10] In a letter to the author.

on a sense of loyalty to the British Crown, and because I regarded internment as an episode to be viewed against the whole background of British jurisdiction over Hong Kong. The incidents in internment could not be regarded in isolation.

"This may sound strange now in the light of the growth of Hong Kong in the past twenty years, but it was imperative to maintain morale, partly through the insistence on a sense of the permanence of British sovereignty to ensure the observance of orderly social conventions, and to engender self-respect.

"I wonder if the stability of Hong Kong is due to this regard displayed throughout the Japanese occupation for the continued existence in internment of British authority? . . ."

The local population gave the British a great welcome when they returned in 1945. In Hong Kong, Chinese businessmen were free to do business under conditions unknown to their fellow countrymen on the mainland. During the Japanese occupation the Chinese population had dwindled by two-thirds; but under the leadership of the Governor, Sir Alexander Grantham, Hong Kong soon recovered from the war.

A "new deal" for Hong Kong was at one time envisaged by the British, but the Chinese did not show the faintest interest and the matter was lapsed.

On a number of occasions, the Kuomintang have tried to harass Hong Kong, but relations with Mao Tse-tung have generally been good, even during the Korean War, when many troops passed through Hong Kong en route for Korea. Mao, after all, has time on his side. When the lease on the New Territories runs out Hong Kong will no longer be a viable proposition, and Mao's successors will obviously never agree to renew the lease. Hong Kong has, therefore, roughly thirty years of freedom before she becomes part of Communist China.

*   o   *

Writing in the seventeeth century, when Britain was, as it is now, only a small island off the north coast of Europe, without vast overseas possessions, Sir Thomas Browne, a Norwich physician with a taste for philosophy, pointed out that "the lives, not only of Men but of all Commonwealths and the whole World, run not upon an Helix that still enlargeth, but on a Circle where, arriving at their Meridian, they decline in obscurity and fall under the Horizon again."

The zenith of the British Empire, and indeed of all Western empires in the East, had been reached and passed before 1942, but then the swift decline began, the rush beneath the horizon.

Life burns on, dictators in East and West emerge like croaking frogs from a marsh to vanish in the mists of time. The good and the just and the brave do not always win the last battle; eventually, there will be nothing left to win. And in the story of twenty years of indecision and petty people in power that led step by remorseless step to the fall of Singapore, the corner-stone that brought down with it the ancient Eastern empires of Britain, France and Holland, only a handful are heroes save by hindsight.

The Japanese are regarded as the villains, for every tragedy must have its villains, but they only did what enterprising European adventurers had done centuries before them. The Japanese were the catalyst and not the cause of the way the world changed. The vast improvements in communications of all kinds, the spread of education, the jet engine, television, short-wave radio; all these have combined to shrink the world. All these would also gradually have led to the end of Eastern empires, whether the Japanese had captured Singapore in 1942 or whether the British had repulsed them. But because they did capture Singapore all these changes were hastily telescoped into a decade instead of proceeding gradually over the years. For the important thing about Singapore was not that the British had lost, but how; not that the Japanese had won, but why.

A gradual political evolution would, of course, have brought immeasurably more blessings to the East. The sudden sharp reversal of fortunes in 1942 left a vacuum of power that Communism, corruption, dictatorship, with their variants and pseudonyms, have since steadily tried to fill.

It is unlikely that either Yamashita or Percival realised the enormous significance of the events that took place at the Ford Motor factory outside Singapore on that Sunday afternoon more than twenty-five years ago. There was no reason why they should. Colonel Tsuji wrote later: "In military operations we conquered splendidly, but in the war we were severely defeated. But, as if by magic, India, Pakistan, Ceylon, Burma, the Dutch East Indies and the Philippine Islands one after another gained independence overnight. The reduction of Singapore was indeed the hinge of fate for the peoples of Asia."

✿   ✿   ✾

And the main actors in this tragedy, with its cast of millions, acted out with all Asia as its stage, how did the years treat them?

Percival endured captivity, even solitary confinement, with fortitude; he was a brave man. He returned to England in September 1945, and found to his surprise many letters and telegrams of good wishes and appreciation for what he had tried to do. He was especially heartened by the number from the United States, where, as he wrote later, "the significance of what happened in the Far East has always been, and still is, more fully understood than it ever has been in our own country."

Some months after his return, he was called to Buckingham Palace where he received, from the hands of King George VI, the decoration of Commander of the Bath, which he had been awarded much earlier in the war. Had he been successful at Singapore, he would almost certainly have been created a K.C.B. —Knight Commander of the Bath.

As he was about to leave, the King asked to see him privately, and discussed with him the fortunes of war "with," as Percival wrote later, "the greatest sympathy and understanding. So the King understood. It made me feel very happy."

General Percival retired from the army and lived quietly in Hertfordshire. His chosen career, through no fault of his, lay in ruins about him. Officers who had been his junior, but who had risen to seniority at a time when British resources were greater, received high honour and public acclaim, but Percival never complained. He bore uninformed criticism stoically, with patience and dignity. He busied himself with the welfare of his former members of his command, who had been prisoners with him in Malaya and Singapore, but there is no doubt that, under his mask of acceptance, he felt deeply the savage irony of chance that had selected him for that impossible command.

The writer saw him shortly before he died, a patient, tall, withdrawn figure, whose misfortune it had been to direct an ill-equipped and wrongly-trained army in a hopeless campaign; to defend a country for whose defence pre-war politicians, influenced and activated by blind, petty motivations and crass ignorance, by indifference on the part of the voters who had elected them, had neglected to pay the insurance premium. Percival knew all this, but kept his silence; he was a gentleman, and the need had been for a rougher, tougher harshness than he could provide. The men in his army only knew him as a name, never as a character. He died in 1966 and there was sorrow at his passing. He was a man who, although not a natural leader, had bravely done his best.

General Yamashita, known for his swift victory as "The Tiger of Malaya," aroused the envy of Tojo, his former colleague, by the brilliant success of his campaign.

He might be, as his biographer has recorded, "Japan's greatest war hero," but, even so, Tojo refused to allow him to enjoy his triumph. Yamashita was actually in Singapore, writing the report of his victorious campaign, which he hoped to present personally to the Emperor, when he was suddenly and secretly posted back to the empty snows of Manchuria. He was not even permitted to visit Japan on the way there, in case he should in some way jeopardise Tojo's own position.[11]

From Manchuria, Yamashita was sent to Luzon to defend the Philippines, a hopeless campaign against growing American

[11] There is a curious parallel here in Churchill refusing Wavell's repeated requests for a brief leave in England—he had not been home since 1938—when he was relieved of his Middle East Command and posted to India, thence to Singapore. Churchill, it has been suggested, also feared that this enormously popular man might somehow provide a focus for criticism of his own conduct of the war.

strength. He did his best with a tired army and poor equipment, for now the tables were turned; Japanese planes and weapons at the end of the war had much the same performance as at the beginning.

On September 2, 1945, he finally surrendered. Of Yamashita's campaign in the Philippines, the American army historian Robert Ross Smith wrote that he "executed one of the most effective delaying actions in the whole history of warfare."[12]

In the following month Yamashita was tried in Manila as a war criminal, on charges concerning the deaths of 57,000 people in Malaya, Singapore and the Philippines. Yamashita, again with great dignity, pointed out that his command had been as big as MacArthur's or Mountbatten's.

"How could I tell if some of my soldiers misbehaved?" he asked later. "It was impossible for any man in my position to control every action of his subordinate commanders, let alone the deeds of individual soldiers. The charges are completely new to me. If they had happened, and I had known about them, I would have punished the wrongdoers severely."

His defence counsel wrote: "The prosecution case boiled down to the fact that Yamashita should have done something about the matter, regardless of whether he had the right or power to do it. This was the most bloody of crimes. The accused must answer for it—simply because he was the accused. There must be revenge."[13]

Tomoyuki Yamashita was found guilty and sentenced to be hanged. After receiving this sentence, Yamashita wrote a verse:

> The world I knew is now a shameful place,
> There will never come a better time
> For me to die.

Early in the morning, when that time came, he was led out to the execution shed. He bowed toward the Imperial Palace, and told the Buddhist priest who was present, "I pray for the Emperor's long life and prosperity forever." Then he died.

[12] *Triumph in the Philippines* by Robert Ross Smith.
[13] *The Case of General Yamashita* by Frank A. Reel.

His Japanese biographer, Shuji Oki, wrote later: "If he had not been executed for Manila, he would surely have been executed by the British Army for his conquest of Singapore. If he had stayed in Manchuria, he would surely have been killed or captured by Soviet forces. Therefore, although he was hanged, the Philippines was the best place for him to die."

Colonel Tsuji, who had first worked out his plan for the conquest of Malaya and Singapore as a result of a dream, eluded Allied investigators. For several years he moved in various disguises through different countries of Southeast Asia, before returning to his home to write a classic, and often poetic, account of the war in which victory had owed so much to him. He is now a member of the Japanese Diet.

General Gordon Bennett, the fiercely individualistic Australian who was shocked by the inability of his troops to hold the attack on Singapore, escaped from that island to Australia, but found to his surprise that, on arrival, he was ostracised by many of his military colleagues. The Prime Minister expressed his confidence in him, the Australian Cabinet welcomed him warmly, but Lieutenant-General Sir Vernan Sturdee, the Chief of the General Staff, told him that his escape was "ill-advised." Gordon Bennett's biographer wrote: "Then he had gone on with his work, leaving Gordon Bennett to stand aside in his room like a punished schoolboy. No other member of the military board had called in to greet the soldier returned from the fight."[14]

After the war, General Percival wrote to the Australian military authorities: "I have to report that Major-General H. Gordon Bennett, G.O.C., A.I.F., Malaya, voluntarily and without permission relinquished the command of the A.I.F. on February 15, 1942, the date on which the capitulation of the British forces in Malaya took place . . ."

As a result of this letter from the former Commander-in-Chief in Malaya, Gordon Bennett faced a Court of Inquiry. Their conclusion ran: "The Court is of the opinion, on the evidence, that Lieutenant-General Henry Gordon Bennett was not justified in handing over his command or in leaving Singapore."

[14] *The Gordon Bennett Story* by Frank Legg.

A commission was then set up to examine the matter further. It reached the same conclusion.

He retired from the Army, felt that he was too old to return to his pre-war career as an accountant, and bought a small orchard. In 1957, he and his wife returned to Singapore for the dedication of the British Commonwealth War Memorial, and he later visited Japan, meeting many of the officers against whom he and his men had fought.

In 1962, he died of a heart attack at the wheel of his car, and was accorded a state funeral. Thousands of men who had served with him in the First and Second World Wars were present.

General Wavell became Lord Wavell and then Viceroy of India. Sir Bernard Fergusson has described how, during the last hours of Singapore, "there was a moment . . . when he was genuinely tempted to stay behind for the capitulation.

"He would certainly be in for a bad time if he did so; but all the world would say: 'Good old Archie Wavell! He stuck with his troops to the end.'

"The alternative was to return to India and face the music, which would certainly mean criticism, and which might entail total loss of confidence and even disgrace. I wasn't really in any doubt as to what my duty was, but just for the moment the other idea had its attractions—such as they were."[15]

In 1947, Wavell returned to England, from which he had been absent for nine years. He wrote to Fergusson of the concern he felt about what he considered was a general lowering of individual honesty in the country, and added: "Unless we can get back to something like our old standards of honesty, family morality, hard work and pride in craftsmanship, I do not feel that we shall maintain our position or regain our former prosperity, which was founded on the above qualities more than on other things. . . ."

He died in 1950. His was the first state funeral to sail up the Thames since the death of Nelson. Crowds lined the streets to watch the passing of one of the greatest of Britain's soldiers,

---

[15] *Wavell: Portrait of a Soldier* by Sir Bernard Fergusson.

a man who, like Percival, had been in the fight too soon for his own self-advancement, who sowed that others could reap, and who never publicly complained.

The views of many were summed up by a policeman on duty with the crowd: "They're making a hell of a fuss of him now he's dead. Why didn't they do so while he was alive?"

o o o

On the night of the surrender, February 15, 1942, Yamashita slept badly. He awoke early, and an hour before dawn he walked out alone toward the defeated city. His Chief of Staff followed him, concerned about his safety, for deserters and gangs of armed looters still prowled the streets.

The night was silent; even the croaking frogs and the lizards slept. The air felt thick with the smell of cordite; black specks still travelled on the wind from the burning oil tanks.

Yamashita walked slowly from his command post outside Bukit Timah to the edge of a wood. His colleague watched him as he turned gravely toward Tokyo and bowed and prayed ceremoniously, in the Japanese fashion, to the Emperor, the Son of Heaven.

Quod erat demonstrandum. Like some old Roman legionary of the past he had done that which he had set out to do. Indeed, he had done infinitely more. He had destroyed forever the white man's authority over Asia.

That night, the arteries of the old empires opened; centuries of supremacy and rule of law began to bleed away. The wounds will never now be staunched.

That Sunday—February 15, Chinese New Year Day, by tradition the day on which Christ overcame the temptations of the devil—was the hinge on which one door closed behind centuries of white predominance and another opened to a new and unknown future. Was it the beginning or the end of the most peaceful and stable period the East had ever known?

This is a question every man must answer for himself, in his own mind, his own heart. But what can find no dispute, what stands no argument, is that after that Sunday in Singapore the world has never been the same.

A Note on Sources

THE growth of the old British Empire in the East, spasmodic and often reluctant, has had many chroniclers. The largest number have recorded the British impact on India, for, by reason of its enormous physical size, its latent possibilities for exploitation and the harmony that existed between British and Indians over the years, India, the jewel in the imperial crown, was easily the most important British possession in the East.

For a picture of the development of British India, the following books are useful. They show its expansion against the manners, morals and customs of the times, so that there is no danger of judging events in the seventeenth, eighteenth and nineteenth centuries by the totally different standards of the twentieth.

It is easy for critics of past imperial performance to ask why this or that was or was not done, because they overlook the fact that standards of transportation and communication which now obtain were not in existence a hundred or two hundred years ago. They ignore the fact that, even today, such are the distances involved in the Indian subcontinent, that a train journey from Bombay to Calcutta is counted in days rather than in hours. And every yard of those railway tracks was laid by Indian labourers working under European supervision, beneath a blazing tropical sun, across deserts, mountain ranges, about a hundred years ago, against endemic risks of malaria, typhoid and other fevers; and also that this monumental engineering task was carried out thousands of miles and six weeks' travel time away from the parent British firms which supplied both the rails and the engineers. Distance and the climate were among the greatest enemies of progress in India. They remain so. These books explain why.

Brecher, Michael, *Nehru, a Political Biography*
Cohen, B. S., *The Development and Impact of British Administration in India*
Collis, Maurice, *Marco Polo*
Eckel, Paul E., *The Far East Since 1500*
Edwardes, Michael, *A History of India from the Earliest Times to the Present Day*

——, *The Last Years of British India*
Furneaux, Rupert, *Massacre at Arritsar*
Griffiths, Sir Percival J., *The British Impact on India*
Hall, D. G. E., *Burma*
——, *A History of South East Asia*
Menon, Vapal Pangunni, *The Transfer of Power in India*
Moon, Penderel, *Divide and Quit*
Newton, Arthur Percival, ed., *The Great Age of Discovery*
Parkinson, C. Northcote, *East and West*
Rapson, E. J., and others, *The Cambridge History of India*
Roberts, P. E., *The History of British India Under the Company and the Crown*
Sinai, I. R., *Challenge of Modernisation*
Spear, T. G. P., *The Oxford History of Modern India*
Stanford, J. K., ed., *Ladies in the Sun*
Steel, Flora Annie, *India Through the Ages*
Toye, Hugh, *The Springing Tiger*
Woodruff, Philip, *The Men Who Ruled India*

Second to India in importance of British imperial possessions in the East came Malaya and Singapore. A clerk in the East India Company, Stamford Raffles, whose name is commemorated now in Singapore by a square and a hotel, saw the possibilities of developing Singapore Island as a trading post for British merchants, in an area owing predominant allegiance to the Dutch, and against apathy, disinterest and sometimes direct antagonism from his superiors in London.

For a study of the growth of Malaya and Singapore, economically, politically and strategically, the following books are valuable.

Coupland, Sir Reginald, *Raffles of Singapore*
Cowan, C. D., *19th Century Malaya*
Grenville, J. A. S., *Lord Salisbury and Foreign Policy*
Gullick, J. M., *Malaya*
Gungwu, Wang, ed., *Malaysia: A Survey*
Kennedy, J., *A History of Malaya*
Moorhead, F. J., *History of Malaya*
Robequain, Charles, *Malaya, Indonesia, Borneo and the Philippines*
Raffles, Lady, *Memoirs of the Life and Public Service of Sir T. S. Raffles*
Tregonning, K. G., *Papers on Malayan History*
Winstedt, Richard, *History of Malaya*
Wurtzburg, C. E., *Raffles of the Eastern Isles*

For accounts of other British possessions, such as Burma and Ceylon, and their importance in the lost mosaic of imperialism, the following are of interest.

Cady, J. F., *A History of Modern Burma*
Collis, Maurice, *Last and First in Burma*
Endacott, G. B., *A History of Hong Kong*
Farmer, B. H., *Ceylon: A Divided Nation*
Palmer, Leslie, *Indonesia and the Dutch*
Pratt, Sir John, *War and Politics in China*
Ting-fang, Wu, "*The Causes of the Unpopularity of the Foreigner in China*," *Annals of the American Academy of Political and Social Science*, Vol. XVII
Wehl, David, *The Birth of Indonesia*
Woodman, D., *The Making of Burma*

Until the middle of the nineteenth century, Japan was virtually unknown to the West, and had been for more than three hundred years. Then, under American and British influence, she leapt suddenly and dramatically into the twentieth century, and as Churchill wrote: "In less than two generations, with no background but the remote past, the Japanese people advanced from the two-handed sword of the Samurai to the ironclad ship, the rifled cannon, the torpedo, and the Maxim gun . . . the transition of Japan under British and American guidance from the Middle Ages to modern times was swift and violent."

The following books give an account of these changes and the failure of the West to recognise their significance.

Adachi, K., *Manchuria, A Survey*
Beasley, W. G., *The Modern History of Japan*
Blount, J. H., *The American Occupation of the Philippines 1898–1912*
Brown, A. J., *The Mastery of the Far East*
Coolidge, A. C., *The United States as a World Power*
Ford, J. D., *An American Cruiser in the East: Eastern Siberia, Japan, Korea*
Griffis, W. E., *The Mikado's Empire*
Jones, F. C., *Japan's New Order in East Asia*
Rawlinson, *England and Russia in the East*
Spender, *The Changing East*
Storry, Richard, *A History of Modern Japan*
Young, A. M., *Japan in Recent Times 1912–1926*
Young, C. W., *The International Relations of Manchuria*

The later books on this list also trace Japanese resentment at the abrogation of the 1902 Anglo-Japanese Treaty during the Washington Disarmament Conference of 1921. This single act caused Japan to feel that she had lost face—and "face" to the Oriental means public humiliation of a magnitude still largely unappreciated by the West—so that the Japanese felt that their only way of redeeming this situation was to prove to the world eventually that the East was not only the equal but the master of those who had thus insulted her.

There are many accounts of the 1920s and 1930s when, with vast unemployment in Britain, a severe economic recession and industrial unrest, which came to a head in the General Strike of 1926, events on the other side of the world such as Japanese rearming, or Singapore lying naked to attack, passed unheeded.

Against urgent domestic economic problems, even the rise of Fascism in Italy, and National Socialism in Germany caused little enough alarm, and so at a time when Malaya and Singapore still lay at least four weeks' sailing distance from England, the British public was understandably and greatly interested in potential crises so far away.

Such glimmers of doubt and alarm at the course of future events that some held could be—and were—dismissed by the mini-pundits of the day, many of whom had never seen the East but who then, as now, lacked neither shrill voices nor platforms on which to use them.

For an account of these years, the following books are useful. There are also many pictorial scrapbooks, and biographies and autobiographies of politicians, statesmen and others who condemn, or attempt to justify, the situation according to the views they held and their wish to show wisdom in hindsight.

Baker, R. S., *Woodrow Wilson and World Settlement*
Bassett, Colonel S., *Royal Marine*
Blakeslee, G. H., *The Pacific Area*
Boyle, Andrew, *Trenchard: Man of Vision*
Buell, R. L., *The Washington Conference*
Chatfield, Lord, *It Might Happen Again*
Dennett, T., *Roosevelt and the Russo-Japanese War*
Dennis, A. L. P., *Adventures in American Diplomacy*
——, *The Anglo-Japanese Alliance*
Golovin, N., *The Problem of the Pacific in the Twentieth Century*
Iyenaga, T., *The Case of Japan in the Peace Treaty*
Kawakami, K. K., *Japan and World Peace*
——, *Japan's Pacific Policy*
Medlicott, W. N., *British Foreign Policy Since Versailles*

Sedgwick, F. R., *The Campaign in Manchuria 1904–1905*
Stanford University, *Japan and the United States 1853–1921.*
(*Revised and continued to 1928*)
Stead, A., *Japan by the Japanese*
Willoughby, W. W., *Opium as an International Problem*
H.R.H. the Duke of Windsor, *A King's Story*
Yanagiwara, S. (translated), *Japanese-American Relations*

The events leading up to the battle for Malaya and Singapore in
1941 and 1942, and the campaign itself, are covered in war histories,
official and otherwise, and also in the published diaries and personal
accounts of soldiers and civilians who were involved.
The following books are of value.

Ash, Bernard, *Someone Had Blundered*
Attiwill, Kenneth, *The Singapore Story*
Bennett, H. Gordon, *Why Singapore Fell*
Brown, Cecil, *Suez to Singapore*
Butler, Professor J. R. M., *Official History of the War in the
Far East*, Vol. II
Butow, Robert J. C., *Tojo and the Coming of the War*
Chapman, F. Spencer, *The Jungle Is Neutral*
Eichelberger, Robert Y., *Our Jungle Road to Tokyo*
Fergusson, Sir Bernard, *Wavell: Portrait of a Soldier*
Gallagher, O'Dowd, *Action in the East*
Grenfell, Russel, *Main Fleet to Singapore*
Grigg, Sir James, *Prejudice and Judgment*
H.M.S.O., *The Official Despatches of General Percival*
Hough, R., *The Hunting of Force Z*
Hunt, F., *The Untold Story of Douglas MacArthur*
Ismay, Lord, *The Memoirs of Lord Ismay*
Ito, Masanori, with Roger Pineau, *The End of the Imperial
Japanese Navy*
Kirby, Major General S. Woodburn, *The War Against Japan*
Krueger, Walter, *Down Under to Nippon*
Legg, Frank, *The Gordon Bennett Story*
Mackenzie, Compton, *Eastern Epic*
MacNair, Harley Farnsworth, *Far Eastern International Relations*
Morrison, Ian, *Malayan Postscript*
Owen, Frank, *The Fall of Singapore*
Percival, Lieutenant-General A. E., *War in Malaya*
Playfair, Giles, *Singapore Goes Off the Air*
Potter, John Deane, *Admiral of the Pacific*
———, *The Life and Death of a Japanese General*
Reel, Frank A., *The Case of General Yamashita*
Rose, Angus, *Who Dies Fighting*

Sherwood, Robert E., ed., *The White House Papers of Harry L. Hopkins*
Snyder, Louis L., *The War: A Concise History 1939–1945*
Strabolgi, Lord, *Singapore and After*
Subbaiah, K. B., and Das, S. A., *Chalo Delhi*
Tsuji, Colonel Masanobu, *Read This Alone and the War Can Be Won*
——, *Singapore: The Japanese Version*
Tuker, Sir Francis, *While Memory Serves*
Wohlsteter, Roberta, *Pearl Harbor, Warning and Decision*
Woollcombe, R., *The Campaigns of Wavell*

With the rapid post-war improvements in international communications and the shrinking of distance as a result of technical advance, such as television and the jet engine, the old European empires of the East, which had remained largely unchanged for generations, would obviously have dwindled and declined. Such a situation, although not its causes, had long been anticipated.

In 1833, 109 years before the fall of Singapore precipitated the wane of Western influence over the East, Macaulay, addressing the English Parliament about India, pointed out that although "the sceptre may pass away from us . . . there is an empire exempt from all natural causes of decay. Those triumphs are the pacific triumphs of reason over barbarism; that empire is the imperishable empire of our arts and our morals, our literature and our laws . . ."

Instead of this gradual and gracious transition of power, as when control in a family firm passes from father to son, Soviet Russia's vested interest in organised chaos—for out of that Communism can come—added to the United States' pathological abhorrence of European imperialism, and, in the words of the Duke of Windsor, "most especially the British kind,"[1] has resulted in independence being given or almost forced on countries that were psychologically and politically unready for it. The results of this, Asia and Africa, are too well known to need repeating here.

For some accounts of these years of imperial decline, the following books provide a basis for research.

Allen, Henry C., *Great Britain and the United States*
Briginshaw, Richard, *Britain's World Rating*
Brimmell, J. H., *Communism in South East Asia*
Carrington, C. E., *The British Overseas*
Chamberlain, John, *MacArthur 1941–1951*

[1] Article in London *Sunday Express*, March 19, 1967.

Collier, Basil, *Barren Victories: Versailles to Suez 1918–1956*
Crozier, Brian, *South East Asia in Turmoil*
Easton, Stewart C., *The Rise and Fall of Western Colonialism*
——, *The Twilight of European Colonialism*
Fleming, Denna F., *The Cold War and Its Origins*
Hamlin, Canon M., *The Return to the Philippines*
Michael, Franz H., and Taylor, George E., *The Far East in the Modern World*
Murphy, Ray, *Last Viceroy*
Palmer, Norman D., *International Relations*
Purcell, Victor, *The Revolution in South East Asia*
Romein, Jan, *The Asian Century*
Rose, Saul, *Britain and South East Asia*
——, *Politics in Southern Asia*
Roosevelt, Elliott, *As He Saw It*
Sinha, Sasadhar, *Indian Independence in Perspective*
Thomson, Ian, *The Rise of Modern Asia*

For any study of the pre-war years in Britain, for the war itself, and for Western post-war failures and mistakes, the six volumes of *The Second World War* by Winston S. Churchill are indispensable reading. The author would like to acknowledge his great debt to them.

Index

Spheres of influence, 49, 62
Spitfire planes, 215
Spooner, Rear Admiral, 243
Stalin, Josef, 86, 161, 184, 287
Stanley Jail, 291–92, 295, 298
Steedman, Lieutenant-Colonel, 225
Stilwell, General Joseph "Vinegar Joe," 272–75
Storry, Richard, 52
Straits Budget, 133
Straits Settlement, 24, 34, 37, 41–43, 47, 101–2, 121, 127, 233–34, 237, 241
Straits Times, 133, 221
Strikes, 137
Sturdee, Lieutenant-General Sir Vernan, 304
Subbaiah, K. B., 138
Submarines, 82, 97, 177–78, 180, 188–90
Suez Canal, 35, 122
Sugar industry, 50, 292
Sugita, Lieutenant-Colonel, 3, 245, 249
Sukarno, Achmed, 277
Sumatra, 32, 199, 217, 240, 242
Sungei Patani airfield, 205
Sungei Ujong, state of, 41, 46–47
Sun Yat-sen, Dr., 65, 98
Super-Spitfire planes, 161
Supplies, military, 10, 127, 212, 224, 239, 252
Swettenham, Frank, 34, 46, 48
Swiftsure, 298
Swordfish torpedo planes, 163, 180–81
Sydney, Australia, 76, 159, 224

Tadasu, Hayashi, 60
Taiping airfield, 205
Taiwan Army No. 82 Unit, 151
Takamori, Saigo, 52
Taku, forts at, 57
Tamils, 136
Tanaka Memorial, 85–86
Tanglin Road, 116
Tanjong Bungah, 110
Tank warfare, 8, 10, 91–92, 113, 149, 156, 162–63, 168, 201, 207, 212, 232, 236, 239, 252–53, 270
Taora, Katsura, 60
Taranto, battle of, 180–83
Tavoy, 269
Taylor, George E., 280
Taylor, H. B., 238
Telephone communications, 8, 20, 167–69, 210, 229, 233–34
Temenggong, chief of Johore, 30–31
Tenasserim, 266–69
Tenedos, 185, 187, 189, 191
Tengah airfield, 174, 235, 240
Tennant, Captain William, 185–86, 188, 191–93
Ten Year Rule, 71–72, 102–3
Terauchi, Field Marshall Count Juichi, 111
Terrorism, 95, 262, 276
Thailand, 161, 164–67, 278. See also Siam
Thai territories, 143

Thomas, Sir Shenton, Governor of the Straits Settlement, 120–21, 127–29, 133–34, 171–73, 202, 206–7, 222, 230, 243–44, 249
Thyssen, Timmerman, 31
Tientsin, 57, 98–99, 290
Times, The (London), 63, 72, 123, 178, 227
Tin, production of, 14, 41, 43, 49, 114, 120, 125, 128–29, 135–36, 258, 277
Toa Renmei Undo movement, 262
Tojo, Admiral Hideki, 6, 63–64, 144–47, 149–50, 155, 224, 302
Tokugawa, 96
Tokyo War College, 8, 10, 105, 147
Tomahawk fighter planes, 268, 270
Tonga Islands, 49–50
Tongking, 51
Torpedo bomber planes, 79, 81–83, 104, 157, 162–63, 177–78, 181, 192–93, 198
Toungoo, 272–73
Trade, in South East Asia, 13, 24, 32, 34–36, 39, 41–42, 49–51, 67, 85, 96–97, 99, 119, 128–29, 141–42
Trade-Union movement, 288
Training, troop, 7, 52, 117, 132, 134, 138, 153, 159, 168, 200–1, 244, 259, 261, 267, 302
Transportation, military, 5, 18, 47, 153, 168, 204, 208, 212–13, 246, 276, 283
Transports, ship, 185, 188
Trans-Siberian Railroad, 60, 149
Treaties, 31–32, 38, 47, 49–51, 61, 64, 69–70, 97, 101, 106, 135, 143, 177
Trenchard, Sir Hugh, 75, 79–83, 176
Trenchard: Man of Vision, 79
Trengganu, 38–39, 114, 125, 143
Trenton, 121
Tripartite Pact, 143
Triple Intervention of 1895, 54, 59
Triumph in the Philippines, 303
Trotsky, Leon, 86
T'sen Yu-ying, Governor of Yunnan Province, 51
Tsingtao, 55, 65, 105
Tsuji, Colonel Masanobu, 4, 116, 151, 153–54, 169, 204, 212, 237, 259–60, 262–63, 301, 304
Tsushima, Straits of, 65
T'ung Chib, Emperor of China, 51
Tu Yu-ming, General, 272
Twenty-one Demands, 66
Typhoid, 205

Underground resistance, 263
United Nations, 280
United States, air force of, 268, 270; and Atlantic Charter, 179; and China, 99, 141, 274, 286–87; colonialism of, 49–50; on immigration, 9, 12; and India, 284–86; internationalism of, 68, 144–46, 279–82; and Japan, 14, 59, 66–67, 141–44, 150–51, 155–56, 258, 289–90; and Manchurian incident, 96; navy of,

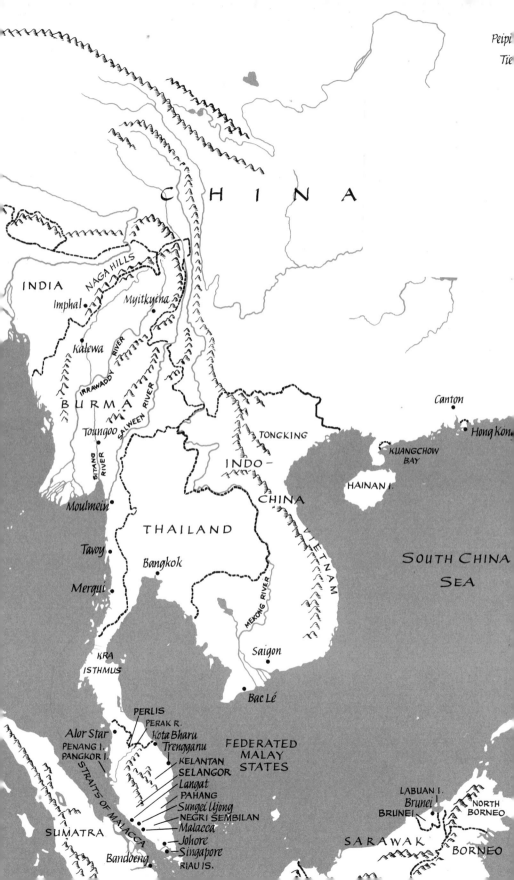